LANGUAGE AND MEANING IN

THE RENAISSANCE

★

LANGUAGE
AND MEANING IN THE
RENAISSANCE

by

Richard Waswo

PRINCETON

PRINCETON UNIVERSITY PRESS

MCM·LXXXVII

Library of Congress Cataloging in Publication Data will be found on the last printed page of this book. Publication of this book has been aided by a grant from the Lacy Lockert Fund of Princeton University Press. The second part of Chapter One appeared in an earlier version as "Magic Words and Reference Theories," *Journal of Literary Semantics* 6 (1977), 76–90. Clothbound editions of Princeton University Press books are printed on acid-free paper, and binding materials are chosen for strength and durability. This book has been composed in Linotron Bembo

ISBN 0–691–06696–5

PRINTED IN THE UNITED STATES OF
AMERICA BY PRINCETON UNIVERSITY PRESS
PRINCETON, NEW JERSEY

Thus the theory of description matters most.
It is the theory of the word for those

For whom the word is the making of the world,
The buzzing world and lisping firmament.

—WALLACE STEVENS

CONTENTS

The reader should know at the outset that this book is not a work of "original" research in either a theoretical or historical sense. I develop no new theory of meaning, but rather use a composite version of some present theories in order to disinter the competing semantic assumptions of the Renaissance. Likewise, I unearth no hitherto unknown texts in the period, but concentrate instead on exploring those assumptions primarily in texts of central importance, acknowledged influence, and broad diffusion, selected from the main areas of Renaissance preoccupation with language: literature, humanist philosophy, polemics for vernaculars, and biblical hermeneutics. Many of the texts are generally well known; those that aren't, like Valla's *Dialectica* or Flacius' *Clavis*, are well known, at least by reputation, to specialists. Although my argument demands close attention to some texts in their original languages (major citations are, of course, translated), I have not scrupled to use decent translations of others, where these were available and I had access to them.

The subject and aim of my inquiry (set forth in part one) require cutting across and bringing together material from long-established and separate academic disciplines. In extenuation of the offense this is likely to give to experts in the various fields trespassed upon, I plead the potential illuminating power of the broad view of the links between cultural domains, as opposed to the deep view of one. If the major link I have found among disparate levels and different concerns in Renaissance uses of and arguments about words—the discovery of the same semantic/epistemological dilemma—be judged to lack the interest and importance I believe it has, I hope the failure will be ascribed to my performance and not the general procedure. Academic overspecialization is something we often complain of and seldom do anything about. The professional rewards are surer, the intellectual risks fewer, if we remain securely within the institutional confines and mystique of expertise. And these practical pressures are increased if we are replowing a field so well tilled, enormous, and polyglot as the Renaissance. The consequences, however, of cultivating only our small and neatly fenced plot are that the issues we raise tend to appear as strangely exotic growths to the people in other plots, behind other fences. It seems, then, worthwhile to look for growths that can have roots in the large and common soil we share. That no single person can possibly master the entire field should not prevent us from trying to comprehend it as wholly and as clearly as we can.

In addition to the parochialism of expertise there is the parochialism of historicism. By this I mean that issues to be investigated are determined not by current but by past concerns. The procedure I follow is the opposite. It so happens that an almost febrile preoccupation with language is shared by a great deal of contemporary and Renaissance thought. To seek relations on this basis between its concerns and ours is to ask the past to speak to the present by using the present to select the questions we put to the past. I briefly defend this procedure in chapter two, and am aware that it is heresy to some historians.* But I fear that the past can be made to speak with no other voice than that of the ventriloquial present. Those who believe that we must let the past speak in its own voice, that the only real historical issues are those that were recognized and formulated in the period under study, condemn it to remain forever mute. For the past has no voice: it exists as habits, institutions, artifacts, and texts. To make any of these articulate requires the voice of a present interpreter. If that interpreter denies that he has a voice, ignoring the cognitive and other interests of his own time and place and pretending that his recon-

---

* A small controversy on this matter was generated by a book review of mine in *Bibliothèque d'humanisme et Renaissance*. See the attack by Paul G. and Marion L. Kuntz, "Truth in History: Waswo's Ideological Relativism versus Kristeller's Empirical Objectivism," *BHR* 44 (1982), 645–48; and my reply, "Learning to Love Relative Truths," *BHR* 44 (1982), 657–60.

struction of the past constitutes its "objective" reality, he bur-
ies the past in the tomb of time and severs any real connection
it might have with the living present. Claimed objectivity is
guaranteed irrelevance. The kind of skepticism I am urging is
neither irresponsible solipsism nor despairing pessimism. We
can only ventriloquize the past, but we do so through sharable
standards of evidence and rational argument. The voices we
hear are and are not our own; projected into and out of other
minds and times, they come back altered to instruct us.

If we lacked the principles of twentieth-century hermeneutics and the sociology of knowledge from which I derive this
viewpoint, we could do no better than adopt that of the Renaissance recovery of the classical past—a past seen with both
the awareness of distance and the desire of intimacy, a past that
lived by being used. The energies of this use and the definitive
modern pathos of the awareness and the desire in writers from
Petrarch to Jonson are described with magisterial eloquence by
Thomas M. Greene's *The Light in Troy*. We are to those writers as they were to their ancient predecessors: we seek to make
them speak to our situation, but only by recognizing their
otherness from ourselves. Niccolò Machiavelli, in rustic exile
from the political world that most mattered to him, donned
courtly attire for his nightly conversations with the philosophers and historians of antiquity. They lived for Machiavelli,
and he makes them live for us, not because he accepted their
premises, but because he made them respond to his own. This
is the real homage that we owe the past: not to believe it but to
use it. We cannot serve it, for it is gone; but we can make it
serve us. This historiography is but an acknowledgment of the
fact concisely remarked by E. H. Gombrich: "There is no reality without interpretation; just as there is no innocent eye,
there is no innocent ear." And there is likewise no innocent
voice.

ACKNOWLEDGMENTS

The greatest intellectual debts I have incurred in writing this book are to the published works of other scholars, which I trust are adequately identified and acknowledged in both the text and notes. Having attempted a synthesis of materials from disparate fields concerning a subject so nebulous as language, I am newly impressed, not only by my own ignorance, but by the network of dependencies that enables us to think at all. If the humanist notion of the "republic of letters" has lost over the centuries much of its lustre as an ideal, it remains a fact. Without our fellow citizens in this admirably borderless state, we could no more reflect, ponder, and write than, without a language, could we speak.

I thank the editors of *Criticism, Journal of Literary Semantics*, and *Bibliothèque d'humanisme et Renaissance* for permission to reprint more and less substantially different versions of articles that first appeared in their pages.

I have profited from the encouragement and criticism of Professors Michel Jeanneret and John G. Blair. Professor Pierre Fraenkel and Dr. Irena Backus of *l'Institut d'histoire de la réformation* have submitted most kindly to my raids on their erudition; Dr. Backus has in addition given me invaluable help with Latin, as did Princeton's anonymous reader of the manuscript. None of these gracious individuals, of course, can incur blame or provide indemnification for such errors as remain.

Finally, I am grateful for associations with colleagues and friends who have informed my thinking in all those subliminal ways that defy recognition by chapter and verse. Such people remain in one's mind over the years as interlocutors and respondents in an endlessly imagined dialogue. They constitute, I suspect, the most vivid sense of an audience that someone working largely in isolation can have, and thus function, I like to hope, not only as a crucial stimulus, giving direction and point to one's arguments, but also as needed curbs, chastening one's more extravagant eccentricities. Though they might find little evidence of their latter function in this book, I trust that Ralph Cohen, William Kerrigan, and Alan Howard have taught me enough in our real conversations to forgive the license I may take with them in my imaginary ones. In addition to his prominent part in these conversations, Austin Quigley has contributed materially to every stage of my investigations. To his engaging and always trenchant lucidity, I owe most.

Instead of dedicating this book to my wife, it is more appropriate that I offer her an apology for the Christmas Eve I spent at the typewriter and a promise that the next project will observe all legal holidays.

GENEVA
October 1985

LANGUAGE AND MEANING IN

THE RENAISSANCE

★

PART I

NOTIONS OF MEANING: THEORY AND HISTORY

A *picture* held us captive. And we could not get
outside it, for it lay in our language and language seemed to repeat it to us inexorably.

—LUDWIG
WITTGENSTEIN

The enormous interest on both sides of the Atlantic in linguistic problems during the past thirty years has generated completely new branches of theoretical inquiry, such as semiotics
and narratology, out of the convergence of critical and hermeneutic philosophy, structural linguistics, anthropology,
and literary criticism. But little of this activity has provoked
any reexamination of traditional assumptions about the most
fundamental power of human language: the reason it is indispensable is that it has meaning. So-called semanticists enjoyed
a brief vogue in the fifties, and the construction of semantic
theories has since become a major concern of some linguists,
philosophers, and computer programmers. But the maps of
meaning produced by these differently directed efforts—to relate signs to the psychology of their users or to describe math-
ematically the rules of their combination into "well-formed"
or "deviant" utterances—are only redrawings of very old ter-
rain. The former effort was part of classical rhetoric; the latter
was part of medieval nominalism. Few of these efforts, then or
now, have questioned very seriously the status of the assumed
semantic unit—the "sign" itself. Until the later work of Wittgenstein, probably the fullest such interrogation was made by

Ferdinand de Saussure, who endowed the concept with the great prestige it has subsequently enjoyed in this century.[1]

Regardless, however, of the sophistication and elaboration of these sundry metalanguages, to call the semantic unit a "sign" is to adopt the "picture" of semantic operations that has lain in Western languages since Plato. A sign is a mark, token, or image of something else. It directs us away from itself to something else; its function is extrinsic, standing for or pointing toward something else; and its existence is posterior to that other thing, a copy or trace or symbol of it. If words are regarded as having meaning as "signs," the picture of the world thereby assumed is that painted by ontological and epistemological dualism, in which language becomes merely an imitation or copy of "reality." This picture has been sufficiently falsified in a great many domains of contemporary thought—from the psychology and physiology of perception to the history of art—[2] to make it genuinely paradoxical that it should continue to prevail in areas of direct concern with the meaning of language. What is more, this paradox itself has not often been observed. One critic, however, has observed it quite accurately. Commenting on Genette's narratological hypothesis "of perfect temporal correspondence between narrative and story," she remarks,

Such an expectation of conformity is encouraged and supported by a conception of discourse as consisting of sets of discrete signs which, in some way, *correspond to* (depict, encode, denote, refer to, and so forth) sets of discrete and specific ideas, objects, or events. It is precisely such a conception of discourse that dominates contemporary

[1] *Course in General Linguistics*, ed. Bally, Sechehaye, Riedlinger, tr. Wade Baskin (New York, 1959; 1st ed. 1916). Page numbers of references to this book are given parenthetically in the text.

[2] See, e.g., the collection of essays in *Illusion in Nature and Art*, ed. R. L. Gregory and E. H. Gombrich (London, 1973). Such dualism has also been rejected by social scientists at least since Durkheim; cf. Ernest Gellner's concise critique of the semantics of "correspondence": "Concepts and Society," in *Rationality*, ed. Bryan R. Wilson (New York, 1970), pp. 24–25.

narrative theory, and it is the dualism at the heart of that model of *language* that provides the scaffolding for the two-leveled model of narrative. (This model of language has, of course, been the major one in Western intellectual history and, in spite of some epistemological doubts and technical modifications introduced recently by various linguists and philosophers of language, it continues to be the model that dominates not only narratology but literary studies generally.)[3]

The principal thesis of parts two and three of this book is that some very grave doubts about this model, along with alternatives to it, became articulate and widely diffused in the culture of the fifteenth and sixteenth centuries. The specific issues, boundaries, and methodology of the investigation are set forth in chapter two. The first chapter attempts to explain the infrequently observed paradox of the domination of the dualistic model, sketching its deployment in history, arguing that it is fallacious as theory, and presenting an alternative kind of theory as more correct and more useful.

The domination of the dualistic model of how language means, which has extended even to a number of fashionable contemporary theories, explains why not much attention has been focused on the Renaissance challenges to it. We need to escape the captivity of this picture before we can perceive the powerful efforts of earlier periods to do so. Escape, moreover, is not merely a matter of knowing a few counter-theories; if it were, there would have been no domination. Such theories have been available at least since the Sophists in antiquity, Valla in the Renaissance, several pioneer philologists around the turn of the nineteenth century, and increasingly in this century in the work of such disparate thinkers as Ernst Cassirer, Ludwig Wittgenstein, Benjamin Lee Whorf, J. R. Firth, and Hans-Georg Gadamer. For the real power of the dualistic model is not theoretical at all; it is emotional. It lies in our vocabulary

---

[3] Barbara Herrnstein Smith, "Narrative Versions, Narrative Theories," *Critical Inquiry* 7 (1980), 225. This article continues Smith's trenchant and salutary critiques of both stylistic and linguistic theories of literature made in *On the Margins of Discourse* (Chicago, 1978).

of discourse because it haunts our psyche, reflecting our anxieties about language, displacing our reactions to the power of words, and satisfying our desires for closure and repose on what Samuel Johnson called "the stability of truth." To escape from this model, we shall begin by reviewing some contemporary challenges to the power it derives from our ambivalent feelings about words.

By including feelings and assumptions in my accounts of past and present semantic theories and debates, I am of course suggesting that these are more important in determining meanings than the theories they generate. The broad classification of semantics as "referential" and "relational" that I shall offer is thus a description and judgment of both formal theories and casual presuppositions in terms of their utility for the exploration of language in all its uses. The semantics I call "relational" is characterized precisely by its refusal to conceive of meaning as reference produced by signs; it is a rejection of the current standard philosophical/linguistic triad of (1) syntactics, (2) semantics, and (3) pragmatics as the study of "signs" with respect to (1) each other, (2) the world, (3) their users. So to compartmentalize semantics is to exclude from "meaning" grammar, syntax, and interpreters, and to fix it as the representation signs offer of their referents. By "semantics" I understand any conviction, expressed or implied, conscious or unconscious, about how language means—any model for, attitude toward, or habit of interpretation. The purely formal limitation of semantics to a system of rules establishing the truth-conditions of statements in the language of logic, or to a system of rules determining well-formed utterances in natural or computer languages, is valid only for the particular and synchronic purposes of philosophy, linguistics, or information processing. Such limitations hamstring history simply by ignoring it. And insofar as the meanings of words are themselves historical, inherited from all the recorded and reconstructed past and modified by the ever-changing present, these limitations falsify what they purport to analyze. I do not underestimate the importance—in fact, I shall stress it—of what can be learned from the synchronic and systematic study of an abstracted *langue*. But since my purpose is to investigate the past, I am primarily concerned with the alternative and competing semantics to be found in actual *paroles*.

I

FROM REFERENTIAL
TO RELATIONAL
SEMANTICS

Quant à *signe*, si nous nous en contentons, c'est —FERDINAND
que nous ne savons par quoi le remplacer, la   DE SAUSSURE
langue usuelle n'en suggerant aucun autre.

In these words the founder of modern linguistics as the study
of *langue* as a synchronic system of functions (distinguished
from *parole* as the diachronic activity of speech) expressed his
misgivings about the ancient and traditional semantic unit of
the "sign." His frustrated desire to replace this term is a wish
to escape from the picture of the world that it implies. Saussure's recognition of the inadequacies of his central term illustrates both how difficult it is to move from a referential to a
relational account of the operation of language and how much
is to be gained by making this move.

Though he retains "sign," he gives a new composite definition of the term carefully designed to purge its traditional assumptions of reference to either prior objects in the world or
mental representations of them. "The linguistic sign unites,
not a thing and a name, but a concept and a sound-image." He
then replaces the last two terms with the famous "signified"
and "signifier" (*Course in General Linguistics* 66–67) and goes
on to stress the wholly arbitrary character of the sign. Saussure, wishing to establish as an academic discipline the study
of language "*in and for itself*" (*Course* 232), thus attempts at the
outset to cut language loose from its presumed obligation to
refer to or represent prefabricated, naturally "given" realities,

exterior or interior. His new terms replace the representational, passive, imitative, secondhand qualities of the standard
nouns ("concept," "image") with participial nouns (*signifié,
signifiant*) that implicitly stress the active agency of signs in
their dealings with the world.[4] What is "signified" by the au-
dible "signifier" is not, in Saussure's terminology, predetermined to "correspond" to a "thing" that exists elsewhere. Indeed, the principal justification for the creation of the
discipline that takes language as its exclusive object of study is
the constitutive role language plays in human cognition:
"Without language, thought is a vague, uncharted nebula.
There are no pre-existing ideas, and nothing is distinct before
the appearance of language" (*Course* 112). For Saussure, language represents neither the world nor a mental process.
Rather, it constitutes both. And it is precisely this insight that
leads him to discover that "sign" poses more problems than
those avoided so far.

Saussure arrives at these in his discussion of linguistic
"value." Value is what is attributed to a word by virtue of its
use in the communally established language game (Saussure
offers an extended analogy between the function of words and
chessmen, *Course* 88–89, 110). And this crucial function of the
linguistic unit in a socially determined system reveals the inadequacy of describing words as "signs": "the idea of value
. . . shows that to consider a term as simply the union of a certain sound with a certain concept is grossly misleading. To define it in this way would isolate the term from its system"
(*Course* 113). Saussure then insists that *signification* depends
upon and must be distinguished from *value* in order to avoid
"reducing language to a simple naming-process." Words have
value only by association with, and dissociation from, other
words: "Language is a system of interdependent terms in

---

[4] The idea of secondhand representation that Saussure is trying to avoid is
clearer in French than in English. To say that a sound has a "signified" rather
than a "concept" matters less in English—where the definition of "concept" is
general idea, notion, or category—than in French—where the definition of
concept is "représentation mentale . . . d'un objet."

which the value of each term results solely from the simultaneous presence of the others" (*Course* 114).

What Saussure is talking about here is of course nothing less than meaning. The examples he gives demonstrate that his distinction between "value" and "signification" is (without benefit of Frege) that between "sense" and "reference."

Modern French *mouton* can have the same signification as English *sheep* but not the same value . . . particularly because in speaking of a piece of meat ready to be served on the table, English uses *mutton* and not *sheep*. The difference in value between *sheep* and *mouton* is due to the fact that *sheep* has beside it a second term while the French word does not (*Course* 115–16).

Saussure thus articulates the liberating principle that the meaning of a word is not its referent, but, anticipating Wittgenstein, its use *in the language*.[5] This crucial qualification, made by Wittgenstein and often overlooked, is built into Saussure's very definition of *langue* as a value-conferring "system of interdependent terms." The qualification prevents the insight that meaning is use from degenerating into what some have since made of it—a crass slogan of behaviorism. The use that is meaning is not any individual's psychological disposition to respond; it gives Humpty-Dumpty no license to declare that words mean what *he* uses them to mean. This use is, on the contrary, explicitly systemic—the function of a part determined by its multiple *relations* to other parts.

Saussure further exemplifies the point by recurring to his rejection of the presumed representational character of the sign: "If words stood for pre-existing concepts, they would all have exact equivalents in meaning from one language to the next; but this is not true" (*Course* 116). After listing some verbs in German and French whose uses, like those of *sheep* and *mouton*, coincide at some points but differ at others (i.e., have the same reference but different meanings), he finds the same nonequi-

[5] For an analysis of the process of negative elimination by which Wittgenstein arrived at this qualified definition, see Garth Hallet, S.J., *Wittgenstein's Definition of Meaning as Use* (New York, 1967).

valence of value in the larger units of the system. "Proto-Germanic has no special form for the future; to say that the future is expressed by the present is wrong, for the value of the present is not the same in Germanic as in languages that have a future along with the present" (*Course* 117). These and other similar examples (all of which presage the later theories of Whorf and Firth) lead Saussure to a final modification of his composite "sign" that completely reverses its traditional semantic role. This role, as I shall shortly review it from Plato onward, was referential: what the sign "signified," or referred to, or represented—a preexisting object or concept—was identified as its meaning. Meaning was thus determined by reference. For Saussure, the opposite is true: meaning (as "value") determines reference (as "signification"): "it is quite clear that initially the concept is nothing, that is[,] only a value determined by its relations with other similar values, and that without them the signification would not exist" (*Course* 117). Hence, what a word "signifies"—its referent as object or concept—depends on its meaning, which is determined not *as* that object or concept but as a function of the relations the word has with other words. Meaning is thereby not placed outside and independent of words, but is coextensive with their operation.

For example, the word "tree" does not signify a certain kind of natural object because it somehow corresponds to that object; it signifies that class of object because it distinguishes that class from similar ones: "bush," or "vine," or "weed." The object as such is not there to be corresponded to until the word divides it from others. It is the use of the word within its *langue* in order to divide the world that constitutes its meaning. And that meaning, in turn, determines a referent whose existence is not given a priori—that is, the world does not present itself to us as irrevocably, or essentially, or naturally, so divided. Language does the dividing. The topography of the planet does not present itself as naturally divided into the political boundaries that have been drawn upon it. Languages are maps of the world; different maps pick out different features of the world for different purposes—to yield different kinds of knowledge about it. There are maps of the earth's nations, geography, geology, rainfall, population, vegetation, railroads, highways, and three-star restaurants. None has any greater or lesser degree of "reality," any larger claim to priority or privilege, than any other.

To return to the "tree": its *definiens* in common use—let's say, the possession of a trunk—is not a metaphysical "essence" of "treeness," a necessary condition of its "being"; it is merely what identifies trees for us as one (highly useful) class of vegetation among many.[6] No referent or *definiens* has the privilege of "essence" for the simple reason that different discourses can reclassify the object in terms of different contrastive categories to which that *definiens* may be wholly irrelevant. This is what botany and carpentry do with "tree": the attribute that counts in common use (its referent or "signification") is ignored by both. Trees have no status in botany, where they are reclassified with all other vegetation on the basis of how they reproduce themselves. Nor have they any interest for the carpenter, who classifies instead their internal material: soft or hard, closed or open grain, are what matter to him. All the features of trees identified by these discourses are equally real: trees have trunks; they multiply as angiosperms or gymnosperms; their wood takes a high polish. No single feature is a privileged "essence." Trees can have as many additional features, all equally real, as we have words to articulate how we perceive or use them—that is, sets of contrastive categories to put them in: trees are beautiful—and threatening; they supply shade—and attract lightning; they supply oxygen—and need water; they add value to property—until they become diseased; they are pillars, targets, billboards, dwellings, playgrounds, landmarks, trysting places, and the bathrooms of dogs. These and

---

[6] We may note that with respect to the members of the class—e.g., palm, pine, poplar—the *definiens* is not a "universal" characteristic, a single shared feature. Banyan trees do not have *a* trunk; their branches grow down and take root. The categories into which ordinary language divides the world are loose, and do not permit the extraction of a single "essential" feature: they consist, in Wittgenstein's famous analogy, of "family resemblances."

any other imaginable features of trees are what "tree" might mean in any given use—to which no clue is given by the "signification" of "tree" in the common *langue*. And even this "signification," as Saussure pointed out, disappears when other discourses subsume trees as parts of larger classes or divide them into smaller ones. The concepts signified by words, as Saussure puts it, "are purely differential and defined not by their positive content but negatively by the relations with the other terms of the system. Their most precise characteristic is in being what the others are not" (*Course* 117).

By thus divorcing meaning from reference and regarding it as a function of the manifold relations of words with each other, Saussure proposed in his domain (independently developed in other domains, as well) what has become one of the major revolutions in twentieth-century thought: the shift from referential to relational semantics, from regarding the meaning of language as a given object of reference to regarding it as a dynamic function of use. This revolution did not begin with Saussure—I shall be arguing that it is a definitive feature of the Renaissance—and it is by no means complete. By its nature, it cannot ever be complete—in the sense of hardening into a universally accepted orthodoxy. For to observe that meaning is not reference, but "a complex of contextual relations,"[7] is not to replace one theory or model with a different one of the same kind; it is a radical redescription of the phenomenon. Meaning as reference is a thing; meaning as function is an activity. No matter what kind of thing is singled out as meaning by the former description—whether what is referred to is a Platonic Form, an object, a mental picture, an intention—it yields perforce a recipe for construing meaning: we can triumphantly point to x and say, "There it is." The latter description permits no such ostensive simplicity; rather than yielding a recipe, it opens an argument. Instead of answering one question, it poses many. Instead of sanctioning one mode of interpretation

[7] J. R. Firth, *Selected Papers . . . 1952–59*, ed. F. R. Palmer (Bloomington, Ind., 1968), p. 173 et passim.

that looks beyond the text to achieve closure, it sanctions multiple modes of interpretation that look at the text to discover the plural and perhaps competing networks of relations that determine its meanings at all levels, from its grammar through its characterization of its own audience to its incorporation of past texts and its use by future ones. For these reasons, the description of meaning as activity can prescribe no single method and thus generate no orthodoxy of interpretation.

As we shall see, the very multiplicity of interpretive strategies sanctioned by relational semantics has aroused, both in the past and in the present, considerable hostility and fear. Part of this reaction, then and now, is encouraged by the vulgarization of the description into polemical slogans that permit the misapprehension of multiplicity as mere chaos. But multiplicity is not the absence of control; it is an expansion of controls. It licenses no solipsistic infinity. Indeed, it enlarges our comprehension of texts by directing our attention to their interplay of relations, which, though various, are determinate and publicly arguable in any given case at any given time. By regarding words as mutually reactive semantic agents instead of passive semantic receptacles or transmitters, the description of meaning as activity invites us to apprehend language itself as a performing art—as doing a great deal more to and for ourselves and the world than merely reflecting either or both. To such enrichment the appropriate response seems to me not fear but grateful enjoyment.

Saussure's brilliant analysis of linguistic "value" implies an additional dimension to the activity of meaning that he does not discuss but that logically completes the description. Saussure initially hits on the idea of value as a way to stress both the social character of the linguistic system and the constitution of its units by relations of comparison and exchange (*Course* 111, 115). Like the value of money, that of words depends on the unlike things they can be exchanged for (commodities/ideas) and the like things they can be compared and contrasted to (other coins and currencies/other words and languages). No such value is absolute or immutable; each is a function of another; all can operate only by virtue of communal assent. In his effort to identify the subjects and stake out the boundaries of a new discipline, Saussure focuses, naturally enough, on the mechanisms by which value is produced in such a system. The dimension he omits is the other part of the exchange—consumption. We are all simultaneously producers and consumers of value in the linguistic economy as in the monetary one. As individuals, we cannot alter or control either system; as a collectivity we can and do—over time and seldom consciously. As individuals, we can, however, consciously seek to maximize our gains and minimize our losses in both economies—but only by mastering their rules to the point that we become able, if we choose, to violate them profitably, creatively, and with impunity. I am developing Saussure's illuminating analogy to make the point that the consumer is the interpreter, that meaning as creative activity in language includes meaning as interpretive activity in language users. As we cannot spend money except in a community where its values are established and accepted, so we cannot make sense except in a community where our words are likewise current. Translations, and currency conversions, into the values of another community are always possible and never exactly equivalent; as students of literature and foreign tourists have long known, such transactions are likely to involve more loss than gain. Whether among members of the same community or different ones, meaning is a transaction between an utterance and a hearer, a text and a performer. It is the act of construing the multiple relations of the linguistic units that compose the utterance or text in terms of the multiple relations that utterance or text may be perceived to have with others—that is, the context in which the interpreter both finds and places it.

The interpreter's liberty to select and impose such contexts, consciously or unconsciously, is of course greater in the case of writing than in speech, where a concrete situation and the presence of the speaker impose constraints and provide opportunities that do not exist in reading. But, although carried out under the different circumstances of talking to someone or

reading a book, the transaction of meaning as a necessary con-
strual of relations is the same in both. It is also the same with
respect to all the units of the system, whatever their size. That
logical distinctions may be made between the meaning of a
word and the meaning of a sentence, or of a text or a genre of
texts, does not alter the process of construing relations that is
performed in each case. The activity is the same in kind as we
proceed up the scale from word to genre; the only change is the
quantitative expansion of the number of relations and the
scope of the systems to be taken into account.

Spelling out the implications of Saussure's crucial notion of
linguistic "value" has thus completed the theory of relational
semantics by including, in addition to those relations constructed in the system—terminological, grammatical, syntac-
tical—those contextual relations constructed by its interpreters. The latter, however, are not considered as outside the
system but as part of it. The description of meaning as "use in
the language" presupposes users—not merely in the sense of a
community of competent speakers but also in the sense of sub-
communities, institutions, and individuals—all of whom supply a wide range of contexts in which meanings are determined, from social practices through professional conventions
to personal beliefs. This dynamic inclusiveness, based on the
identification of its subject not as an object but as an activity, is
what makes relational semantics so various and therefore useful, so revolutionary and therefore liable to misunderstanding.
Though it can be presented as a formal theory (Saussure's is
the most succinct version I know), relational semantics is in
some basic ways an antitheory—that is, a denial that what normally counts as theory in philosophical or scientific discourse
can apply to the elucidation of meaning. Relational semantics
neither predicts any results nor prescribes any procedure for
arriving at them. It shows us where to look without telling us
what we're going to find. It locates meaning not as the product
of a systematic investigation but as the operation of a systemic
practice—what Saussure calls the "social fact." Instead of prescribing what is to be produced, it describes the activity of

production and consumption. In one vital and negative respect, however, relational semantics plays the role usually expected of a theory: it furnishes—is indeed founded on—a principle of exclusion.

It excludes precisely what Saussure was attempting to eliminate from his careful redefinition of the composite "sign"— the whole dualistic picture of the world that lies in the Western vocabulary of discourse. And the rejection of this picture is what gives the shift from referential to relational semantics its increasing importance and profound implications in many domains of twentieth-century thought. Saussure found "sign" defective in two ways: (1) by its presumption of standing for or corresponding to preextant entities in the world; (2) by its presumption of independent status as *the* semantic unit. The second defect reduces language to a mere nomenclature, ruling out of any consideration as *meaning* all that relational semantics rules in: the interdependence of terms, the structure of grammar, the entire existence of language as historical product and social practice always embedded in contexts of human purpose. The revolution here consists in declaring semantically relevant, in bringing together and seeing as determinant of *meaning*, all the kinds of disparate and mundane observations made about language since the beginning of recorded writing about words but almost never integrated to become an explicit semantics. Observations such as: historical changes in the forms and meanings of words; their context dependency; their systemic functions; their possession of multiple referents; their ability to constitute knowledge, shape feeling, and mold behavior; their domination by social usage. All of these hardly arcane linguistic phenomena have been remarked more and less casually since antiquity; some furnished the subject matter of grammar and rhetoric. But as observations they remained largely isolated, not seen, until the Renaissance (and then only temporarily), to be mutually relevant or to cohere sufficiently to provide a sustained challenge to the dominant model of meaning.

And this model is the first defect of Saussure's "sign": the ineradicably potent assumption that words represent things that are, as such, already there to be represented. This defect reduces language to a mere copy of whatever is supposed to be "reality," identifying the *meaning* of words as the things they refer to, and postulating an absolute, dualistic division between words and things. This is the referential semantics of venerable tradition; the revolution of its rejection is that of much of the analytic, critical, and hermeneutic philosophy of our time. The motives and consequences of this rejection, as derived from the later work of Dewey, Heidegger, and Wittgenstein, have recently been argued at length by Richard Rorty.[8] His argument is a full-scale rejection of the post-Cartesian notion of knowledge as accurate representation and its concomitant correspondence theory of truth. And it is based on the linguistic insight that a number of contemporary thinkers from quite different traditions share with Saussure: that language does not reflect one world but shapes many, and that meaning is consequently not the discovery of "unique referents" but the examination of "current practices."[9]

To urge the abandonment of the search for a class of "privileged representations" that alone counts as knowledge or truth in philosophy, history, or science, and to acknowledge the genuinely cognitive contributions of ordinary speech, art, myth, and literature, are made possible by the move from referential to relational semantics. Not until language is released

---

[8] *Philosophy and the Mirror of Nature* (Princeton, 1979). The careers of the particular philosophers Rorty selects exemplify the shift I am describing here from a different viewpoint: each attempted in his early work to discover the all-commensurate discourse, the final vocabulary that would yield apodictic knowledge of objects, then "each of the three, in his later work, broke free of the Kantian conception of philosophy as foundational, and spent his time warning us against those very temptations to which he himself had once succumbed. Thus their later work is therapeutic rather than constructive, edifying rather than systematic" (p. 5).

[9] *Ibid.*, p. 374. His argument, having collapsed all the dualisms in the post–seventeenth-century obsession with epistemology and its pictorial depiction of mind as mirror, ends with a cogent plea for the reconceiving of philosophy itself as edifying, hermeneutic conversation.

from its sole semantic obligation to represent can this hierarchy of privilege that sustains a dualistic universe begin to
crumble. Only when meaning is redescribed as an activity can
the constitutive role of language in human cognition become
visible. One philosopher, citing Wittgenstein, Ryle, and Firth,
summarizes the redescription: "Meanings, we have learned,
are not entities or objects corresponding to expressions; they
are the *uses* of expressions; they are the work expressions
do"—and draws its consequence: "Our world—remembered,
imagined, or perceived—is organized by the language we
speak."[10] An introductory text to contemporary philosophy
presents as a general consensus the view that meaning cannot
be intelligibly discussed as a thing or a "class of things."[11] Another philosopher, criticizing all forms of referential semantics, rejects any theory of meaning that poses it as a "what"
question, an identity sentence that "designates something."[12]
The same rejection has imposed itself on information theory,
where "meaning is defined as a relationship, not an absolute
property," which is called a "selective function."[13] The fascinating efforts to create intelligent machines that "understand"
natural languages require programs that are modifiable by the
"interaction" of the semantic "relations" built into the pro-

[10] W. Haas, "The Theory of Translation," *Philosophy* 37 (1962), 212, 215.
This article is the best treatment of its subject I know of. Haas points out incidentally (214–15) that the readmission of reference into the semantics of use
via the so-called use-to-refer is still inadequate to account for the meaning of
such expressions.

[11] Daniel M. Taylor, *Explanation and Meaning* (Cambridge, 1970), p. 129.
Many linguists and semanticists persist, despite Saussure, in so considering it:
see Bernard Harrison's review of Jerrold Katz, *Semantic Theory*, in *Mind* 83
(1974), 599–606. That it cannot be so considered is one of the few shared positions in the polemics collected in *Readings in the Philosophy of Language*, ed.
Jay E. Rosenberg and Charles Travis (Englewood Cliffs, N.J., 1971).

[12] Max Black, *The Labyrinth of Language* (London, 1968), p. 162. See also his
articles on "Dewey's Philosophy of Language" and "Wittgenstein's Views
about Language" in *Margins of Precision* (Ithaca, 1970).

[13] Donald M. MacKay, *Information, Mechanism and Meaning* (Cambridge,
Mass., 1969), pp. 128, 85.

gram.[14] What has been learned about meaning in the attempts to teach computers to understand and deal with it seems generally to vindicate one rather unpopular school of linguistics, which has long called for "the abandonment of the dualist view of meaning involving such phrases as word and idea, thought and its expression, form and content" and located meaning "in the statement of the internal relations of the structures and systems in a language, and the extended relation of these within generalized contexts of situation."[15] Finally, the move from referential to relational semantics has generated new kinds of intellectual history as the study of how language at any given time constructs and transforms the world.[16] Michel Foucault takes this study to be the analysis of discursive practices or formations, the rules of which "define not the dumb existence of a reality . . . but the ordering of objects," and in which words are not seen as groups of referential signs, "but as practices that systematically form the objects of which they speak."[17]

To deny that reference is meaning is to accept the creation of

[14] Burton Raphael, "SIR: Semantic Information Retrieval," in *Semantic Information Processing*, ed. Marvin Minsky (Cambridge, Mass., 1968), p. 56.

[15] J. R. Firth, "A New Approach to Grammar," *Selected Papers*, p. 118. The terms "structure," "system," and "context of situation" have technical meanings in Firth's theory, which are elucidated in this paper and others in the same volume.

[16] This is the formulation of Karl-Otto Apel, *Die Idee der Sprache in der Tradition des Humanismus von Dante bis Vico* (Bonn, 1963), which he derives from what he calls the congruence of Germanic "transcendental" language philosophy (Herder, Humboldt, Cassirer) and Anglo-Saxon "pragmatic behaviorism" (Wittgenstein, Morris). He has since published an English summary of his program: "The Transcendental Conception of Language-Communication and the Idea of a First Philosophy (Toward a Critical Reconstruction of the History of Philosophy in the Light of Language Philosophy)," in *History of Linguistic Thought and Contemporary Linguistics*, ed. Herman Parret (Berlin, 1976), pp. 32–61.

[17] *The Archaeology of Knowledge*, tr. A. M. Sheridan Smith (New York, 1972), p. 49. We may observe that "practices" as forming their "objects" have been detected in literature and art long before such operation was seen as also characteristic of language.

a multiplicity of meanings by the use and interpretation of words as a social practice in contexts and for purposes. And to deny that reference is reference to a ready-made, preestablished world of objects or concepts is to accept that multiplicity of meanings as constituting the various worlds we know or live in. Together, these convictions—both manifest in Saussure's critique of the "sign"—compose the shift from referential to relational semantics as it has been occurring in this century. Its revolutionary importance is that by redescribing what language does, it redescribes what the world is. By apprehending meaning as an activity of language and its users, it reorients our perception of the world and of ourselves, and redefines the aims of that perception—knowledge and truth—not as waiting to be found in a realm beyond or above or beneath language, but as being made by the semantic activity of language. Our assumptions about how language means seem the most basic we can have, for they impose themselves on everything language talks about. If those assumptions are dualistic, separating meanings from the use of words (i.e., by locating them in the things words "represent"), then language will present us with a self-contained exterior world before which it is obliged to become transparent, as if thought existed apart from its expression, as if facts existed apart from values, as if our minds existed apart from our bodies. If those assumptions are monistic, identifying meanings with the use of words, then language will show us the interpenetration between itself and a world before which it can be anything but transparent—as thoughts, facts, and minds are themselves brought into existence by the language that embodies them.

This profound alteration of our linguistic/semantic assumptions can be stated, and can be discovered in history, with respect to either of its linked terms. With respect to meaning, the shift is from regarding it as referential to regarding it as relational. With respect to language, the shift is from regarding it as the transparent vehicle, the plain or fancy container of an independently fixed content, to regarding it as a creative agent that constructs its own protean meanings. In short, from language as cosmetic to reality to language as constitutive of realities. In these latter terms the shift can be detected in the practice of some of the greatest writers and poets in the West between Gorgias and Petrarch. But it is never accompanied, during this period, by a sustained body of theoretical reflection on its former terms, a general and conscious awareness that meanings are relational and not referential. I have been barely sketching this awareness as it permeates and seeks to alter our consciousness today. The body of this book will attempt to demonstrate that the same awareness, the same shift in semantic assumptions, also became pervasive and revolutionary in the Renaissance, where, stimulated for the first time by theoretical reflection, it then ramifies into various practical concerns for using and arguing about words, and becomes most generally evident in the greatest literature of the period.

That the shift from referential to relational semantics has been made independently by a variety of thinkers in a variety of domains both then and now is what makes it interesting and offers persuasive evidence for its validity. In both eras, however, the perceptual and conceptual revolution entailed by the shift remains proposed and not achieved. It need hardly be said that the theories of relational semantics I have outlined, despite their wide acceptance and growing influence, remain highly controversial—as indeed they did in the Renaissance. The belief in that single, solid world of preconstituted things for our minds to picture, our languages to represent, and our sciences to control dies very hard. One reason it does so is the prestige that empirical science has acquired by its great success at that control. On the other hand, it has been increasingly questioned, at least since Heisenberg enunciated his famous "uncertainty principle," whether that control in any way depends on the "accurate representations" that are supposed to correspond with nature and yield objectively certain knowledge.[18]

---

[18] The great questioner is of course Thomas S. Kuhn, *The Structure of Scientific Revolutions*, 2d ed. (Chicago, 1970); a more radical critique is Paul Feyerabend, *Against Method* (London, 1975). These and other challenges are discussed and defended by Rorty, pp. 344–58. It is worth noting that Kuhn

The confidence in such correspondent knowledge, which of course requires a referential semantics, was being newly formed in the later Renaissance. And its formation was indeed a powerful motive to close down the kind of linguistic investigation that developed a relational semantics and to encourage other kinds—notably the seventeenth-century search for a universal, more perfectly transparent language and grammar. Intellectual historians of a Whiggish persuasion have long been fond of telling the heroic story of the emergence of empirical science during the Renaissance. At the present time, when we are somewhat disillusioned by the results of that science and distrustful of its methodological premises, I shall be telling a very different story of how the Renaissance preoccupation with language developed, in theory and practice, semantic premises that contested and contradicted those of that science.

But there is, I believe, a deeper reason for the abortion of the revolution proposed by the shift from referential to relational semantics—a reason that underlies the scientific faith in a self-contained object-world that language is obliged to represent. Such a world is, after all, far older than the observations, techniques, and dogmas that have facilitated its exploitation since Bacon and Galileo. Empirical science had only to build upon and so greatly reinforce the dualistic picture of the world that already lay, as Wittgenstein observed, in language itself—that is, in the referential semantics assumed by the traditional vocabulary of discourse. Saussure, we recall, could find no term to replace "sign." And here is the immense difficulty of making the shift: it requires us to criticize and find alternatives for the very categories, given to us by language, that we use to talk about language.[19] We cannot redescribe meaning as an activity

---

confesses a general debt to, and Feyerabend makes a pleased if belated discovery of, B. L. Whorf, who saw language as constitutive of more than many are willing to accept.

[19] For example, that one can use the verb "mean" to mean "refer" does not entail that all, or indeed any, meaning is reference. Once I find out (by asking, "What do you mean?") the subject matter of your utterance, I have still to find out its meaning, i.e., what you're saying *about* that subject matter. Likewise,

of construing relations if we take the semantic behavior of words to be that of signs. Saussure could and did—but only by so redefining "sign" that its traditional behavior all but disappeared. The word as sign arbitrarily and by itself stands for or refers to something elsewhere that is not arbitrary at all but given by nature, which is its meaning. For Saussure, the word as sign arbitrarily, but only in relation to other signs, stands for or refers to something equally arbitrary, which is determined only differentially by its relation to other signs, thus has no "positive content," and is not its meaning. Its arbitrariness is all that remains of the traditional "sign," since its operation of signifying (standing for or referring to) is denuded of its usual ontological postulate by Saussure's careful confinement of that operation within the sign itself, between its constituent parts. The reference is not made to the thing (in the world) by the name (in language) but rather to the word's concept by the word's sound (both in language). Despite the fact that Saussure has modified the sign virtually to the vanishing point, eliminating the ontic status of its referent and completely reversing its semantic role, the term remains because there is no other.

The term remains, and with it the risk that careless readers will take it, as usual, to locate meaning in some extralingual elsewhere—anywhere but where Saussure insisted it was. In due course, we shall see how Lorenzo Valla and Martin Luther coped in their different ways with the same enormous difficulty of redescribing meaning as an activity other than "signification" in a vocabulary that had already described it as that, and only that.[20] Why, having defined it practically out of ex-

---

that one can also use the verb "mean" to mean "intend" does not entail that meaning is intention. Language, however, is always *inviting* us to find its meaning beyond itself—elsewhere, in things or minds.

[20] This difficulty is of course a major theme in Wittgenstein's *Philosophical Investigations* (hereafter *P.I.*), tr. G.E.M. Anscombe, 3d ed. (Oxford, 1968), to which conventional reference is made by section number. The "picture" that language inexorably repeats (115) assures us that we are "tracing . . . the

istence, didn't Saussure get rid of "sign"? Why, if there is no other term, couldn't he content himself with none? Having shown that the semantic operation of words is the opposite from that of signs, why couldn't he say that words are not signs at all, but simply words? Signs do not constitute what they refer to; words do. Saussure made this vital distinction clear, but went right on calling words "signs." For his pioneering purposes, there were practical and tactical advantages in so doing; but his own discomfort about it is symptomatic of the larger questions: whence comes the pressure to exile meanings from language, to see words as signs representing a semantic elsewhere? Why does the dualistic model of meaning and picture of the world lie in our vocabulary of discourse? Why has language historically persisted in misrepresenting itself as representing things?

★

The answer to these questions is to be found, I believe, in the ambivalent feelings human beings have about their supposedly unique faculty of speech: we both fear and revere the power of words. Separately or in combination, these opposite motives—detesting the power of speech or worshipping it—can produce the same kind of semantic theory that exiles meaning from language into whatever realm words are taken to stand for. But the very notion of "standing for"—the ancient identification of the word as a sign—is a displacement of the power intuitively felt in the use of words themselves. Long before we have notions of reference or representation, we have intuitions of "correspondence"—not in the sense of a statement matching a picture, but in the sense of the magical identity of the word and the thing. That the latter sense develops into the former is not accidental. The power of language, first felt as the immediate, magical control of objects or persons, becomes in our philosophical and literary traditions defused, diffused, and

---

thing's nature" while we are "merely tracing round the frame through which we look at it" (114).

displaced into other realms by theories of reference. The clear-
est evidence of this displacement is that such theories inevitably require, and some even assert, a connection between words
and things that is, simply, magic.[21] The history of referential
semantics shows that it does not explain how language means,
but either escapes or celebrates its power to do so.

Despite our familiarity with the variety of sophisticated
metalanguages available today, we need to remind ourselves
that many of the feelings we still have about the use of words,
the ways we respond to language in daily life, do not differ in
kind from those of Homeric heroes or Old Testament patri-
archs. Though we no longer recite our titles and genealogy
when we are introduced, the importance of nomenclature is
still sufficient to command large expenditures for investigation by public relations firms and market researchers. And
though our culture no longer regards anything with sufficient
awe or fear to prohibit the pronouncing of its name (as the
names of God and his angels were unpronounceable by the ancient Hebrews), certain words are still taboo in many circumstances. The flouting of such taboos in the American and European student protests of the late sixties is the most vivid
recent usage of words that elicited the ancient and violent terrors of the curse. Both the cogency of the attack and the fury
of the response are comprehended in Wittgenstein's remark
that language is "a form of life."[22] For it embodies and trans-
mits the rituals and codes that in part constitute the life of a society. It does this, moreover, by giving order to the exterior
world of objects in which the society exists, so that the deliberate and public violation of a linguistic taboo is a direct assault

[21] A convincing attack on referential (which he calls "modern empiricist")
theories is made by Bernard Harrison, who observes incidentally what I shall
sketch historically: that such theories "postulate a purely magical connection
between *explicans* and *explicandum*": *Meaning and Structure: An Essay in the Philosophy of Language* (New York, 1972), p. 105. A much fuller historical account
is given by Roy Harris in a meticulous analysis of Western conceptions of language, which he classifies as "surrogationalist" (referential), "instrumentalist"
and "contractualist": *The Language-Makers* (London, 1980).

[22] *P.I.* 19.

not on issues or policies, or even individuals, but on the whole system of order in the society, the entire form of its life. If the thing is forbidden in genteel society, the word that names it is forbidden too. If to pronounce a name is to summon up or control an object, the name of God will be unpronounceable. Speak of the devil, and he will appear.

The immemorial sense of a magical connection between words and things endures today not only in the myths and rituals of preliterate cultures.[23] It also persists as an explicit principle in the main tradition of English poetry and criticism for the last two centuries.[24] The Romantic tradition, of course, does not fear this magic that converts word to thing—it glorifies it. The magic is worked by the genius of the poet, who is seen as uniquely capable of creating in words an "image" or "symbol" that is itself some kind of transcendent reality. This implicit self-flattery of the poet (and by later extension of the critic) was not, however, apparent in the most famous and influential statement of this view—Coleridge's definition of "a Symbol" as "characterized . . . above all by the translucence of the Eternal through and in the Temporal. It always partakes of the Reality which it renders intelligible; and while it enunciates the whole, abides itself as a living part in that Unity, of which it is the representative."[25] The part embodies the whole, the sign the signified: it *is* what it represents. A contemporary critic in the tradition sees this identity as characteristic of poetry itself, which is a "magically monistic effigy that is not merely an empty sign through which we are directed to things, but rather both the sign and the substantive thing itself."[26] The literal "miracle" that accomplishes this unification

[23] See Robin Horton, "African Thought and Western Science," in *Rationality*, ed. Wilson, pp. 155–56.

[24] The tradition and its insistence on linguistic magic have been well outlined by Frank Kermode, *Romantic Image* (1957; rpt. London, 1971).

[25] Samuel Taylor Coleridge, "The Statesman's Manual" (1816), in *Lay Sermons*, ed. R. J. White (Princeton, 1972), p. 30.

[26] Murray Krieger, *A Window to Criticism: Shakespeare's Sonnets and Modern Poetics* (Princeton, 1964), p. 6.

was, before its post-Romantic secularization, the Word of God, about which Coleridge was speaking when he defined the "Symbol." The vocabulary of the critic—the image that is both "sign" and "thing"—is as old and as durable as St. Augustine; its traditional use in Western Christianity was to describe the incarnation and the sacraments.

The persistence in both our developed, postliterate culture and traditional, preliterate ones of the magical correspondence between words and things is due, most simply and fundamentally, to our continuing recognition of the quite mundane power of language to affect us in ways that seem to defy explanation. Whether in poems, obscenities, religious rituals, or everyday life, words activate our adrenaline, our fantasies and terrors. They are in fact so potent that we cannot believe it. That mere words, evanescent sounds in thin air, should be capable of so disturbing and delighting us seems impossible. Hence the wishful rationalization of the nursery jingle: "Sticks and stones will break my bones, but names will never hurt me." We fly to a spurious consolation in the palpable solidity of *things*. They, not words, are where the power really is. And it is from this very dubious point—the incredulity, distrust, and ambivalence we feel toward the power of words—that theory begins. In our moods of cool skepticism (like Plato) or impatient rebellion (like Juliet) we ask, "What's in a name?" And we have almost never had the courage to answer, "Everything."

Such ambivalence seems to me to account for the prevalence of reference theories of meaning long after other ways of analyzing the operation of language become available, and also to suggest the inadequacy of those theories. For to get meaning out of language and into "things" of whatever kind creates more problems than it solves. It creates the dualistic gap between words and things that no theory can bridge without recourse, overt or concealed, to the felt, magical power that—once displaced from words to things—prevents the theory from explaining how language works. Notions of semantic reference have proliferated in Western culture in symbiotic confusion with our perception of the magical potency of the *logos*: reference, as we shall see, requires magic. Magic, as the *felt* correspondence of word to thing, simply gets transposed into the *theorized* correspondence of two separate orders of being. The naive magic that frankly seeks to exercise the power of words over the world has at least the virtue of not dividing them. The sophisticated magic that seeks to exorcise that power by making that division must then exercise itself in backhanded ways in order to overcome the division it has made. Our ambivalence toward the power of words has produced semantic theories that either deny that power or attach it to something else. Such theories are caught in a vicious circle of their own making, basing themselves on an absolute division that then requires a reconnection they cannot rationally make—at which point magic enters to assert it.

The paradigm of this procedure in the West is the Socratic method of defining terms. The questions are of course formulated so as to posit an objective ontology at the outset— *what* is "beauty," "virtue," etc.—and the long debate begins on the ontic status of abstract universals as opposed to that of particular objects. The method is to go through the characteristics of objects to which the quality is attributed, seeking some shared features to be hypostatized into an Idea or Form. The meaning of a word is presumed to be the thing it names; therefore the abstract term must, to be meaningful, name some kind of "thing." Simple though this explanation may appear, it very quickly runs into epistemological trouble. For merely to know names is not to know things (*Cratylus* 436–39),[27] since the proper objects of knowledge are not particular things but the hypostatized "things," the existence of which is required by the initial questions. Thus language has meaning by referring to things, but can arrive at knowledge only by referring to a certain class of things, one which indeed presents formidable

[27] The Platonic texts used are *The Dialogues*, tr. B. Jowett, 3d ed. (New York, 1892), vols. I, II, IV; and *Epistles*, tr. Glenn R. Morrow (New York, 1962).

difficulties to being known, since it consists (in this world) of "things" like shadows on a wall.

Plato could hardly be a better example of ambivalence to language: as a poet, he brilliantly exploited the dramatic and fictional resources of dialogue, parable, and myth; as a moralist and political theorist, he had a profound distrust of the other skilled users of language in his society, the poets and the Sophists. Seen in this light, Plato's whole dualistic line of thought is an attempt to set real knowledge beyond mere opinion, to preserve real meaning from the mere "jugglers" of words (*Gorgias* 459–61; *Sophist* 232–35). Plato himself makes the connection between his entire epistemology and its concomitant distrust of language in the seventh *Epistle*, which draws the further consequence that such knowledge of real being as we can glimpse cannot possibly be written down. The "weakness of language"—its alliance with the mere properties as opposed to the being of objects (342e–43a)—will not permit it. Real knowledge is finally mystical; it is an illumination arrived at in the dialectic between master and disciple, which though it may begin with rational discourse must ultimately pass beyond it, as Socrates so often passes in the dialogues from argument to myth. In one such myth he deplores the invention of letters because the written word and its apprehension merely by silent reading cannot hope to achieve the mutual enlightenment of the living dialogue: books can fall on deaf minds, they are defenseless (*Phaedrus* 275–76).

If individual words are taken as the semantic units of language, and if things are posited to exist quite apart from words, and if meaning is sought in those things, then a theory of meaning will have to explain the connection between them and words. That some words somehow refer to some sort of things (leaving aside the begged question of their ontic status) is obvious. That this reference, or "signification," or "representation" constitutes the meaning of the words is what needs explaining. The word means the thing: but how does it do so? What kind of relationship is this and how does it work? Even at the lowest of Plato's levels—the designation by the word of the particular sensory object the knowing of which is not real knowledge—this relationship is problematic. Do words mean things by virtue of having some intrinsic relation to the things; are they "natural" reflections of the objects they designate? Or is the connection wholly arbitrary and conventional? Socrates rather enjoys demonstrating in the *Cratylus* that both can be the case. (Some semanticists and psychologists are still demonstrating it.) If the connection of word to thing cannot be firmly determined even in the case of ordinary objects, it will be totally elusive in the case of the extraordinary ones. The very existence of the latter is necessitated in the first place only by the assumption that seeks the meaning of words in things. If we cannot find a thing in the world to point at in order to make our use of words like "beauty" meaningful, then the things must be posited to exist elsewhere. Not only is the theory circular, but it simply cannot establish the required connection, which can only be supplied by the mystical process of mutual enlightenment. The best it can offer is an assurance that if we spend enough time in conversation with Socratic sages we may be able to glimpse the Forms, and then our words will be connected, however imperfectly, with their proper objects and hence have meaning. The connection, in short, is magic. It is above and beyond natural processes, human speech, and reason. The connection in this kind of theory always has to be magic, which is why reference theories can explain nothing. They require a connection that must simply be asserted. In this case, and in some others, the connection is relocated first—shifted from words/sensory objects to words/ extrasensory objects. But it does not matter where it is located; nor does it matter if the connection is sought not with objects but with "images" or "ideas" (in the Lockean sense). To locate meaning elsewhere than in language is to begin an infinite regress, which can be halted only by supernatural fiat.[28]

Just such a fiat was shortly to be supplied, of course, in the

---

[28] Taylor gives a clear example of such inevitable regression in the case of mental images: *Explanation and Meaning*, pp. 143–44.

Greek-inspired Christian doctrine of the divinely creative *logos*. Plato's pervasive dualism as well as his ethical bias were especially appeaing to that equally ambivalent and brilliant professional teacher of language, St. Augustine. Disturbed, like Plato, by the egotism and abuses of popular oratory, Augustine discovered, unlike Plato, a kind of language that had a special guarantee of its meaning. Ironically, he discovered it in just the form that Plato denied it could take—in the written scriptures. And he found that it could best be apprehended in just the way that Socrates most doubted—by silent reading.[29] Augustine described the operation of scriptural language in Book Two of *De Doctrina Christiana* by adopting from Latin rhetoric the standard dichotomy of "sign" and "thing." A sign is anything that makes something else come to mind. Some signs occur in nature and some are "given," among which are words. Ordinary words simply signify things, whereby they have meaning (literal and figurative); but the words of the Holy Spirit *are* the things themselves. What is more, those things can in turn signify other things: only God can use things the way people use words. The Bible is the only book in which things—the objects whose designation confers meaning—can in turn designate other things, by which they are made doubly meaningful. In this way Augustine presents scriptural allegory and typology as the implicit models of maximally achieved meaning, achieved of course by the divine will and located in the things that will has created. Though these models offer interesting and contradictory opportunities for interpreting meaning, their theoretical assumptions are clearly Platonic and result in the view of human language as mimetic in Plato's

---

[29] In *De Magistro* xi–xii (*Concerning the Teacher*, tr. George G. Leckie [New York, 1938]), verbal instruction is directly opposed to inward illumination. In *De Trinitate* xv.xx (*Later Works*, tr. John Burnaby [Philadelphia, 1955]), the Word of God, as true knowledge, is silent thought. See also his famous description of Ambrose reading (*Confessions* vi.iii) and the analysis of Joseph Mazzeo, "St. Augustine's Rhetoric of Silence," in *Renaissance and Seventeenth-Century Studies* (New York, 1964).

sense: our language acquires meaning by referring, however imperfectly, to "images of an eternal and intelligible reality."[30]

The flight from words to things, with God as the ultimate magic to assert the connection that constitutes meaning, has now established the theoretical framework within which language will be discussed until the eighteenth century. The guarantee provided by identifying the authority of the necessary magic effectively sidesteps the crucial issue of the connection between words and whatever else is assumed to supply their meaning. With meaning thus given, as conferred by reference, semantics can proceed to debate the nature of the something else referred to. Theory has no need to question the connection, but merely relocates what it is a connection to.

The first major relocation occurs when late medieval nominalists replace universals with particulars as the objects that confer meaning. These philosophers took a detailed interest in the logic of quantifiers (which endeared them to twentieth-century analytic philosophy) and of grammar; but the whole polemic of substance-concepts in which they were engaged precluded any real inquiry into meaning.[31] Their argument with the realists was conducted on the mutually shared ground of referential semantics: the only questions concerned the ontic status of the objects to which words referred and the exact "mode" of that reference.[32] Indeed, the nominalists denied Plato's ontology as well as the sillier semantic consequences drawn from it by earlier medieval writers.[33] They also took formal notice of "syncategorematic" terms (like prepositions and conjunctions) that were seen not to refer. But their pri-

[30] Mazzeo, p. 23; on ambivalence of interpretive procedure, p. 17.

[31] Jan Pinborg, *Logik und Semantik im Mittelalter: Ein Überblick* (Stuttgart, 1972), p. 179.

[32] Armed with Frege's solution to the problem of how "signs of generality" signify, Michael Dummett can criticize the solution "which attributed to them the power of standing for objects" offered by the nominalist kinds of *suppositio: Frege: Philosophy of Language* (London, 1973), p. 20.

[33] For example, by Fredegisius of Tours, who insisted "that there must be something corresponding to the word 'nothing' ": F. C. Copleston, *A History of Medieval Philosophy* (New York, 1972), pp. 69–70.

mary effort with respect to language was to elaborate kinds of
suppositio, which, whatever other confusions surround it,
seems to be the notion of reference as "standing for."[34] That a
word was a sign whose meaning was the object or concept signified remained the unquestioned basis of their concentration
on the nature and extent of that object or concept. Taking *significatio* for granted, they created, with *suppositio*, a taxonomy
of referents and ways of referring. Their effort assumed the semantic operation of language as mimesis, attempting only to
make its imitation of the posited ontological order and/or the
universal concepts in the mind far more transparent and rig-
orous than it was for Plato.[35]

The same effort to make language a more perfect mirror of
the wholly separate object-world was resumed by empirical
science in the seventeenth century. The new intensity of the effort was in part a reaction to all the contrary tendencies—the
various challenges to referential semantics that will be chronicled in this book—that emerged in the Renaissance. But the
dominant assumption remains that the meaning of words is to
be sought and found outside language itself—above, beyond,

---

[34] Copleston gives as succinct an account as seems possible of the doctrine
in William of Sherwood and Peter of Spain, pp. 234–36, and in Ockham, pp.
244–46. The more thorough survey of Norman Kretzmann describes "the divisions of supposition" as "syntax-dependent referential functions of a term's
signification": "History of Semantics," in *The Encyclopedia of Philosophy*, ed.
Paul Edwards (New York, 1967), VII, 372. Another scholar, however, denies
that any single definition can be given of *suppositio* because of its embedding in
obscure dichotomies and the chaotically contradictory uses of the verb *suppo-
nere*, which he lists: Oswald Ducrot, "Quelques implications linguistiques de
la théorie médiévale de la supposition," in *History of Linguistic Thought*, ed.
Parret, pp. 189–227. In the same volume, Pinborg takes *suppositio* as "approx-
imately" reference, and attempts to distinguish its forms: "Some Problems of
Semantic Representation in Medieval Logic" (pp. 254–78); these are seldom
clear, in part because he uses "supposit" as if it were an English verb.

[35] Apart from the nominalists', the other late medieval effort to do this was
that of the speculative grammarians, or *modistae*, in whom its absurdity is
much clearer: they simply asserted that the logical and ontological structure of
the world *was* that of the parts of speech. See the temperate strictures of Copleston, pp. 269–70, and the more thorough critique of Jacques Chomarat,
Grammaire et rhétorique chez Erasme (Paris, 1981), pp. 215–23.

or through it. Neither the variation in what confers meaning (particular objects, universal concepts, mental images) nor the variation in the manner of the conferral ("signification" by divine sanction, "representation" by mental reflection)[36] alters the theoretical conception of meaning as reference. And the connection required by the notion of reference remains unexplored; when one postulated connecting agent withdraws from the semantic field, another replaces it, as divine magic gives way to the mental magic of the visual picture. The direct correspondence of word to thing assured by God becomes the indirect correspondence of word to thing via the memory-image of sensations (the Lockean "idea"). The philosophical changes between the realism and nominalism of the Middle Ages and the empiricism and rationalism of the seventeenth and eighteenth centuries are considerable; but they change nothing at the level of semantic theory, where words are still presumed to mean by referring to whatever lies over the dualistic divide.

The formal discipline that deals most comprehensively with language from antiquity to the eighteenth century perpetuates the same theory, not as a philosophical presumption, but as a pedagogical principle. Rhetoric, conceived in the Middle Ages and the Renaissance as a decorative art, regards meaning as separable from and prior to the words that "clothe" it. As the art of designing that clothing, rhetoric directly exploits the widest range of the powers of language—and is ambivalent about the very verbal skills it seeks to inculcate. Rhetoric never quite recovers from the distrust and scorn that Plato had for the Sophists. Even when its prestige is expanded by Renaissance humanists, their revived insistence that the good speaker must necessarily be a good man betrays all the anxieties about the use of words that result in the dualistic exile of meaning from the treacherous medium that expresses it.[37] Beside the

---

[36] On the visual, mentalist mode of representation in the seventeenth and eighteenth centuries, see Michel Foucault, *The Order of Things* (New York, 1970).

[37] The ambivalence of rhetoric toward its own aims will be discussed in chapter 4.

linguistic dichotomy of word/thing or sign/signified stands the rhetorical one of style/thought or manner/matter, neatly lined up with the other dualisms that constitute the theoretical frameworks of ontology (human/divine, flesh/spirit), epistemology (sensible/intelligible), and moral psychology (passion/reason). Although the balance of power between rhetoric, grammar, and logic shifts at the Renaissance, and although rhetoric in practice uncovers problems not accountable for in its own terms, those terms persist in formulating the relationship of language to meaning as cosmetic and not constitutive.

The same terms continue to prevail even when the Romantics reverse this tradition, embrace the power of words instead of dreading it, and come to regard language as constitutive of meaning. The importance of this point can scarcely be overrated, for its implications continue to dominate much present inquiry into language. The Romantic revolution in semantics did indeed insist that language made meaning; but it did so only by reaffirming the ancient dichotomy of word/thing and by relocating the magic that connected them. Thomas De Quincey clearly summarizes this development when he writes of "style" that it

is contemplated as a thing separable from the thoughts; in fact as the *dress* of thoughts . . . But there arises a case entirely different, where style cannot be regarded as a *dress* or alien covering, but where style becomes the *incarnation* of the thoughts. The human body is not the dress or apparel of the human spirit: far more mysterious is the mode of their union. . . . Imagery is sometimes not the mere alien apparelling of a thought, and of a nature to be detached from the thought, but is the coefficient that, being superadded to something else, absolutely *makes* the thought as a *third* and separate existence.[38]

An admirable insight, versions of which still abound in literary criticism; but its very terms perpetuate the traditional dualistic vocabulary and its requisite magic. Monism must be forced by fiat from dualism; a third thing must be produced from the

[38] Thomas De Quincey, *Selected Essays on Rhetoric*, ed. Frederick Burwick (Carbondale, Ill., 1967), p. 262. The italics are De Quincey's.

"mysterious" union of the first two. John M. Ellis has analyzed the mystification of the term "style" that results in modern criticism and linguistics when the dichotomy it implies is
being rejected.[39] In De Quincey's comment, however, it is rejected only in the case of a special kind of language—literature.
He admits cases, presumably in ordinary language, where, indeed, style is clothing. Literature (in the later tradition, mainly
poetry) is privileged. And its privilege resonates with religious
veneration: "style" is "incarnation," the archetypal assertion
that spirit can become body, word become thing. What we
might call the Augustinian circle is complete: the special semantic character of the Bible, whence Coleridge drew his famous "Symbol," has simply been transferred to literature.
This transference in the realm of semantic theory quite naturally parallels the other and better known ones: poetry becomes religion; poets become differentiated from ordinary
folk by the possession of sacred sensibilities; critics become
priests, initiates into these mysteries, and purveyors thereof to
the rest of mankind.

We continue today to suffer exhortations to regard the use
of language in literature as somehow different in kind from all
its other uses. The paradox of ascribing such mysterious privilege to literature, its producers, and its professional interpreters is that the privilege is secured by a cancellation of just that
semantic power that ordinary language constantly exhibits.
The myth of the sacred—the necessary magic that makes
words constitute meaning only by converting them into
things—achieved its reductio ad absurdum in Symbolist poetics, where words were treated as if they *were* things. That is,
their status as lexical units and their semantic combination by
means of syntax were ignored as much as possible; they were
presumed merely to have the same "physical presence" as discrete hunks of stuff.[40] The analogue of this position in modern

[39] *The Theory of Literary Criticism: A Logical Analysis* (Berkeley, 1974), pp.
172–75.

[40] Kermode analyzes the Symbolist impatience with "discourse" and the
wish to write poetry "with something other than words," *Romantic Image*, p.

criticism is the endless repetition of Archibald MacLeish's dictum, "A poem should not mean / But be." Just as, taken in one direction, Augustine's rhetoric (the silent apprehension of significant things) eliminates words, Symbolist semantics eliminates meaning. These paradoxes are partly explicable, I think, as the expression of our fundamental ambivalence toward language: to delight in it can be at the same time to destroy it.

To say this is not to ignore the powerful hermeneutics that Augustine bequeathed to the Christian world, or to claim that Symbolist verse is meaningless. It is rather to observe that the logical implications of the referential vocabulary are to annihilate what it sets out to illumine, a consequence that demonstrates, if nothing else, its inadequacy as theory. These implications, moreover, were drawn by believers in the respective traditions, not by hostile critics. Protestantism, a movement powerfully inspired by Augustine, produced such diverse adherents as Robert Browne, who wished to dispose of both logic and rhetoric, and, by a more circuitous path, Brigham Young, who wished to abolish language altogether.[41] The Symbolists gave us Imagism, Vorticism, Dada, and more recently the *nouveau roman*. However the particular programs of these various movements may be importantly related to their social and economic or political circumstances, they still share a way of regarding meaning that either relocates it out of existence or seeks explicitly to destroy it.

These historical developments in semantic theory have particular importance for students of literature. It is a supreme and unfortunate irony that the ancient referential dualism should have gained implicit dominance in belletristic contexts around the turn of the nineteenth century, at just the time

---

151. The same dislike of discourse and a similar presumption that words should evoke the naked, unrelated surfaces of "things" persist in the avant-garde program of such writers as Alain Robbe-Grillet, *For a New Novel*, tr. Richard Howard (New York, 1965), pp. 19–22 et passim.

[41] Browne, *Treatise upon the 23. of Matthewe* (Middelburg, 1582) in *The Writings of Robert Harrison and Robert Browne*, ed. Peel and Carlson (London, 1953), pp. 175–84; Young, *Journal of Discourses* I (Liverpool, 1854), 70.

when it was being abandoned by other students of language. The Romantic alienation of the artist from his society had as its counterpart in the English scholarly world the mutual estrangement of philosophers, philologists, and literary critics. In the linguistic researches of Stewart, Monboddo, and Sir William Jones, the representational model of meaning was being replaced by notions of structure, of contextual use, of the relation between utterance and hearer, of rule-governed formal systems.[42] But few if any of these ideas, which were to become the stock-in-trade of linguistic and critical philosophy in our own century, found expression in discussions of literature. The subsequent Victorian hostility between "science" and "culture" made it increasingly unlikely that students with different interests in the same subject, language, would learn anything from each other. One consequence of this antagonized separation of academic disciplines is the survival in literary criticism of theoretical assumptions and assertions that are embarrassing because they have elsewhere been so long discredited. To describe the operation of language in poetry as the mystical conversion of sign to thing is to offer exactly the same kind of explanation that is offered in describing plague and famine as God's punishments for sin. Both explanations invoke the causal action of a mysterious force: that of genius or the deity. Both may of course be true, since they are neither demonstrable nor falsifiable. And for this reason, they are equally empty as explanations. The only difference between them is that the former still passes current among literary scholars, while the latter could not be offered with a straight face to an audience of physicians or nutritionists.

I have argued that reference theories of meaning require an assertion of mystery to reunite what they divide, and also that they ultimately lead to the obliteration of what they purport to describe. I have further attributed the prevalence of such falla-

[42] These developments are well described by Stephen K. Land, *From Signs to Propositions: The Concept of Form in Eighteenth-Century Semantic Theory* (London, 1974).

cious theories to the general ambivalence in Western culture toward the power of language and, more specifically, to the post-Romantic transference of semantic uniqueness from Scripture to secular poetry, along with the concurrent fragmentation of academic disciplines. The impulse to distrust the power of language or to worship it—in the former case to find its meaning in some other thing, in the latter to find it in the word-become-thing—seems to me the root of that "bewitchment of our intelligence by means of language" against which Wittgenstein called philosophy to battle.[43]

The consequences of that bewitchment have been the dualisms that isolate meaning from language and language from the world. And the refusal of these consequences is the perceptual and conceptual revolution proposed by the shift from referential to relational semantics as it first occurred in several cultural domains in the Renaissance and as it is reoccurring in even more of them today. The dualistic picture of the world and the dualistic model of meaning are like the chicken and the egg: they propagate each other so that we cannot tell which came first—nor does it matter. The consequence of referential semantics is also its premise; it implies the divided universe that it postulates. As a contemporary philosopher, W. Haas, has written,

If we wish to explain meaning by "extralingual reference," then we must insist on a complete and permanent dualism of two orders of things—linguistic expressions on the one hand, and extralingual things on the other. We must accept the fiction of *isolated references*. This dualism cannot be substantiated in any way; and it makes no difference whether the extralingual things are ideas in the mind or physical facts. For "reference" to make its sign-producing link, words and other things must be supposed to be permanently divided. . . .

---

[43] *P.I.* 109. Ellis's seminal book, *The Theory of Literary Criticism* (which builds on Wittgenstein's later work), has demonstrated not only how the dualism of reference theories has produced a futile series of false choices in the theory of interpretation but also how it prevents much contemporary work in linguistics from being useful to literary study: pp. 9–10, 203–05 et passim.

there is no such division, hence no such link, hence no theory of meaning in terms of such a link.

What there is instead, as Haas goes on to say, is an "active interplay" between words and things, which both constitutes meanings and shapes the world.[44] Such "interplay" is the multiplicity of relations in relational semantics, which are not conducted by divine mysteries or profane mystifications between two separate orders of being, but which are constructed in language by its users as a social and historical practice that simultaneously forms ourselves and the worlds we inhabit. We need no magic to bring together what is already joined: the expression and its meaning, the word and the thing. To call this creative commerce "interplay" suggests, of course, Wittgenstein's famous and repeated characterization of language as a game: though made possible by rules, it is not everywhere circumscribed by them, so that the possible strategies of play are unbounded.[45] The freedom of individual players is accommodated, but only by the mutual acceptance of communal constraints, which can be altered by gradual evolution or conscious choice. Moreover, any game can be played, and can be seen and described as being played, well or badly. Wittgenstein's ludic analogy and Saussure's economic one are the most richly suggestive redescriptions of how language means which I have called relational semantics. It will be observed that while this kind of theory excludes referential semantics as mistaken, it also accounts for it: reference is a game that can be played, an economy that can be established. We may then decide that the game is not worth the candle nor the commodity worth its price.

There are other descriptions of the creative commerce made visible by regarding language not as cosmetic to but as consti-

---

[44] W. Haas, pp. 217, 223. The philosophical importance of Haas' work as a linguist is well outlined by the editors of his Festschrift, D. J. Allerton, Edward Carney, and David Holdcroft, *Function and Context in Linguistic Analysis* (Cambridge, 1979), pp. 4–21.

[45] *P.I.* 7, 23, 65–71, 83–86, 654–56.

tutive of meaning. One of them describes language as dreaming our desires.[46] That is, different languages along with all their different uses—from repeating a myth to replicating an experiment—are systems that simultaneously articulate both the designs of a human community upon the world and its wishes for itself. Seen in this light, the game of reference is a dream of our desires for certain knowledge of and privileged access to a monolithic reality. The traditional referential vocabulary of discourse is the dream of Western languages about themselves, what they aspire to but cannot attain. We may sympathize with the aspiration without accepting it as fact. What is to be gained by the shift from referential to relational semantics—along with a genuine explanation of how language works—is an awareness of the multiplicity of the functions of language that, by refusing absolute privilege to any single one, would help to make our culture less schizophrenic. To ac-

---

[46] As Susanne Langer argues in a fine essay, "The Lord of Creation," *Fortune* (Jan. 1944), pp. 140–142, based on her *Philosophy in a New Key* (Cambridge, Mass., 1942), Ch. 5. Her version of the constitutive view derives in turn from Ernst Cassirer, *The Philosophy of Symbolic Forms, Vol. I: Language*, tr. Ralph Manheim (New Haven, 1953; 1st ed. 1923). The most powerful recent development of it comes from the German tradition of hermeneutics: Hans-Georg Gadamer, *Truth and Method* (New York, 1975; 1st ed. 1960), the implications of whose work have been well developed by David Couzens Hoy, *The Critical Circle: Literature, History and Philosophical Hermeneutics* (Berkeley, 1978). A brilliant demonstration that all seeing is seeing "as," and that philosophy has historically attributed the structure of language to that of the world is made by Colin Murray Turbayne, *The Myth of Metaphor*, rev. ed. (Columbia, S.C., 1970). One of the most influential treatments in English of the idea that languages do not copy but articulate "the world of our experience" is that of E. H. Gombrich, *Art and Illusion*, (n.p., 1960).

In linguistics proper, the constitutive view (a minority position) offered by Saussure and developed by J. R. Firth, is perhaps best known from the work of Benjamin Lee Whorf, *Language, Thought, and Reality*, ed. John B. Carroll (Cambridge, Mass., 1956). Attacks from various angles—but all in the interest of a more "creative" concept of meaning than the referential—have recently been made on the dominant Chomskian school by Harrison, *Meaning and Structure*; Ian Robinson, *The New Grammarians' Funeral* (Cambridge, 1975); Geoffrey Sampson, *Making Sense* (Oxford, 1980); and Roy Harris, *The Language Myth* (London, 1981).

knowledge the different purposes of different discourses is to perceive, for example, that science and art are not incompatible ways of knowing the world, and that the spurious titles to privilege each has asserted impoverish both by enclosure in a false autonomy. Science as the sole purveyor of facts—answerable to no social control—and art as the exclusive supplier of values—responsible to no community—are games of reference gone haywire, claiming for the objects of their discourses a transcendental status that declares them untouchable by ordinary discourse. Such lofty privilege is made immediately untenable by the realization that discourses *form* their objects, and that ordinary discourse is perfectly capable of examining the purposes for which these discourses have been conducted. Such examination, much of which has been made of science, would free it from the positivist delusion that it is neutral and value-free. Such examination, rather less of which has been made of art, would free it from the aesthetic delusion that it is autonomous, free from social pressure or political interest. To see languages as constituting meanings is to see that science determines values and that art constructs facts—that neither could possibly function otherwise, since determining values and constructing facts are what all discourse simultaneously does.

I return briefly to the case of literary criticism, which relational semantics would free from its pretension to assert the sacred status of its objects. The modern view of poetry does this by invoking the "miracle" of the word becoming substance,"that magically monistic effigy that is not merely an empty sign through which we are directed to things, but rather both the sign and the substantive thing itself." Taken by itself, this statement of monism by magic precludes either analysis or argument; it can only be opposed by a counter-statement. If Krieger says that poetry is a mystic effigy, I may say that it is an emanation of the World-Soul; someone else might say that it is the diversion of a decadent bourgeoisie. Evidence of a sort for all these assertions may be found in various qualities or characteristics of poetry that we might select.

We can point in the first case to the multiple significance of puns or metaphors, in the second to the continued use throughout the ages of sundry archetypal "motifs," in the third to the presentation of certain social values. Insofar as statements of this kind purport to be definitions (if their form be taken as an identity sentence), their procedure is incorrect.[47] Insofar as they are descriptions, they are just like the proverbial blind men touching different parts of the elephant—one could hardly imagine they were describing the same thing. The lists of "qualities" each might adduce remain mutually exclusive, providing no way by which any list could refute, support, or be at all relevant to another. And insofar as they purport to supply a semantics for poetry, they merely, after the manner of their kind, locate its meaning elsewhere. No matter whether they find it in the operation of a magic symbolism, or of a metaphysical principle, or of a socioeconomic process, it is placed beyond language and beyond debate.

We must, however, put such assertions in their context, and ask how Krieger's succinct version of Romantic literary semantics functions in his actual treatment of Shakespeare's poems. We find that he traces patterns of sound, of imagery, and thematic ideas, some of which are seen to emerge from aesthetic and ethical traditions of the Renaissance. The critic quite properly assumes that the poems in their historical context constitute their own meaning and tries to show us how they do so. In his initial review of many modern postulations of the monistic "body" of poetry, its miraculous "corporeality," he exemplifies this quality by a pun of Donne's that demonstrates the use in poetry of "reference-breaking devices that depend on and are inseparable from its phonetic and linguistic form."[48] Hence the statement that the poetic word is a substan-

---

[47] See Ellis's lucid account of the vital distinction between establishing a category and describing the characteristics of its members, between the "reasons why" x is y and the "causes of" x's inclusion in y, pp. 39–40.

[48] Krieger, *A Window to Criticism*, pp. 14–16. In *Theory of Criticism: A Tradition and Its System* (Baltimore, 1976), he has reaffirmed this view, while observing that it is rather "embarrassingly" like the "language of sacramental

tive thing functions with respect to the actual analysis to say that the sense in which the word *is* a physical thing—that is, a sound—partly constitutes its meaning, particularly in combination or juxtaposition or contrast with other sounds. As an observation, if not as theory, this principle has been long enough in the possession of poets to have become a truism.[49] It is nevertheless of sufficient importance to justify some care in its formulation. We may recognize, as critics since the Romantic period have almost universally done, that sound (along with grammar, syntax, and the whole sociohistorical context of life) is constitutive of meaning without it being in the least necessary to postulate a supernatural agency either to supply the word with what it has already by virtue of its (manifold) relations with other words, or to convert the word into something else. More importantly, we may also recognize that the sound of words is semantically functional in language itself; that this phenomenon in no way makes poetry different in kind from other forms of discourse.

That the difference is simply one of degree is clear in the well-known contemporary formulation of the principle by Roman Jakobson, who calls the "poetic function" of language that which "*projects the principle of equivalence from the axis of selection into the axis of combination.*" That is, words are chosen less on the basis of parallel definitions and more on that of parallel sounds, by whatever means (grammar, meter, rimes, tropes) these may occur. Jakobson's introductory example is the slogan "I like Ike."[50] The extent and complexity of such aural combination may be maximized in poetry, where "verbal equations become a constructive principle of the text. . . .

---

presence," assuring us that he can still use it to describe poetry "without being trapped by its consequences," pp. 210–11. The trap, however, lies in its assumptions.

[49] Ezra Pound called it "melopoeia," *ABC of Reading* (London, 1934), and found it particularly in the troubadours, whence Dante had drawn its first explicit modern statement, *De Vulgari Eloquentia* II.

[50] "Linguistics and Poetics," in *Style in Language*, ed. Thomas A. Sebeok (Cambridge, Mass., 1960), pp. 357–58.

Phonemic similarity is sensed as semantic relationship."[51] But the operation of the basic principle is, of course, not confined to poetry and, therefore, neither defines it nor awards it any special or sacred status.

The use of referential semantics to make such a claim (by asserting the magic word/thing) thus turns out in practice to refute it. What is claimed as the mystical uniqueness of poetry is but one of the semantically constitutive powers (sound) that it shares with all language. The self-contradiction of such claims should encourage us to demystify our talk about literature by recognizing that no cultural product has a transcendent status above or beyond the discourses that constitute and reconstitute it. This recognition is made possible by a relational semantics, which requires no magic other than the potency that the use of words has always had for human beings. It requires only that we admit this power, not trying to evade, exalt, or transfer it, and that we understand its operation to be contingent on a great variety of human purposes, collective and individual, which, though they may be unbounded, are still construable in any given case. To admit this is also to admit what at least 2,500 years of wrangling over semantics have demonstrated: meaning is always construable and never definitive; the transactions that create and re-create it are as embedded in society and time as language itself. Thus to see meaning as requiring interpretation, and language not as representing an ontology but as creating one, is to acknowledge the ambivalent potency of the *logos* for both the logic of argument and the skill of artistry. This acknowledgment was the principal achievement of the Sophists whom Plato so despised.[52] To reaffirm it here by having argued back across the centuries of dualistic bewitchment of our semantic concepts is to illustrate that meaning is a function of the meeting between one historical "occasion" (*kairos*, as Gorgias said) and another. Language can indeed

[51] Jakobson, "On Linguistic Aspects of Translation," in *On Translation*, ed. Reuben A. Brower (Cambridge, Mass., 1959), p. 238.

[52] See the fine analysis of Gorgias by Mario Untersteiner, *The Sophists*, tr. Kathleen Freeman (Oxford, 1954), pp. 157–201.

transcend time, can communicate to generations yet unborn, as Renaissance poets so tirelessly insisted. But it does not do so by somehow plugging in to an imagined eternal order of things; it does so by our willingness, our need to reapprehend it as part of our own unending effort to understand.

2

THE RENAISSANCE
SEMANTIC SHIFT

The imaged Word, it is, that holds   —HART CRANE
Hushed willows anchored in its glow.
It is the unbetrayable reply
Whose accent no farewell can know.

In the early years of the fourteenth century Dante commenced a large work in vernacular prose in order to explain the four levels of allegorical meaning contained in his Italian love lyrics. He completed four of a projected fifteen books designed to subdivide all knowledge, or "philosophy," and present it as commentary on the poems. During one course in this vast "banquet," Dante offers a formal digression in defense of the immortality of the soul. After citing a number of ancient and medieval authorities, he makes a syllogistic argument (derived from Aquinas) that because nature has implanted in man's reason a hope for life after death, that life must necessarily exist. It would be unthinkably illogical for it not to exist; since nature has created a "perfect" (i.e., complete) world, and since the mind (*ragione*) of man is the most perfect thing in it, what is found in one must be found in the other. If not, the universe would be absurdly self-contradictory: "It would then follow that nature had acted against herself in placing this hope in the human mind (since it is said that many have passed from the death of the body to live in another life)—and this is also impossible."[1]

---

[1] *Il Convivio* (II.8[9]), ed. G. Busnelli and G. Vandelli, 2d ed. (Florence, 1968), I, 162: "Ancora, seguiterebbe che la natura contra se medesima questa

Almost exactly three hundred years later the English poet Fulke Greville composed a Senecan closet drama about Turkish politics. Toward the end of the play the Fifth Chorus neatly expresses an opinion on nature and immortality contrary to Dante's:

> Forsake not Nature, nor misunderstand her:
> Her mysteries are read without faith's eyesight:
> She speaketh in our flesh; and from our senses,
> Delivers down her wisdoms to our reason.
> If any man would break her laws to kill,
> Nature doth, for defence, allow offences.
> She neither taught the father to destroy:
> Nor promis'd any man, by dying, joy.[2]

The overt philosophical differences between these passages are of course those that have traditionally characterized the Renaissance as the great transition from the medieval to the modern world. Dante's normative concept of nature gives way to the descriptive concept promoted by empirical science; the Thomistic concord between reason and faith gives way to their Protestant and Baconian opposition; and the presumed congruence between the human mind and the structure of the universe ("reality") disappears, as Dante's epistemological confidence gives way to the epistemological anxieties that become the central preoccupation of philosophy in the seventeenth century and after.

These large conceptual shifts are the commonplaces of intellectual history. Properly qualified and understood as general trends, not as unidirectional and irreversible progressions, they may serve to indicate the boundaries and context of my concern. This concern, however, is with a more fundamental and implicit shift that underlies these intellectual trends. It is a shift in attitudes toward language and in assumptions about its

---

speranza ne la mente humana poste avesse, poi che detto è che molti a la morte del corpo sono corsi, per vivere ne l'altra vita; e questo è anche impossibile."

[2] *Mustapha*, "Chorus Quintus," in *Selected Poems of Fulke Greville*, ed. Thom Gunn (London, 1968), p. 149.

operation and efficacy. What these are may be inferred from the kind of argument for immortality that Dante is willing to accept and Greville is not.

Dante's conviction that the hope guarantees the fact is grounded not only in the substance of religious belief and philosophical tradition, but rests more deeply on the unquestioned identity or equivalence between what is said (*è detto*) and what is real. Nor is this merely a matter of accepting the testimony of authority. It depends rather on the felt necessity, articulate since Plato, for words to "correspond" to things. Dante's reasoning is fully analogous to the Socratic method of investigating language. Because words are regarded as necessarily "referring" to preextant, objective "things," the existence of such "things" can be deduced from that of the words that name them. In this way Plato deduces the existence of the Forms from terms like "beauty" and "virtue," which, since they can refer to no single sensory object, must refer to another class of object—the "intelligible." The postulation of such objects is quite literally one way of making language "capable of being understood." Thus Dante, having been careful to locate the "hope" of immortality in the noblest part of the mind—reason, the conceptual faculty—can perform on that hope the same kind of deduction that Plato performs on concepts. If we have the notion—in speech, writing, and our mind—then the thing itself must exist somewhere.

Three centuries later, it is apparent that the validity of this equivalence between word and fact is no longer assumed. We may have a notion of joy in the hereafter, but nature has no longer promised it. The "correspondence" between word and thing may still, of course, be regarded as desirable (indeed, the more passionately desired because it has been threatened); but it is no longer felt as necessarily given. Language can no longer automatically supply it; it has become problematic. That human reason (*ratio*) and human speech (*oratio*) can themselves create what may not in fact exist becomes newly and universally troubling in the seventeenth century. For Francis Bacon, Greville's friend and mentor, this problem is the motivation for his reform of all learning. His famous "Idols" explicitly accuse both the mind and its language of being deficient. "For the mind of man is . . . like an enchanted glass, full of superstition and imposture." Words, far from guaranteeing facts, are much more likely to impose "false appearances" on us.[3] Bacon's whole confident and ambitious program is designed to remedy just these deficiencies, to make the mind and its language properly conform to things. The "correspondence," which for Dante was a given, is for Bacon a distant but exhilarating goal, something to be achieved only by unremitting effort. The difference between these two systematic thinkers at opposite ends of the Renaissance is not over the operation of language (it works, or should work, by referring to preextant things) but over its efficacy.

But the difference is not trivial. It is one dimension of the shift in attitudes toward language that characterizes the Renaissance. We may gauge the depth of its importance by briefly surveying another of its manifestations: the changing feelings of poets, the most proficient users of language, about the new medium that they struggled to legitimize throughout the Renaissance—their vernacular languages.

Dante was of course the pioneer in this struggle. His treatise, *De Vulgari Eloquentia*, is full of acute analyses of Italian lyric forms and cogent observations on the aural qualities of words in both Italian and other Romance languages.[4] His primary argument here is for the establishment of an "illustrious" vernacular, composed of features shared by many of its dialects (a kind of *hoch* Italian), that could serve as the medium for a national literature. The time for this idea had not yet come, and the treatise remained virtually unknown until Trissino used it in the linguistic polemics of the early sixteenth century.[5] The reason Dante's program for the vernacular lay fal-

---

[3] *The Advancement of Learning* (II.xiv.9, 11), ed. G. W. Kitchin (London, 1915; rpt. 1973), pp. 132, 134. The full exposition of the "Idols" is in *Novum Organum*, I.24–68.

[4] Tr. A.G.F. Howell, *Latin Works of Dante* (London, 1904).

[5] A good, succinct account of these is given by Robert A. Hall, Jr., *The Italian Questione della Lingua* (Chapel Hill, 1942).

low for over two centuries is clearly suggested by his having written the treatise in Latin.

For all his genuine devotion to and unprecedented use of Italian, Dante was enough a man of his own time to regard Latin as incontestably superior. In the *Convivio* he must justify at length his choice of an admittedly inferior instrument to explicate his poems. He bases the superiority of Latin on the simple observation that it is fixed and permanent while vulgar tongues are constantly changing or "corruptible": "Lo latino è perpetuo e non corruttibile, e lo volgare è non stabile e corruttibile." Because of this stability, Latin is nobler and more powerful than vernaculars, and is therefore "sovereign" to them. Consequently, it is unfit to "serve" the analysis of their products. Throughout this argument, Dante quite calmly makes precise observations of change in the vernacular: words may be born, alter, and die in the short space of fifty years; if citizens dead for a millennium should return to their cities, they would find an entirely foreign tongue spoken there. For Dante these facts further establish the "beauty" of Latin as the harmonious relation of its parts, which is "more properly" achievable than in vernaculars because the latter are governed by usage, but Latin by the rules of grammar: "peró che lo volgare seguita uso, e lo latino arte."[6]

The superiority granted, Dante can proceed to the didactic justification of using Italian to offer his banquet of wisdom to all who hunger for knowledge, the "unlettered" (in Latin, of course) and "lettered" alike: "Onde con cío sia cosa che molti più siano quelli che desiderano intendere quelle non litterati che litterati, seguitasi che [lo latino] non avrebbe pieno lo suo comandamento come'l volgare, che da li litterati e non litterati è inteso."[7] The vulgar can better fulfill its task, which is to explain the poems to their readers. The gift of its commentary will be more widely shared, its banquet more liberally spread.[8]

---

[6] *Il Convivio* (1.5), I, 33–36.

[7] *Ibid.* (1.7), I, 44–45.

[8] *Ibid.* (1.9–10), I, 58–60.

The very terms of the titular metaphor reveal that Dante is committed to the vernacular as an instrument, a means for present instruction. For all his patriotic and acute sensitivity to it, he remains undismayed by its mortality. It is to be consumed like food, which contains nourishment. The "bread" of the prose commentary will make the "meat" of the *canzoni* more appetizing and digestible.[9] The nourishing knowledge thus conveyed or contained is more important than the means of containment. The vernacular may fade, alter, and decay; but what it "refers to"—the entire cosmos—will endure. Dante is thus making the "intelligible" universe available to his "unlettered" countrymen. To increase its accessibility and attractiveness is ample reason for employing the vernacular.

By the seventeenth century, however, the mortality of vernaculars is no longer regarded by poets with such equanimity. Not only has the efficacy of language as a means of access to objective reality been called into question, but poets have been exposed to a different kind of commitment to the language they speak. The example of Dante's own work had inspired continental writers to value and produce vernacular literature. Although opposed by the humanist veneration of Latin in this particular theatre of war between ancients and moderns, the major European vernaculars had won predominance in theory and practice by the end of the sixteenth century. Into vulgar languages were incorporated both the actual achievements (via translation and production) and the theoretical rules (via systematization in grammars and "*ars*") of Latin. They demonstrated, as we shall see, a parity of power. Hence the eventual and impassioned affirmation of the ultimate power of language, specifically of writing, to transcend time. Of the several explosive celebrations of this newly acquired ability of vernaculars, the richest in implication are Shakespeare's:

> Not marble, nor the gilded monuments
> Of princes shall outlive this powerful rhyme . . .
> 'Gainst death and all oblivious enmity

[9] *Ibid.* (I.I), I, 8–9.

> Shall you pace forth: your praise shall still find room
> Even in the eyes of all posterity
> That wear this world out to the ending doom.
>> So, till the judgment that yourself arise,
>> You live in this, and dwell in lovers' eyes.   [Sonnet 55]

> But thy eternal summer shall not fade
> Nor lose possession of that fair thou ow'st,
> Nor shall Death brag thou wander'st in his shade,
> When in eternal lines to time thou grow'st:
>> So long as men can breathe or eyes can see,
>> So long lives this, and this gives life to thee.   [Sonnet 18]

>> Yet do thy worst, old Time: despite thy wrong
>> My love shall in my verse ever live young.   [Sonnet 19]

>> His beauty shall in these black lines be seen,
>> And they shall live, and he in them still green.
>>> [Sonnet 63]

Far from being a consumable container, valued for what it conveys, the poet's mother tongue has itself acquired supreme value: it can confer what would otherwise not exist. It is not food, but a monument, claiming precisely the power that until the Renaissance was reserved to ancient languages, and claiming it by taking over such monumental metaphors from their loci classici in Ovid and Horace.[10] Inspired by Ronsard, Samuel Daniel asserts the power unconditionally:

> These are the arks, the trophies I erect,
>> That fortify thy name against old age;
> And these thy sacred virtues must protect
> Against the dark and time's consuming rage.

[10] These are cited in W. G. Ingram's and Theodore Redpath's edition (from which I quote) of *Shakespeare's Sonnets* (New York, 1968), p. 128. The infrequent appearance of such metaphors in classical Latin poetry is contrasted to their reiteration in Renaissance verse by J. B. Leishman, *Themes and Variations in Shakespeare's Sonnets*, 2d ed. (1963; rpt. New York, 1966), pp. 27–91. The achieved articulation of such claims is not diminished by the same poets' finding them, in other poems, unsustainable—as demonstrated in Shakespeare's case by Anne Ferry, *All in War with Time* (Cambridge, Mass., 1975), Ch. 1.

He also asserts it, quite unlike Ronsard, in a much more conditional way, which suggests how potentially vulnerable this new commitment is, how dependent on a kind of willed faith:

> This *may* remain thy lasting monument,
>   Which *happily* posterity *may* cherish;
>   These colors with thy fading are not spent,
>   These *may* remain when thou and I shall perish.
> *If* they remain, then thou shalt live thereby;
> They *will* remain, and so thou canst not die.[11]

Both the Renaissance vernacular promise of literary immortality and its classical sources presuppose the survival of the written or printed text, which, of course, distinguishes them from the most ancient version of the topos in oral literature, where the aim is to preserve the memory of the hero's deeds in an unwritten narrative whose actual words and formulae are fluid. The Renaissance claims, however, are distinct from those of the classical period in explicitly requiring not only the survival of the text as a physical object (the monument that outlasts brass and stone; the unfading "colors" of its "black" lines) but also of readers who can comprehend it—whose "eyes" and "breath" receive a new importance. This requisite comprehension is not a matter of scholarly reconstruction; the posterity so continually invoked is that of *speakers*. It is a speech community, the idea of which, developed in humanist philology, had helped make vernaculars respectable in the first place.[12] Shakespeare makes a monument of tongues:

> Your monument shall be my gentle verse,
> Which eyes not yet created shall o'er-read;
> And tongues to be your being shall rehearse
> When all the breathers of this world are dead:

---

[11] *Delia*, 1592, quoted from *Poetry of the English Renaissance*, ed. J. W. Hebel and H. H. Hudson (New York, 1929), pp. 245–46. My italics, of course; "happily" means "by chance."

[12] This process will be described in ch. 4.

You still shall live—such virtue hath my pen—
Where breath most breathes, even in the mouths of men.

[Sonnet 81]

This new emotional investment in the enduring efficacy of the vernacular and the power of its poets was destined to be short-lived. Such a commitment was too easily destroyed by just the kind of linguistic observation made by Dante. But when seventeenth-century writers make it, they do so in an elegiac tone, with a sense of loss.

This sense is especially acute in England, not because the new kind of commitment was stronger there than elsewhere in Europe, but because historical accident provided English writers with a more vivid example of vernacular mortality. The speech and scansion of Chaucer, England's greatest "modern" poet, were in fact lost to his own community of descendants, as those of Dante and Petrarch were not to theirs. Edmund Waller writes "Of English Verse":

Poets may boast, as safely vain,
Their work shall with the world remain;
Both bound together live or die,
The verses and the prophecy.

But who can hope his line should long
Last in a daily changing tongue?
While they are new, envy prevails,
And as that dies, our language fails.

When architects have done their part,
The matter may betray their art:
Time, if we use ill-chosen stone,
Soon brings a well-built palace down.

Poets that lasting marble seek
Must carve in Latin, or in Greek;
We write in sand; our language grows,
And like the tide our work o'erflows.

Chaucer his sense can only boast,
The glory of his numbers lost;

Years have defaced his matchless strain;
And yet he did not sing in vain . . .

The consolation that Waller goes on to find sufficient for Chaucer is that he obtained his mistress while he lived, which is all he hopes for his own verse, that "it prove / But as long-lived as present love."[13] In this context as in many others, when compared to the performance of the preceding generation of poets, Cavalier verse is a poetry of lowered expectations. The lowering is quite self-conscious—a graceful retreat from the boastful illusions of one's predecessors. But it is still a retreat, a giving-up of something that is not replaceable. Instead of mastering his language ("such virtue hath my pen"), the poet must surrender to it as to an inevitably destructive force, an unstoppable "tide." The poet's uneasiness is apparent; he cannot simply accept the fact of linguistic change as Dante did. His feeling toward his medium is not only one of loss but of betrayal. Dante held no high expectations of his medium, though he helped to make them possible, and did not feel betrayed by it. He was more committed to the end than to the means.[14] As Renaissance poets became more committed to their means, its inadequacies became more disturbing. One cannot feel betrayed unless one has first trusted. By Waller's time the ordinary process of vernacular change has become blamable: it is a threat, a failure, a defacement. The poet's native language is only fit for temporary satisfactions because it will collapse.[15]

A generation or so later, all these sentiments are sufficiently commonplace to receive elegantly modified expression in Pope's *Essay on Criticism*:

[13] *English Augustan Poetry*, ed. Paul Fussell (New York, 1972), pp. 27–28. The poem was first printed in 1668.

[14] All language is of course inadequate to Dante's ultimate end, the beatific vision, as he reminds us repeatedly in *Paradiso* XXXIII.

[15] The obsessive concern of seventeenth- and early eighteenth-century writers with the instability of the vernacular is demonstrated in Richard Foster Jones's pioneering study of linguistic attitudes, *The Triumph of the English Language* (Stanford, 1953), pp. 263–69.

> Be thou the first true merit to befriend;
> His praise is lost who stays till all commend.
> Short is the date, alas, of modern rhymes,
> And 'tis but just to let them live betimes.
> No longer now that golden age appears
> When Patriarch-wits survived a thousand years:
> Now length of fame (our second life) is lost,
> And bare threescore is all ev'n that can boast;
> Our sons their fathers' failing language see,
> And such as Chaucer is, shall Dryden be.
> So when the faithful pencil has designed
> Some bright idea of the master's mind,
> Where a new world leaps out at his command,
> And ready Nature waits upon his hand;
> When the ripe colors soften and unite,
> And sweetly melt into just shade and light;
> When mell'wing years their full perfection give,
> And each bold figure just begins to live,
> The treach'rous colors the fair art betray,
> And all the bright creation fades away!   (ll. 474–93)[16]

The pace of change accelerates: Dryden will soon join Chaucer. The poetic option mentioned by Waller—to write in Latin
or Greek—is ignored by Pope; the vernacular is the only
choice. And its "failings" are most tantalizingly described in
the traditional Horatian vocabulary that assimilates verbal and
visual art: the pencil, idea (as "image"), colors and figures of
both rhetoric and painting create a "new world" that ripens
and mellows into perfection only to disappear. Though Pope's
metaphors are primarily visual, the sound of the passage is de-
licious, especially as the shorter vowels, spondaic irregulari-
ties, and quick rhythm of the two penultimate lines give way
to the broader vowels, absolute metrical regularity, and slowly
paced finality of the last line. It is hard to assess the attitude
here. The treachery of the medium is being asserted—but so
melodiously that we may suspect the beauty of the lines to be
sufficient unto the day. There is more acceptance of the inevi-

---

[16] Quoted from *English Augustan Poetry*, ed. Fussell, p. 293.

table than uneasiness with it; there is no overwhelming tide and no defacement, but a "natural" process of growth and dissolution. There is likewise no surrender or retreat: Pope's artist/poet, like Pope himself, is clearly in command. The poet seems to be at home in the reduced temporal horizons of his medium. His own language may be all he has, but although it will dissolve, he can still use it splendidly.

A summary of these shifting poetic attitudes toward the efficacy of vernaculars may suggest their connection with other predominant anxieties of the Renaissance.

DANTE: My language will pass away, but it can reveal eternity to my contemporaries.

SHAKESPEARE and DANIEL: Time will swallow all that I love, but my language, while spoken, will preserve it.

WALLER: Time will swallow my language, too; all that we may achieve will be lost. (POPE: But we can still achieve it pro tem.)

The pattern here is that of new energies released, new attachments formed, new possibilities envisioned—only to become a prey to devouring time.[17] The Renaissance obsession with time is in part grounded in its changing attitudes toward language, for it was in language that humanist philologists had discovered time as history.[18] And, in turn, it was history, by observing the fact of change in all languages, that made it possible to liberate and dignify the vernaculars, to perceive their status and potency as equal to those of Latin or Greek. And it was history that finally cast down what it had raised up: the new faith in the enduring power of spoken language.

The process, however, of raising up this patently vulnerable

[17] The literary thematics of time as both bourgeois commodity and destructive force have been catalogued at length by Ricardo J. Quinones, *The Renaissance Discovery of Time* (Cambridge, Mass., 1972).

[18] The rise of modern historiography in the period is excellently surveyed by Peter Burke, *The Renaissance Sense of the Past* (New York, 1970). For an analysis of the emergence of history from philology in the work of Valla, see Donald R. Kelley, *The Foundations of Modern Historical Scholarship* (New York, 1970), pp. 9, 25–36.

new faith was not simply the expression of nationalistic pride nor the self-promotion of poets anxious to flatter their subjects and themselves. In fact, the explicit Renaissance assertions of the enduring efficacy of vernaculars imply an altered view of the operation of language itself. We can observe in these altered poetic attitudes a change in the assumed relation between language and meaning. For Dante this relation is ontologically bound: that is, the meaning of words depends on the a priori being of objects. For Shakespeare and Daniel this relation is ontologically autonomous: that is, the meaning of words depends on the act of speaking them. Dante's argument for Christian immortality assumes that words have meaning by corresponding to preextant things; Shakespeare's assertion of literary immortality assumes that words have meaning by creating something that would not exist without them.[19] Without a speaking posterity, the memory of the master/mistress would fall into oblivion. The meaning of the poem is not its object of "reference," but the very act of praise committed in reciting it. The former assumption is that language is cosmetic to meaning; the latter that language is constitutive of it.

This is the shift from referential to relational semantics in terms of the opposed models of language it implies: from the "model of the garment" (the cosmetic view) to "the model of the melody" (the constitutive view).[20] The difference is that between regarding language as the clothing or container of thoughts, feelings, objects, and meanings that have a separate existence elsewhere and regarding it as constituting those thoughts, feelings, objects, and meanings in the very act of articulating them—just as a melody is constituted by, and is in-

[19] The assumption is not original with Shakespeare, who is used here to exemplify one direction of its fullest development. Similar assumptions of semantic autonomy have been detected in the troubadours by Eugene Vance, "Love's Concordance: The Poetics of Desire and the Joy of the Text," and in Petrarch by John Freccero, "The Fig Tree and the Laurel: Petrarch's Poetics," *Diacritics* 5 (1975), 34–52.

[20] I borrow this concise version of these traditional metaphors from Max Black, *The Labyrinth of Language*, pp. 65–66.

separable from, its sounds and the relations among them. Although this difference is manifest in the ways that Dante and Shakespeare regard their own verse, the theoretical opposition between these views is a product of all the subsequent reflection on language that has crystallized clearer issues out of what remained for Renaissance thinkers and writers a rather murkier solution of assumptions. Their own theoretical choices, though they involved issues isolated since, were made within conceptual fields widely different from ours. To inquire, therefore, how it happened that a constitutive view of the relation between language and meaning emerged in the Renaissance is to ask the past to answer a kind of question that it would never have posed.

To be put in this ordinary and inevitable position is the necessity, privilege, and danger of all historical investigation. Necessary, because we are confined within our own skins and the cognitive interests of our own time and place; we are in part products of our own history, individual and collective.[21] The questions that interest us, and the way we pose them, will perforce differ from those of the past. Privileged, because we are thus at liberty to ask the past any question that we like; and we can select the questions with the great advantage of hindsight, of acquaintance and experience with what happened after the period in question. As present inquirers, we are literally older than those whom we study; we have seen more of the temporal world than they have (though age alone is of course not wisdom). Dangerous, because this very privilege of age tempts us to see the past only as a biological metaphor: it is but our own youth. We extract from it the linear development of our best loved (or worst hated) selves; we observe in it only the organic causation of whatever idea, institution, or form of art we approve (or disapprove) at present.[22] This temptation has been

[21] This point is a commonplace of the sociology of knowledge; I take its application to the interpretation of the cultural past from Jürgen Habermas, *Knowledge and Human Interests* (Boston, 1971), p. 181.

[22] Foucault's whole enterprise is an assault on and an alternative to the "biological, evolutionist metaphors in which the difficult, specific problem of

especially seductive in the case of the Renaissance, producing the still conventional view of the period as the "birthplace" of everything from empirical science through parliamentary democracy to the doctrine of art for art's sake. Our tendency to trace the triumphant growth of mighty modern oaks from pregnant Renaissance acorns has been abetted by our willingness to accept the period's own estimate of itself. Although the notion of "rebirth" as a full organic flowering was not applied to the period as a whole until the nineteenth century (the *OED* cites the first such use of the term in 1845), it was Renaissance humanists who insisted that they were giving birth to a new and purified learning that would flourish under the pedagogical cultivation they so eagerly prescribed. The situation was aptly summarized by C. S. Lewis: "Our legend of the Renaissance is a Renaissance legend. We have not arrived at this conception as a result of our studies but simply inherited it from the very people we were studying."[23]

The danger of this temptation, however, may not be obviated even when perceived. Lewis's perception, for example, led him merely to reverse the emphasis on the terms of the same biological metaphor: the cultural historian "must even try to forget his knowledge of what comes after, and see the egg as if he did not know it was going to become a bird."[24] The corrective urged here is that of Rankian historicism; instead of focusing on the process of egg becoming bird, we are to discover how the egg "really" looked when it was still but an egg.[25] This kind of historical *ding an sich* has proven quite as

historical mutation is usually dissolved," *The Archaeology of Knowledge* (New York, 1972), p. 209.

[23] *English Literature in the Sixteenth Century* (New York, 1954), p. 56. Charles Trinkaus has pointed out that we are still succumbing to this legend as well as to the biological metaphor: "Humanism, Religion, Society: Concepts and Motivations of Some Recent Studies," *Renaissance Quarterly* 29 (1976), 677, 686.

[24] Lewis, *English Literature*, p. 5.

[25] To the credit of his candor and the damage of his argument, Lewis later admits his inability to recover just this "original" perspective on the formally rhetorical literature of the period. When he observes with perfect accuracy that

elusive as the ontological one. Moreover, as applied to the documents or art works of cultural history, the biological model does not disclose their continuity, but simply imposes its own. Lewis perceived this too; and his warning to the cultural historian is still appropriate: "He must beware of schematizing. He must not impose either on the old things that were dying out (not all old things were) nor on the new things that were coming in (not all of them to stay) a spurious unity."[26]

To inquire how assumptions about language and meaning altered during the Renaissance, and to seek both the causes and consequences of these changes, presupposes neither "origin" nor "growth" in the organic sense. The inquiry will discover in the principal domains of the Renaissance preoccupation with language a shared set of tensions and problems that arise from the competition between the cosmetic and constitutive views of the language/meaning relation. To examine this competition is to plot a shift in semantic attitudes that is highly irregular and sporadic, but nonetheless pervasive: complete in some areas, refused in others, but somehow contested in all. Thus formulated as a conflict between semantic assumptions, the issue selected for investigation imposes no predetermined model of change or subsequent development upon the data. For example, we may find explicit theories of semantically constitutive language in Valla or Luther without regarding them as seeds that were inevitably to blossom in Wittgenstein. We may find the assumption of constitutive semantics in Shakespeare or Cervantes without claiming an unbroken chain of influence from them to Wallace Stevens.

Cultural change, to insist on the obvious, is a sloppy business; its accurate description is not likely to be tidy. Ideas and literary works are not people; the history of their life cycle is not that of a predictable, biological continuum. They appear, are hailed or ignored, imitated and misconstrued, used for

---

"of the praise and censure which we allot to medieval and Elizabethan poets only the smallest part would have seemed relevant to those poets themselves" (*ibid.*, p. 61), he wholly discredits his earlier historicist pretensions.

[26] *Ibid.*, p. 63.

often contradictory purposes, are enshrined, attacked, or forgotten, perhaps to reemerge sooner or later, intact or fragmented, in similar or remote contexts, with the same or with quite different emotional resonance. Such, in brief compass, was the fate of the simple observation of vernacular change as made from Dante to Waller. If something like a pattern emerged from our initial glance at one set of linguistic attitudes, what it revealed was a kind of discontinuity quite unlike any metaphor of biological growth. Such discontinuity and ambivalence will also be found to permeate other areas of linguistic concern, both theoretical and practical. The question of how meaning is to be sought, how words are to be interpreted, was not then and is not now to be answered from within the confines of any single academic specialty.[27] Change in so fundamental a matter as the understanding of language proceeds at different paces on many different fronts, none of which can claim any necessary, causal priority. The issue selected for investigation does not postulate any particular conformity between, for example, altered ways of apprehending the meaning of Scripture and of secular literature; it merely alerts us to the possibility of some interaction between the semantic principles of explicit debates about language and the semantic assumptions of its literary and other uses. Although in principle there is no limit to the kinds of uses that may be considered, in practice the limit is imposed by the ignorance of the investigator.

To analyze the shift in Renaissance attitudes toward language in terms of both explicit and implicit semantics—disengaging the practical consequences of theory and the theoretical assumptions of practice—is what distinguishes this study

[27] An interdisciplinary cornucopia of theories and kinds of research concerning language is reviewed by George Steiner in the course of a cogent argument that the understanding of all language is a process of "translation" and that literature is not a marginal but a central phenomenon of speech: *After Babel* (Oxford, 1975), Chs. 2, 3. Karl-Otto Apel also makes the point that literature is of central relevance for understanding past conceptions of language: *Die Idee der Sprache* (Bonn, 1963), p. 67.

from other treatments of linguistic change in the period. One of the best of these poses the problem in a way that is both broader and narrower than the issue I have outlined here.

The Renaissance fell heir both to the medieval preoccupation with texts and to its lingering predilection for oral performance. In terms of the presence of the word to man, the Renaissance is one of the most complex and even confused periods in cultural history, and by the same token perhaps the most interesting up to the present in the history of the word. An exacting devotion to the written text . . . which has been the seedbed of modern humanistic scholarship, struggled in the subconscious with commitment to rhetoric and to dialectic, symbolic of the old oral-aural frames of mind, and maintained the old oral-aural anxieties and a sense of social structure built . . . on personal loyalties rather than on objectification of issues. Humanist rhetoric as such was opposed to scholastic dialectic, and yet both belonged to the oral-aural culture which typography was destined to transmute.[28]

Father Ong's general concern is with changes in the technological media of communication as giving rise to the sensorial reorganization of the world. Within this framework of transition from oral through written and typographic to electronic culture (the history of the Western sensibility from antiquity to the present), the Renaissance is a crucial and complicated episode. The breadth of such a framework, employed with Ong's habitual precision, restraint, and qualification, allows him to suggest many interesting relationships, such as the association of divine witness and the physical presentation of language made in his carefully ambivalent use of the phrase, "presence of the word." In addition, the framework is sufficiently capacious and complex to have explanatory power. It nicely accommodates, for example, the changes we have traced in poetic attitudes toward the efficacy of the vernacular. In Father Ong's terms, the vulnerable and short-lived faith in the staying power of vernaculars is explicable as the retention of old oral-

[28] Walter J. Ong, S.J., *The Presence of the Word* (New Haven, 1967), pp. 61–62.

aural habits in the new medium of print. Shakespeare's "black lines" that can keep their subject "green" only by being spoken are a perfect illustration of Ong's central contention that the initial effect of the new visual orientation of print is to intensify the old oral orientation to the potency of the word as sound. Such intensifications are necessarily temporary, occurring precisely at the transitional points of the framework, "where a new development at first only exaggerates a condition which it will later eliminate."[29]

The narrowness of this still useful and, I believe, insufficiently exploited framework, however, is that it overlooks the extent to which an atavistic attitude may be at the same time a revolutionary semantics. To see the Renaissance insistence on the enduring power of written speech only as a throwback (which of course it was—a conscious transference of the power of Latin) is to ignore the semantic dimension, the new context, of the old assertion. If the action of speaking can create what would not exist without it, we are in a semantic world that would at least have been new to Dante. And it would not be the only occasion when the Renaissance, seeking to revive something old, like classical art or Augustinian piety, created something very new indeed. Another difficulty with Ong's framework in this case is the degree of causation attributed to the medium: it does not seem to be the "new development" of print that eliminated the boastful faith in vernaculars, but rather the very old observation of their inevitable change.

It is possible, however, that this old observation gained new force in a context that was indeed a result of printing. This context is suggested by Elizabeth Eisenstein, who makes even greater claims for the medium as causal agent. Although allowing that the Renaissance got under way before the invention of printing, she argues that many of its achievements were

---

[29] *Ibid.*, p. 239. Wider extensions and convenient summaries of Ong's cultural stages may be found in his *Rhetoric, Romance, and Technology* (Ithaca, 1971). His *Interfaces of the Word* (Ithaca, 1977) continues to extend the examples without further developing the concepts.

"reoriented," if not made possible, by print.[30] One such achievement would be the "fixing" of the distance between the past and the present, the formation, via print, of a "rational-ized" concept of history out of earlier observations. Such a "reorientation," like Father Ong's notion of the transitional moment between word-processing technologies, could also explain why history (as initial stimulant to vernacular imita-tion of classical achievements) raised up the poetic faith in ver-naculars that it subsequently (in revealing the "fixed" gap be-tween Latin marble and vulgar sand) cast down. On the other hand, why didn't the "fixity" of the printed text permit sub-sequent poets the confidence that their works would last? Pre-sumably because the poets were not yet fully responding to language as printed text, but still hearing it as speech. Eisen-stein also offers many shrewd estimations of the effects of print on science and Scripture, ironically observing that as it made the former clearer, it made the latter muddier.[31]

Despite the vast scope of her inquiry, however, she never considers what would seem the most immediate consequence of printing, Ong's main theme: the impact of the transforma-tion of the means of communication on the very object that is communicated—words. Surely the first thing we should ex-pect to alter as a result of an alteration in the means of repro-duction is the product itself, along with an alteration in our habits of consumption and use. Words, to be sure, are a slip-pery "product," and changes in the way they are consumed—that is, apprehended and interpreted—cannot be easily docu-mented by the kinds of evidence that social and intellectual his-torians usually seek. Ong demonstrates such changes by anal-ysis and argument of a more literary, psychological, and anthropological kind. In any case, the question of how far either the nature or degree of such changes in the Renaissance can be attributed to print remains open and fascinating. Ong's

[30] Elizabeth L. Eisenstein, *The Printing Press As an Agent of Change* (Cam-bridge, 1979), I, 186ff., 300–301.
[31] *Ibid.*, II, 699–701.

framework, however, has the advantage of a wide perspective that can correct the major weakness of Eistenstein's. Locating his primary changes as those from orality to writing (whether in ancient Greece or modern Africa) and from print to electronics (today), he does not insist, as she does, on the feeble resources of a culture based on manuscripts as opposed to those of one based on printed books—both being forms of writing. As such, the change from one to the other is secondary in Ong's view; they share much, especially in the Renaissance, for the crucial alterations brought about by print are not fully manifested until the later eighteenth century. Eisenstein, however, seriously underestimates the capacities of scribal culture.[32] However much forms of knowledge and consciousness in the Renaissance may have been redirected by the agency of print, the fact remains that those forms took shape in the culture and societies that existed before the printing press. Petrarch, the Florentine humanists, and Lorenzo Valla had both the technical and intellectual means to revalue antiquity, to invent the "middle" ages, and to explore language as the mediator of all human experience—activities that provided the foundation for the subsequent development of Renaissance pedagogy, history, philology, literature, and religion.

The shift in semantic assumptions that was occurring in these and other disciplines cannot be described or accounted for as a consequence of print, although print contributed to its diffusion. Indeed, the sheer exponential increase in the number of readers made possible by printed books created, as Eisenstein says, widespread revolutions out of what, in scribal culture, were occasional debates among the learned. Recalling this long-acknowledged agency of print in the social diffusion of ideas, new and old, reminds us that controversy, and not consensus, is then likely to prevail. It certainly prevailed in all the areas of linguistic concern that were central to the period.

[32] This criticism is impressively documented in the review article by Anthony T. Grafton, "The Importance of Being Printed," *Journal of Interdisciplinary History* 11 (1980), 265–86.

Ong's analysis retains a valuable appreciation of the impassioned confusions about language in the Renaissance, and thus avoids both overgeneralization and oversimplification. These faults occur when scholars try, for whatever reason, to characterize the period, or a century within it, as having some single view or concept of language. An example is Michel Foucault's declaration that the epistemological field within which language operates in the sixteenth century is one of "correspondence," in which knowledge is the interpretation of signs that are ontologically bound, of words that are virtually coextensive with things. For the sixteenth century, we are assured, language was "not an arbitrary system" but part of the traditional book of nature.[33] Like many generalizations, this one is valid enough for making certain large contrasts, and is quite misleading if accepted as exclusively true. Foucault merely uses it as a contrastive introduction to his real subject, which is the changed mode of signification or representation in which language operates in the seventeenth and eighteenth centuries. But if the sixteenth-century concept of language could in fact be thus exclusively characterized, then one would have to account for its miraculous, overnight alteration at the dawn of the seventeenth. If the only view of language available in the sixteenth century was that of analogical correspondence, then Shakespeare and Daniel could not have written the sonnets that they did, and Francis Bacon would not have made the complaints that he did. If it is true that the idea of language as an "arbitrary system" was by no means generally accepted in the sixteenth century, it is also true that this idea had been continuously advanced by different kinds of theorists since the middle of the fifteenth. In short, the imposition of a single view of language on the period both falsifies the gradual processes of change and wholly obscures their consequences, that is, the tensions between competing theories or divergent assumptions, which, as Ong suggests, constitute the most interesting energies of the period.

[33] *The Order of Things* (New York, 1971), pp. 32–37.

My purpose, then, is to focus on the tensions (which Foucault might call "discontinuities," and to which he urges us to attend) produced by the emergence of a constitutive view of the relation between language and meaning that is at odds with the prevailing cosmetic conception. The word, of man and of God, is one of the primary energies of the period that is liberated. Free, it causes problems so tremendous that they must finally be evaded. Words, for Bacon and Locke, must be rebound to things of some sort, and the whole issue subsides for a while only to explode again in the Romantic period. It is still, of course, exploding. The pattern of energies released only to be denied, of positions attained and then retreated from, which we shall observe in explicit debate and implicit usage, will not picture the changes with which we are concerned in any neatly developmental way, but will instead show us how, and how tenuously, such development as there is takes place. If indeed the Renaissance promises of vernacular immortality were but throwbacks to an oral world of magic words, there would be no development at all. It is rather because the poems have, in the course of reviving a classical topos, articulated a new understanding of the operation of language itself that the tensions endure in literature if not in theoretical debate. When Pope, for example, writes that "The sound must seem an echo to the sense," there is no question about priority: the old cosmetic view is assumed; meanings preexist words. But when Pope's artist commands a "new world" (if but a temporary creation) to leap forth, this assumption is contradicted: language is not echoing something, but creating it. A new world created by human language would not have been conceivable to Dante— except as blasphemy. How it became respectable is my subject. I venture to summarize the shift that made this possible by rewriting a famous couplet of Pope's:

> True wit is Nature to advantage dressed,
> What oft was thought, but ne'er so well expressed.

On the contrary:

> True wit is nature to cognition brought,
> What once expressed, can then be called a thought.

★

To propose that the legitimized creation of "new worlds" in literature owes something to altered assumptions about how language means is of course to deny a basic premise in modern formalist theory—that of the "autonomy" of art. The fullest flowering of this doctrine in the slogan *l'art pour l'art* is the product of one of the most potent biological metaphors by means of which the nineteenth century saw itself as the heir of the Renaissance. Predicated on the eighteenth-century discovery of "aesthetic experience" as distinct both from cognition and ordinary life,[34] the burgeoning new field of "aesthetics" found the seeds of its own development in various assertions and achievements of the Renaissance. The period's art, in short, was seen as emancipating itself from medieval constraints and acquiring value for its own sake. No longer bound merely to serve theology, metaphysics, or ethics, art of all kinds could begin its triumphant march toward pure Crocean hedonism.[35]

The primary agent of this metamorphosis was often taken to be the consequently much-studied phenomenon of neoplatonism. In particular there was its doctrine of divine inspiration or poetic furor, of which Ernst Curtius wrote: "As it did with so many other coinages of the Greek spirit, the Middle Ages took this one from late Rome, preserved it, and copied it to the letter, until the creative Eros of the Italian Renaissance

[34] A full history of Kant's subjectivist aesthetics and its critique in twentieth-century phenomenology is given by Gadamer, *Truth and Method*, pp. 39–90.

[35] This view is still widely accepted by Italian scholars: see the essays of Umberto Eco, "Sviluppo dell'estetica medievale"; Antonio Viscardi, "Idee estetiche e letteratura militante nel Medioevo"; and Cesare Vasoli, "L'estetica dell'Umanesimo e del Rinascimento," in *Momenti e Problemi di Storia dell'Estetica* I (Milan, 1968).

reawakened the spirit in the letter."[36] In general there was its conception of self-realizing form, most cogently explicated and traced in both art and science by Ernst Cassirer. With clear historical self-consciousness, he found that the Renaissance dissolution of the bond between the beautiful and the good "paved the way for the autonomy of aesthetics, which then received its theoretical foundation more than three centuries later."[37] Though some Renaissance poets did indeed claim divine inspiration, and though some thinkers did indeed labor to legitimize artistic creation per se, we may still doubt whether their efforts justify the autonomy attributed to them by a much later aesthetics, as well as question the status of such claims and whence they derive. We may, in other words, examine the bases on which and the purposes for which these discourses formed their privileged objects. Renaissance assertions of artistic autonomy will therefore be seen in their proper role as statements to be interpreted—not as the means, principles, or limiting horizon of interpretation. Such claims, as made explicitly for poetry, assert that its dignity and value derive from two different, but often combined, grounds: its universality or its divine inspiration. I shall briefly examine each in turn.

That poetry contained all knowledge—the idea that produced all the popular systems of theologia poetica—was just what Dante had set out to demonstrate from his own lyrics in the *Convivio*. It was Dante's enthusiastic defender, Coluccio Salutati, who gave the idea systematic exposition in a huge treatise, begun in 1391 and concluded only by his death in 1406, aptly titled *De Laboribus Herculis*. Salutati begins by straightforwardly lifting poetry out of its traditional subordinate place in medieval education (where it was but a branch of grammar). He declares that poetry (specifically "poeticam narrationem") includes, uses, and explicates not only the tri-

[36] *European Literature and the Latin Middle Ages*, tr. Willard Trask (New York, 1953), p. 475.

[37] *The Individual and the Cosmos in Renaissance Philosophy*, tr. Mario Domandi (New York, 1964; 1st ed., 1927), p. 163.

vium and quadrivium but also all philosophy, hence it is greatest in dignity. The ostensibly unique means by which poetry
achieves this status is specified in Salutati's definition of the
true function of the poet: to designate one thing by another
("vero officium poetarum est per unam rem aliud desig-
nare").[38] It is quite simply the use of symbols, whereby one
thing stands for or represents ("sumitur" and "ponitur" are his
usual terms) something else, that liberates poetry from grammar and rhetoric and constitutes its own proper art.[39] Any use
of language that can be construed to employ a "simula-
crum"—a likeness, figure, imitation, representation, shadow—is, for Salutati, poetry.

In this way he is able to buttress its dignity by locating its
origin exactly 235 years after the creation of the world (Genesis
4:26): when Enos called the name of the Lord, he must have
done so in figurative words that signified something else, since
human invention could not find the "proper terms" for the
inexpressible.[40] Having provided these impeccable Christian
credentials for it, Salutati can proceed to find poetry everywhere, identified and justified at once by the ancient expedient
of allegorical interpretation. To cite Augustine and to find in
the mythological fables of ancient poets foreshadowings of
Christian truth is only the beginning, for if poetry is to be
really universal, it must symbolize everything. Thus Christian
allegories combine freely with Euhemeristic, moral, psychological, and scientific ones. Poetical narratives about Jupiter,
for example, use him to "represent" a man, a star, air, fire, a
natural or supernatural force, the will of God, fortune, the ra-

---

[38] Ed. B. L. Ullman (Zurich, 1951), I, 19. Poetry also contains all the normative Pythagorean proportions, all harmony celestial and mundane: I, 23.

[39] *Ibid.*, I, 72.

[40] "Nam cum scriptum sit Enos incepisse vocare nomen domini, nec possi-
bile sit propriis et humane inventionis vocabulis de deo loqui, quoniam, cum
undique infinitus et inenarrabilis sit, a nobis explicari non possit, figuratis et
aliud ab eo significantibus verbis proculdubio fuit illa vocatio; ut ex tunc fas sit
dicere nostram . . . poeticam incepisse." *Ibid.*, I, 81–82.

74 NOTIONS OF MEANING

tional will.[41] Anything is grist for such a mill, Dante and Petrarch as well as Homer and Virgil. Salutati can go on indefi-
nitely (and did so until he died), shucking away the husk of the
fable to reveal its inner kernel of truth. Though his claims are
extreme (few other humanists if any wished to give poetry so
high a station) his procedures are exemplary of the whole tradition that valued poetry as the symbolic vehicle of some universal theology, from Fulgentius on Virgil nine centuries before to the Florentine Academicians on Petrarch a century
after.

It was a bold stroke of Salutati's to attempt to supply poetry
with its own "proper art" in order to qualify it for autonomous
existence in the noetic economy of the day. But it was neither
cogent nor convincing, since the "art" he selected—the figurative use of words—served merely to perpetuate, by vastly
expanding, the entire medieval view of poetry as instrumental
to something else. Although he enlarged the scope of both the
method (admitting all kinds of allegories, not just the ethical)
and the material to which it applied (modern poets as well as
ancient), it seems impossible to regard such an increase as an
"innovation."[42] It is simply more of the same very old thing.
The mere multiplicity of significations that Salutati permits
does not at all endow poetry with its own "free" mode of operation.[43] Because that operation is defined as figurative speech
in traditional Augustinian terms, it remains bound to serve
and to mean—by "standing for"—something else. Poetry is
universal not by virtue of working in any new or distinctive
way, but by sharing the old operation attributed to language
itself: it can be a container of anything.

Although this old kind of universality fails, both logically
and in practice, to secure the desired "autonomy," what seems
new (and what seems to have misled earlier scholars who were

[41] *Ibid.*, II, 87–108.

[42] As does Charles Trinkaus, *In Our Image and Likeness* (London, 1970), II,
703.

[43] As is claimed by Nancy S. Struever, *The Language of History in the Renaissance* (Princeton, 1970), pp. 51ff.

looking for a concept of "aesthetics" as well as more recent in-
vestigators in search of a new consciousness of language) is of
course the desire itself. Salutati appears to want something that
his traditional vocabulary of discourse cannot provide. He
wants to reverse an order of value, to defend and legitimize poetry, including that in the vernacular; but he is hampered by
the terms and assumptions of referential speech, which persist
in conceiving as instrumental what he wishes to be self-justi-
fying. In this situation he is again exemplary of subsequent
generations of Renaissance thinkers, some of whom will find
different means to assert the revaluation of literature. But most
of these will similarly fail to arrive at a new conception to support the new evaluation. And when a new conception is at least
partially worked out by Lorenzo Valla, it will be largely ignored as theoretical polemics about words continue the partisan warfare of crying up one branch of *studia humanitatis* at the
expense of others without ever becoming fully aware of their
linguistic premises. It is in this context that assertions of "autonomy" arise, which should make clear that to revalue something is by no means necessarily to reconsider it.

Certainly no reconsideration was made possible by the other
major means of revaluation, the revived doctrine of divine inspiration. Whatever the psychological interest or classical
prestige of this idea, its usefulness to defend and legitimize artistic creation was obvious and extreme: it put the issue beyond debate altogether. By assuring "autonomy" for art on
the basis of its origin, there was no need to redefine its operation. The latter could continue to be described, with the same
consequences as for Salutati, in the instrumental vocabulary of
traditional rhetoric.

These consequences are most apparent in the work of the
Pléiade, the group that made the fullest and most concerted
use of divine fury in order "to free poetry from the obligation
of conforming to extra-poetical scales of value."[44] Grahame
Castor has demonstrated how this emphasis arose from the

---

[44] Grahame Castor, *Pléiade Poetics* (Cambridge, 1964), pp. 24, 199.

difficulty of using the inherited instrumental terms—invention, imagination, imitation—to assert the intrinsic, autonomous worth of poetry. "The concepts which the Pléiade had to
use in presenting their case were still part of the system in
which . . . the poet's true situation was in doubt."[45] To "invent" what was there before; to "imagine" what could never
be; to "imitate" what really existed somewhere else—whether
all these activities were construed in Platonic or newly fashionable Aristotelian ways, all placed the poet at a great ontological
and epistemological disadvantage to advocates of other
branches of humane letters, such as philosophy and history.
But such inferiority was reversed at a stroke by regarding the
poet as a classical or Christianized *vates*: his claim to a higher
kind of truth than that attainable by the philosopher or historian became inviolable, while his language remained comfortably explicable by the same rhetoric as theirs. Thus Pierre de
Ronsard, after insisting that the muses only inspire the noblest
souls with the loftiest conceptions, is careful to stress that their
expression is not random nor "fantastic" but rather "well-or-
dered and disposed" by all the embellishing techniques of elocution.[46] Thus Pontus de Tyard is careful to distinguish "fu-
rie" (mental disease) from "fureur" (the four variants of which
he borrows from the *Phaedrus*), and to declare at length that the
poetic variant includes the study of all arts and sciences.[47] In

[45] *Ibid.*, p. 185. The contradictions between theories of inspiration and the
whole Horatian tradition of conscious rhetorical skill were apparent throughout the period; they are well described by Henri Weber, *La Création poétique au
XVIᵉ siècle en France* (Paris, 1956), I, Ch. 3. He observes that "Quand les poètes
de la Pléiade ont cherché à concilier théoriquement . . . l'imitation et l'inspiration . . . ils ont abouti plutôt à d'ingénieux artifices qu'à des conseils pra-
tiques et efficaces," p. 160.

[46] "Abbregé de l'Art poëtique françois" (1565), in *Oeuvres Complètes*, ed.
Paul Laumonier (Paris, 1949), XIV, 5, 13–15. The ambivalence of the concept
of "imitation," which Ronsard takes in the Platonic sense, is apparent
throughout the treatise, along with his effort to push the old derivative notion
of "invention" toward its modern, creative sense by requiring the poet "inven-
ter de nouveau," p. 35.

[47] *Solitaire Premier* (1552), ed. S. F. Baridon (Geneva, 1950). Tyard's expo-

such ways as these was the divine fury tamed for drawing-room rhetorical presentation.[48] Though it was an impressive polemical weapon for poetry lovers and writers, it offered no alternative to the traditional instrumental vocabulary of discourse, but was merely an escape hatch from the valuation that vocabulary implied.

It was of course in the nature of the case that inspired language was hardly discernible from any other kind. One could demonstrate interminably how much wisdom poetry contained (and could urge this *copia* as evidence of inspiration); but one remained unable to verify its source. Similarly, we can today read hundreds of invocations to the muses without being able to discover in the poems themselves any particular use of language, any concrete effect, that seems to require production by a muse instead of a person. A possible Renaissance exception to this rule (the only one I know of) is the verse of John Milton. Milton, in contrast to other poets who dutifully or polemically courted the muse, appears genuinely to have believed himself a *vates*, that is, a thoroughly Christian prophet, and to have produced verse that is "unpremeditated" in ways that no formal rhetoric can fathom.[49] Such an exception, however, re-

---

sition of course combines the dignity of inspiration with that of universality in the systematic neoplatonic association of the muses, graces, and planets with intellectual disciplines (the trivium and quadrivium) and harmonic modes. The whole reproduces with a few additions (and the omission of the angelic orders) the universal system of the *Convivio* (II.6). Numerous diagrams that illustrate such omnivorous poetic theology are reproduced and discussed by S. K. Heninger, Jr., *The Cosmographical Glass* (San Marino, Calif., 1977), Ch. 4.

[48] Orpheus himself, one of the favorite topoi in the polemic, became domesticated in the pragmatic Ciceronian ethics of humanist pedagogy as the vehicle of the wisdom/eloquence equation, a useful example for schoolboys and preachers. See Kirsty Cochrane, "Orpheus Applied: Some Instances of His Importance in the Humanist View of Language," *Review of English Studies* 19 (1968), 1–13.

[49] That he did so is the erudite and persuasive argument of William Kerrigan, *The Prophetic Milton* (Charlottesville, Va., 1974). In addition to a comprehensive history of conceptions of prophetic inspiration, Kerrigan offers co-

sulting from the psychological force of an individual's life and beliefs, can offer no exit from the blind alley in which Renaissance writers found themselves when they asserted the intrinsic worth of poetry in a terminological system that implicitly denied it. What an individual impelled by powerful convictions may accomplish is, for better or worse, not dependent on their conceptual coherence or explanatory usefulness.

That poetry symbolizes all knowledge, or that it is divinely inspired (or both together, with either as cause of the other) are proposals for the revaluation of verbal art, not principles that can guide its study or explain its operation. The kind of "autonomy" claimed by such proposals in the exigencies of controversy is not to be found and remains in the proposals themselves contradicted by the analytical methods and concepts employed.[50] Allegorical interpretation made poetry a slave, imitation made it a second-hand copy, and elocution made it a schoolroom exercise; inspiration did not alter the theory of these operations, it just gave them a magical truth-sanction. The Renaissance lover of literature perceived in the allegories that poets actually composed, in the imitations they practiced, in the techniques of elocution they used, a new value that the received theories of these matters could not justify. We may observe his affecting and contradictory situation with sympathy, but we should not make the mistake of accepting these theories and trying to make them do what he could not. We should rather remain aware that in virtually all the literary and artistic debates of the Renaissance there was "a notable discrepancy between theory and practice."[51]

---

gent evidence from the procedure of the poems. See especially his analysis of temporal structure in *Samson Agonistes*, Ch. 5.

[50] "Autonomy" is manifestly not sustainable even in the exceptional case. If Urania did in fact pour *Paradise Lost* nightly into Milton's ear, his verse still remains less amenable to pure "aesthetic" treatment and more deeply involved in the revolutionary events of his own life and time than has been congenial to the taste of many twentieth-century formalists.

[51] This is the amply documented judgment of John M. Steadman, *The Lamb and the Elephant: Ideal Imitation and the Context of Renaissance Allegory* (San Marino, Calif., 1974), pp. viii, 236.

The main reason for this discrepancy in the case of verbal art is that even the theories that seek to revalue it remain confined by the mimetic assumptions or assertions of referential semantics. The revaluation sought will simply not fit in the old conceptual frame—even when it is stretched as far as Salutati tried to stretch it. If language stands for things, then the language that stands for the most prestigious things (the figures and symbols of Scripture that are Salutati's model or the philosophical and theological abstractions that Dante and the Pléiade wished literature to englobe) will become that which literature is obliged somehow to reproduce. Only when language is seen as doing something other, indeed something more, than representing—and when these other activities are seen not as aberrant deviations from a norm but as valid and significant in themselves—can the operation of literature be reformulated as having an intrinsic value not dependent on its resemblance to or incorporation of more directly representational kinds of discourse. Such a reformulation very seldom occurs in the strictly literary disputes of the period, almost all of which remain within the received linguistic/conceptual framework of sign/thing.

The breakthrough was made in broader areas of linguistic concern—beginning with the examination of changes in the Latin language, which produced the discipline of historical philology. The "rebirth" of the classical past through the acutely self-conscious midwifery of Renaissance humanists created an awareness of the historical context of usage in language that gradually came to be treated as semantically constitutive. That language itself had a past was not unknown to prior generations. But it remained for the Renaissance to explore, under the pressure of concerns as much political as belletristic, some of the implications of this fact. When Lorenzo Valla formulated the temporal distinctions in syntactic and lexical usages of Latin between ancient Rome and medieval Europe, he was making the kind of observations that resulted in real challenges to the received semantics of reference. He offered such challenges by reconceiving the subjects of the medieval trivium—grammar, rhetoric, and dialectic—as the integrated investigation of discursive practices that shape the human world. Although the philosophical, theoretical import of this challenge was hardly understood, its basis in his own historical interpretive practice was widely diffused in debates about the scope and importance of rhetoric, in the status of Latin vs. that of the vernaculars, and in the Protestant revolution in biblical hermeneutics. The kind of semantic observations thus diffused owed nothing to the received conceptual framework: the vocabulary of sign/thing per se offered no way to conceive of meaning as constituted by temporal and social contexts. Reference theories, true to their Platonic origin and Christian development, postulate meaning not just as a substance, but as an eternal one. Renaissance debates about language, therefore, also present a considerable discrepancy between theory and practice. When language is talked about, it is consciously regarded as the clothing of preexistent meanings; but when language is employed to reflect on its various functions—to recommend a style, to praise a vernacular, to teach the figures of speech, to urge a method of interpreting Scripture, or to compose literature—it is often implicitly regarded as constitutive of meaning.

This situation has occasioned the following dilemma in much modern scholarship, both English and Italian: if we pay most attention to what Renaissance writers say about language, we are likely to dismiss it as jejune and simplistic cliché. If, on the other hand, we pay most attention to what they do with language, we may attribute to them theoretical positions that they had not in fact attained.[52] The most comprehensive

[52] The overly negative estimate was characteristic of an older generation of literary historians: e.g., Francesco De Sanctis, *History of Italian Literature*, 2 vols., tr. Joan Redfern (New York, 1931; 1st ed. 1870); Donald L. Clark, *Rhetoric and Poetry in the Renaissance* (New York, 1922); C. S. Baldwin, *Renaissance Literary Theory and Practice* (New York, 1939). The overly positive estimate arose in part as a reaction against them by such historical critics as Rosemond Tuve, *Elizabethan and Metaphysical Imagery* (Chicago, 1947), and has since become intensified in some intellectual historians: e.g., Cesare Vasoli, *La dialet-*

modern study of language in the Renaissance is able to perceive this dilemma precisely because it approaches the subject
by means of a composite relational theory of meaning. Professor Apel sees that the pragmatic concerns of Ciceronian rhetoric are the de facto employment of a language-based epistemology. He also sees that the awareness of this is limited
throughout the period by the presupposition of Greek object-
oriented philosophy in which word equals thing. Of the expanding enthusiasm for this rhetoric, he writes:

The beginnings of the philological and hermeneutic arts, including
empirical linguistic science, will in fact arise in this way, but the implicit language philosophy of humanism is never thereby called into
question. It tends ever outward, defining itself rather as mere empiricism or pedagogy, as is most clearly to be traced in its separation,
since Salutati, from formal logic and Averroistic natural science. The
reader of this polemical and programmatic literature constantly
awaits a decisive, thoroughgoing epistemological and philosophical
argument, which he, like the humanist himself, thinks he perceives in
the Ciceronian "topics." But he waits in vain.[53]

In other words, the relational theory shows us how practice
exists before theory, how forms and contexts of language may
be treated as constituting nonreferential meaning before they
are defined as doing so. It can thus prevent us from either accepting at face value the past's concept of itself or attributing
to the past our own conceptual awareness.

Renaissance theories of literature seldom describe its operation in any new way that can justify the new value they wish
to attribute to it. And when they do, they borrow such redescription from other and wider realms of controversy about
language. From philosophy, from vernacular speech, and
from Holy Scripture appear ways of apprehending the mean-

---

tica e la retorica dell'Umanesimo (Milan, 1968); Nancy S. Struever, *The Language
of History in the Renaissance.*

[53] *Die Idee der Sprache*, p. 153. I shall argue that the wait is not entirely in
vain, that the object-oriented "implicit language philosophy" is indeed called
into question in various ways.

ing of words that liberate them from their single obligation to represent things. Because some of these broader controversies offer a genuine reconsideration of their subject, and because that subject is the medium of literature, they can reveal the substantive changes wrought by the Renaissance in ways of regarding the use of the writer's only tools—words.

PART II

ARGUMENTS ABOUT
WORDS

The usage of men is the maker of words.

[A language] was not derived from reason, but from use . . . it is not based on reason but on example; there is no law of speaking, but only observation.

—LORENZO VALLA,
1437, 1451

Languages are not born like trees, some of which are fragile and weak in their nature, others healthy and robust and better made to carry the weight of our human conceptions. But all their power is born into the world from the will of mortals. Languages of all countries are of the same value, and are formed by men to one end with one judgment.

—SPERONE SPERONI,
1542

Usage belongs to the community.

—JACQUES PELETIER,
1555

Statements like these can have a beguilingly modern ring to the twentieth-century linguist who is interested in the history of his discipline. One such scholar has urged "that linguistic thought in the sixteenth century was more original, more advanced, and certainly more interesting than is generally recognized." Pointing out that the Renaissance first singled out "living" languages as worthy of scholarly attention, Herbert Izzo deplores its "continued neglect" in histories of linguistics during the last thirty years.[1] The grounds of this appreciation

---

[1] Herbert J. Izzo, "The Linguistic Philosophy of Benedetto Varchi, Six-

were, however, apparent long ago in the pioneer work of Robert A. Hall, Jr., and have not changed. The modern linguist can find in the Renaissance campaign to legitimize vernaculars not only the acceptance of historical change and the social function of language as principles but also the attempt to apply them by observing loan-words and developing theories of regular phonetic and morphological change.[2] Although the appreciation is perfectly just, one reason for the neglect complained of is not hard to find: it is simply that all these nascent theories underwent no subsequently continuous development. The historian of ideas, especially when influenced even tacitly by the search for biological continuity, can find nothing very edifying in the spectacle of a fairly widespread body of theory that was ignored for about two centuries, only to have its line of investigation then resumed in different contexts and from different premises. It was Hall who postulated this gap and explained it by invoking the dogmatic and unhistorical attitude toward language of the seventeenth and eighteenth centuries, which sought fixed standards of value and strict categories of

---

teenth-Century Florentine Humanist," *Language Sciences* 40 (April, 1976), 1–7. Another such scholar attributes the neglect to the fact that linguistic theories do not exist per se in the period, and must be disinterred from other contexts: Raffaele Simone, "Sperone Speroni et l'idée de diachronie dans la linguistique de la Renaissance Italienne," in *History of Linguistic Thought and Contemporary Linguistics*, ed. Herman Parret (Berlin, 1976), pp. 302–303. Simone points out further that this neglect has resulted in the false assumption of "uninterrupted continuity" between medieval and "Cartesian" linguistics, which ignores the whole challenge presented by the Renaissance recognition of diachronicity to "la tradition invétérée du 'parallélisme logico-grammatical.' " Many essays in this volume justify his point: what now occupies historians of linguistics is debate about Chomsky's use of past ideas to support his present ones. Since these concern universals of grammar and deep structure, the whole Renaissance emphasis on languages as social and historical products is hardly congenial.

[2] "Linguistic Theory in the Italian Renaissance," *Language* 12 (1936), 96–107. Hall's general argument here, expanded in his later monograph, *The Italian Questione della Lingua* (Chapel Hill, 1942), is that linguistic science began in the sixteenth, not the nineteenth, century. In the later work he observes also the appearance of an organic theory of linguistic change, which postulates phases of growth, maturity, and decay, that is "exactly comparable . . . to Humboldt," p. 36.

grammar.[3] In the theory of language and, perhaps even more, in that of history, there are good reasons for perceiving the age of neoclassicism or enlightenment as an interregnum between the shared concerns of the Renaissance and the Romantic period.[4] Such "discontinuities," however, to which the work of Michel Foucault has alerted us, can also be exaggerated. In the case of language, if we look beyond theory at the literature and pedagogy of the Renaissance, we shall see that the new conceptions so attractive to the modern linguist were by no means without effect. And if we look at the whole context in which those conceptions themselves arise, we shall not find it at all surprising that, as concepts or theories, they tended to lie fallow. For they were unable, for various reasons, to overthrow the static referential bias in all reflection about words. In this sense, the neoclassic period and the enlightenment do not break from the Renaissance but rather continue one of its major tendencies, which is to conceptualize (if not to use) language as cosmetic to a fixed and universal reality.

Before proceeding to examine the theoretical and practical challenges to this tendency, we need to notice their basic context—the foundation of what I have earlier called "the traditional vocabulary of discourse." Historical self-consciousness is forced upon us by the observation that this vocabulary includes no single term for what we today automatically understand by "language"—that is, a unitary, all-inclusive concept of any systematic means of communication.[5] For example,

---

[3] *The Italian Questione*, pp. 46–48.

[4] Peter Burke draws some suggestive parallels, after using Hume to exemplify the eighteenth-century search for "universal principles of human nature" in history: "The nineteenth-century discovery of the past was curiously like the Renaissance discovery, of which—after a gap—it was a continuation, an intensification. Philology again played a crucial role, with Niebuhr in the place of Valla. A historical school of law came into existence once again, with Savigny, 1779–1861, in the place of Alciati and Cujas. Savigny, who taught at Berlin, saw law as a gradual development or growth like language; his greatest pupil was the philologist Jakob Grimm." *The Renaissance Sense of the Past* (New York, 1970), p. 144. Burke mentions also the revived study of the Bible as an historical document in both eras.

[5] The first such extension of the word in English—from a body of words to

such a term is conspicuously absent from the indices of the pe-riod's scholarly works I have looked at. Here one finds instead the following list of major and separate terms:[6]

linguae:	"tongues," the speech of a particular group—local, national, or professional
oratio:★	"speech," the faculty and its product
sermo:★	"discourse," often as written argument, "phrase" or "expression"
verba:†	"words," units of meaning; also
	voces: "words," units of sound or "terms";
	vocabulae: "terms" or "names";
	signa: "signs," which along with the foregoing "stand for" (*ponuntur* or *supponunt*) "things" (*res*);
	partes orationis: "parts of speech," words as units of grammar
significatio:	"meaning," usually found in things
sensus:	"meaning" or "sense," also found in
propositiones:	"propositions," complete utterances or
sententiae:	"sentences," which can equally be the meanings in the utterances

★ These are interchangeable.

† All of these can have "properties" (*proprietates*), which may indicate any-thing from morphology to significance described as "essence" (*essentia*).

In an index it is most unlikely that any of these terms will have a cross-reference to any other. Moreover, when you look up

---

something else—is given by the *OED* from Shakespeare, *Troilus and Cressida*, IV.v.55: "There's language in her eye, her cheek, her lip." One would think that such an apparently obvious metaphor would have occurred to an earlier poet; but I have not found him.

[6] This is not remotely comprehensive, but simply one particular indication of how the period conceived of language. Many of the terms, of course, had been given different and highly technical meanings in medieval logic, which Renaissance humanists generally held in contempt, knew only from commen-taries, or didn't know at all. As Rita Guerlac reminds us in her excellent intro-duction to *Juan Luis Vives Against the Pseudodialecticians* (Dordrecht, 1979), much work of the thirteenth century, now regarded as the heyday of medieval philosophy, remained in manuscripts unknown until the last hundred years (p. 42).

the references given, you are as likely to find an isolated mention or use of the term as a substantive discussion of it. The mere occurrence of the terms, independently of each other, seems as worthwhile recording as their elucidation. If this is but the result of pedantic zeal, it is zeal in the service of a habit of mind that conceives of language in a distinctly atomistic way. As the number of terms for them suggests, *words* are the central focus of interest. There is not the slightest attempt to gather under a single heading the places where all the sundry units, operations, and significances of "language" are treated.

The title of this section is a reminder that the Renaissance as a whole lacked any single generalized modern concept of language: either as an entire system of lexical items and rules for their manipulation (linguistic), or as expressing the "inner form" of national or communal life (Romantic), or as the general use of signs or symbols (psychological, scientific), or as an unbounded social game (Wittgensteinian). The complication is, of course, that actual analysis of discourse of all kinds may be seen to adumbrate all these concepts. These adumbrations are fascinating in themselves, and I believe that their consequences are indispensable for understanding the period and its literature. But it must be remembered that they remain adumbrations—indistinct prefigurements and not direct progenitors—of positions whose much later articulation is what first permits us to see their shadows in the Renaissance.

3

THE CHALLENGE FROM
PHILOSOPHY

i. Lorenzo Valla

For ordinary language has no exact logic.   —P. F. STRAWSON

Lorenzo Valla is probably best known today for having proved
that the "Donation of Constantine," a document purporting to
record the fourth-century emperor's cession of temporal dominion in the West to the popes, was a much later forgery. The
epochal significance of Valla's proof was appreciated by its
English translator: "for the first time, he used effectively the
method of studying the usage of words in the variations of
their meaning and application, and other devices of internal
criticism which are the tools of historical criticism today."[7]
The more or less systematic "method" was indeed the innovation. Though others, like Nicholas of Cusa and Reginald
Pecock, had independently urged the inauthenticity of the
document, Valla was able to demonstrate it decisively. The
structure and argument of his treatise derive from what Valla
shared with all the generations of humanists beginning with
Petrarch: an immersion in classical histories and a passionate
admiration of classical Latin style. The former provides the
dramatic approach to the subject, the latter the observations of
linguistic usage that constitute the evidence.

To show that Constantine would logically never have given,
and St. Sylvester never have accepted, temporal power, Valla

[7] Christopher B. Coleman, tr., *The Treatise of Lorenzo Valla on the Donation
of Constantine* (New Haven, 1922), p. 3. Page numbers of references to this edition, which includes the Latin, are given parenthetically in the text.

writes long speeches for them that give full scope to his own sarcastic criticisms of contemporary reality, as when he has Sylvester ask rhetorically whether the Vicar of Christ should keep soldiers and wage wars. The drama continues even when the speeches are ended and Valla goes on in his own voice to a linguistic examination of the document by railing directly against its author, calling him names and occasionally insulting him more adroitly. What Valla is observing in this lively way is primarily the anachronistic use of particular words. Having detected a few un-Roman terms, he exults: "What else are you doing, wretch, except showing that you have the will to deceive but not the ability?" (Quid agis aliud, infelix, nisi ut iudices te voluntatem fallendi habere, facultatem non habere? 88.) His ridicule slides easily back and forth among matters of chronological fact, usage, and style (mainly in the grammatical sense). At one point he announces style as the topic and goes on to castigate the confusion of terms for the raiment and gear of Roman emperors and later kings (105–109), concluding, "God confound you, wickedest of mortals, who attribute barbarous speech to a cultivated age!" (Deus te perdat, improbissime mortalium, qui sermonem barbarum attribuis saeculo erudito! 110.) This archetypal humanist outrage at "barbarous discourse" is here simply a matter of diction, the choice of individual words. Matters of syntax and verb tense are also noticed, but the focus remains on the author's use of terms, about which Valla wonders, "Which shall I reproach more, the stupidity of the ideas or of the words?" (Utrum magis insequar, sententiarum an verborum stoliditatem? 114.) But he is not at all concerned to maintain this implied separation of words and meanings, especially, no doubt, since he is arguing that the document is trash in every possible respect. All of these are summed up in the final inference that "illa loquendi barbaries" betrays its later composition (120).[8]

[8] We should note in passing another main feature of Valla's treatment that makes it historically important, his skeptical attitude to evidence, which in this case is nourished by his contempt for barbarous, i.e., medieval, speech. He stresses the unknown provenance of the "Donation" and attacks through-

The *Wirkungsgeschichte* of the *de falso credita . . . Constantini Donatione declamatio*, which shows us its historical importance, is instructively disproportionate to its *Entstehungsgeschichte*, which shows us its place in the body of Valla's work. This place is not prominent, for he never even bothered to publish it (i.e., to arrange for its copying by professional scribes). Its immediate purpose, to attack the secular ambitions of the papacy, is made explicit in the direct addresses to the pope with which Valla begins and ends the treatise. Writing in about 1440 while in the service of King Alphonso V of Aragon and Sicily, who was then trying to acquire Naples (which he did in 1442), Valla begins by warning the pope that his title to these lands is poor. He concludes with a lengthy attack (170–83) on contemporary territorial claims of the Church and on the ancient papal hostility to Rome (with whose nobility Valla liked to identify), threatening the pope with another *declamatio* if he ignored this one. The threat never had to be made good. Alphonso conquered Naples, and a few years later Valla himself entered the service of the new pope, Nicholas V. Thus the political circumstances that inspired the treatise, and which account in part for the dramatized immediacy of its racy personifications, altered; and Valla was content to let it rest in the oblivion of its original occasion.

A different set of circumstances was to initiate its revival some sixty years after Valla's death in 1457. Although first published in 1506, the *declamatio* attracted no attention and no ecclesiastical condemnation until after Ulrich von Hutten perceived its utility for the nascent Reformation and issued two editions of it in 1518 and 1519. Its appearance on the *Index* thirty years later merely verified the extent to which Valla's historical philology, via his antipapal criticism, had become identified with the Protestant cause.[9] Thus his modern fame

---

out the "impudentissima fabula" of the legendary "Acts of Sylvester," of which it was allegedly a part (pp. 76, 125ff.).

[9] These facts are presented by Wolfram Setz, *Lorenzo Vallas Schrift gegen die Konstantinische Schenkung . . . Zur Interpretation und Wirkungsgeschichte* (Tübingen, 1975).

rests in large part on this crucial but later association—the humanist legacy to Protestantism of textual analysis and the methodological awareness that the past is different from the present.

In his own day Valla was most widely renowned as the author of the *Elegantiae*, an elaborate account of the grammar, diction, and style of classical Latin. This work was the foundation of his philology; he augmented it and carefully prepared its publication over a period of years.[10] Scores of later editions throughout Europe attested to its enormous influence and popularity and established Valla as the supreme humanist whose purpose was to recover the eloquence of Roman antiquity. The method of this recovery partially implies the new conception of language with which Valla challenged his contemporaries.

This method is nothing more nor less than an empirical survey of actual usage, constantly exemplified from scores of classical writers. Despite his open contempt for nonclassical Latin (especially that of Boethius), his whole approach, which might well attract the admiration of modern linguists, is more descriptive than prescriptive. He is recommending "elegance" according to the *venusto usu* of the ancient past; that is, his standard of judgment is completely historical, not derived from any a priori postulation of grammatical "rule," but based wholly on the observation of change in every aspect of usage: grammatical, syntactic, and semantic. How revolutionary this approach then was may be gauged by the anger it aroused in some of his fellow humanists. Poggio Bracciolini, for exam-

---

[10] A usefully annotated bibliography of Valla's work is given by Mario Fois, S.J., *Il pensiero cristiano di L. V.* (Rome, 1969), pp. 641–44. The most thorough concise account of Valla's career and the entire sequence of his writings is given (in Italian) in Ari Wesseling's introduction to his edition of Valla's *Antidotum Primum* (Assen, 1978). Fuller information must still be sought in the nineteenth-century monographs reprinted in facsimile in vol. 2 of Valla's *Opera Omnia*, ed. E. Garin (Turin, 1962), vol. 1 of which is a facsimile reprint of the Basle edition of 1540. The *Elegantiae*, extant in many editions, will be cited parenthetically by book and chapter numbers; other citations of Valla's work will give in addition to these the page numbers of Basle, 1540.

ple, was outraged by Valla's refusal to see grammar in the traditional, rationalistic, prescriptive way, and could not comprehend his historical perspective.[11] Although Valla uses the traditional categories of grammar as a partial means to organize his work,[12] he does not take them in a prescriptive sense, but simply as a framework within which to observe all kinds of change—in classical Latin as well as that between antiquity and the Middle Ages. Again and again he identifies a typically medieval construction, such as the use of *quod* as a conjunction, to call it "boorish and crude" (III.52)—not because it violates a rule, but simply because it was not used in the same way by the ancients. Variations in the usage of the ancients themselves are noted with care and perfect equanimity: "elsewhere in this kind of construction [the adverb] is omitted," and "everyone knows this, but not everyone uses it correctly" are typical observations.[13] Valla is not remotely interested in prescribing a system of rules, no matter how derived; his concern is to describe actual ancient usages in order to purge them of later "Gothic" and "Vandal" accretions. Setting out thus to restore classical semantic precision to various legal, theological, and grammatical terms, his general practice in the last four books of the *Elegantiae* is to discuss them in pairs that have related or opposed meanings. In this and in countless other ways throughout the work he displays his awareness that the company a word keeps—that is, its total context: use in relation to other terms, grammatical form, historical circumstances—constitutes its meaning.[14]

[11] See the analysis of their quarrel on this issue by Salvatore I. Camporeale, *L.V.: Umanesimo e teologia* (Florence, 1972), pp. 180–92.

[12] In its final form, the *Elegantiae* comprises six books: I, on nouns, verbs, and participles; II, on other parts of speech; III, on the meaning of terms in civil law; IV, on the meaning of other terms (many theological); V, on verbs and verbal idioms; VI, on other grammarians' opinions.

[13] "Aliquando in huiusmodi genere sermonis omittimus *Post*, sic . . ." (III.54) "*Alter* de duobus dici, *Alius* de multis, notum est omnibus, licet non omnes recte utantur" (III.60).

[14] Illustrations are legion, if to us banal—e.g., "*Commendo te regi*, id est, *committo*. *Commendo te apud regem*, id est, *laudo*" (III.46)—but the awareness is cru-

By themselves, the procedures by which Valla examines language in the two works that made his reputation, both then and now, would be a significant challenge to the traditional ontologically bound grammar and semantics of his age. But these procedures were neither the fortuitous accident of intuitive common sense nor (as scholarship has until recently tended to assume) the simple result of a fastidious, belletristic taste hostile to the rigors of scholastic philosophy. They were, on the contrary, the result of a sustained, deliberate, and reasoned attack on the fundamental linguistic premises of that philosophy.

It was as a self-taught philosopher that Valla began his career, as ambitiously as possible, with two works that address the most basic philosophical questions of his time: the nature of the good, *De voluptate ac de vero bono*, and of the true, *Dialecticae disputationes*.[15] The title Valla gave to the first version of the latter work is a more accurate indication of its hubristic scope: *Repastinatio dialecticae et philosophiae*. His aim is to "re-dig" the foundation of all knowledge, which makes his first step the toppling of the entire edifice that had been built on Aristotle. The first book of the *Dialectica* is therefore an attack on the validity of the ten Aristotelian logical "predicaments" or categories, which Valla reduces to three, and on the various scholastic "transcendental" terms, which he reduces to one.[16]

cial and is a fair adumbration of the principle of "collocation" developed by J. R. Firth, "Linguistic Analysis as a Study of Meaning," in *Selected Papers 1952–1959*, ed. F. R. Palmer (Bloomington, Ind., 1968).

[15] Although we are not concerned with the first of these, it is worth noting that it was responsible for the misprision of Valla, both in his own time and in the nineteenth century, as a vulgarly "Epicurean" libertine—an impression that the studies of Camporeale and Fois are centrally concerned to correct.

[16] The substance of this attack, its basis in Quintilian's view of language usage, and its intensification by Valla in the successive versions of the *Dialectica*, are all succinctly described by Camporeale, pp. 153–62. The chronological order of these versions was identified by Gianni Zippel ('Note sulle redazioni della 'Dialectica' di L. V.," *Archivo storico Provincie Parmensi*, series 4 [1957], 301–15) whose reconstructed text of the final version has recently appeared: *Laurentii Valle Repastinatio Dialectice et Philosophie*, 2 vols. (Padua,

The reductions are made, and the whole radical critique offered, on the grounds that such terms violate the "common
custom of speaking" (communem loquendi consuetudinem,
I.xvi; 678) and should be replaced by those that adhere "more
simply and more suitably to the natural sense and common
use" (simplicius et ad naturalem sensum usumque communem
accommodatius, I.xvi; 679) of words.

Whether they approve of it or not, recent scholars have perceived the destructive dimension of Valla's effort, understood
variously as the "unification" of dialectic and rhetoric, or the
replacement of Aristotle by Quintilian, or the "subordination"
of both logic and philosophy to rhetoric.[17] Its constructive dimension, however—the extent to which Valla's critique implies and develops an alternative conception of the relation of
language to meaning, truth, and the phenomenal world—has
been much less widely appreciated. The most acute appreciation, which gives Valla his full weight as a philosopher, is the
excellent study by Hanna-Barbara Gerl, *Rhetorik als Philosophie: Lorenzo Valla.*[18] Before reviewing her conclusions, we

---

1982). Because this composite version has never before appeared in print, I
shall continue to cite Basle, 1540, with reference as necessary to passages
added in the last manuscript version.

[17] Cf. Cesare Vasoli, *La dialettica e la retorica dell'Umanesimo* (Milan, 1968),
pp. 63ff.; Jerrold E. Seigel, *Rhetoric and Philosophy in Renaissance Humanism*
(Princeton, 1968), pp. 160ff.; John Monfasani, *George of Trebizond: A Biography and a Study of his Rhetoric and Logic* (Leiden, 1976), pp. 304–05.

[18] Munich, 1974. Her approach completes a reversal of scholarly attitude toward this aspect of Valla's work in the last generation. For example, in 1948
Charles Trinkaus called Valla's dialectics "feeble" (*The Renaissance Philosophy
of Man*, ed. Cassirer, Kristeller, Randall [Chicago, 1948], p. 149), but in 1970
allowed that present "concern with 'philosophy of language' makes further
study of Renaissance works of this genre imperative" (*In Our Image and Likeness* I, 380n). Both Camporeale and Gerl have since begun to supply this demand for Valla, though the *Dialectica* is rich enough to deserve more independent and detailed analysis. Trinkaus' latest opinion is that Valla was
"possibly the most original mind of the Italian Renaissance": *The Pursuit of Holiness in Late Medieval and Renaissance Religion*, ed. Trinkaus with Heiko A.
Oberman (Leiden, 1974), p. 361. An excellent defense of Valla's dialectics as a
genuine philosophical alternative to syllogistic scholasticism has been offered

must look at some extended examples of Valla's habitual method in the *Dialectica* in order to see how his negative critique moves into, and ultimately depends upon, a newly developed idea of how language works.

Setting out to deny that "transcendental" terms (like *bonum, verum, unum*) are universal in either meaning or reality, Valla takes up the term "one":

Aristotle mantains that one is not a number but rather the beginning of number—as if the beginnings of things were not parts of those things and consequently the things themselves: who reads the beginning of a book reads the book; who touches the head of a man touches the man; who sees the commencement of a pond sees the pond; who hears the introduction of a speech hears the speech. Such matters as these must not be referred to the chicanery of the sophists, but to the usage of men, which is the maker of words. Everyone calls number singular and plural—we speak of things as one or several in number—in which manner Aristotle himself has spoken more than once. [Here follows an example of two women who share eggs from commonly owned hens, designed to show that even one egg still makes a "number," on which Valla concludes:] Thus housewives sometimes have a better sense of the meaning of words than the greatest philosophers. For the former employ words for a purpose, the latter for a game, as Aristotle does when he says that number is numbered or is countable. Along with the housewives, I deny that this is intelligible; I count what is counted, not number itself. Thus a [standard of] measure is not measured out, nor is it measurable; nor is a [standard of] weight weighed out nor weighable; but by the measure itself and by the weight, we measure out and weigh other things. The true or the truth is properly knowledge, or the conception of anything at all, and is like the light of the mind that also extends itself to the senses. I maintain that this light belongs to the mind itself, just as sight and power of seeing belong to the eyes; it is not a light that comes from outside, such as the sun. Yet, as the sun displays the colors of bodies to the eyes, so God exhibits the qualities of things to the mind. Plato elaborated this somewhat differently in the *Republic*, when he said that truth is like the sun, and knowledge or conception like the full, un-

by Lisa Jardine, "Lorenzo Valla and the Origins of Humanist Dialectic," *Journal of the History of Philosophy* 15 (1977), 143–64.

impeded sight of it. But since there is falsehood in ourselves, why is there not also truth? Certainly when we affirm anything to be false or true, it is referred to the mind of the speaker, because it is in his mind that truth or falsehood resides. For false bread, false wine, false prophet are, we affirm, by no means bread, wine, or prophet; and true bread, true wine, true prophet are nothing other than bread, wine, or prophet. Thus truth and falsehood are in ourselves, that is, in our mind. Sometimes they are not manifested in the mind but in the mouth. Therefore an utterance can be false while the mind is not mistaken—when someone speaks otherwise than he feels—and can likewise be true while the mind is mistaken—when someone deceives not another, as before, but rather himself.[19]

[19] I.ii; 649: "Aristoteles negat unum esse numerum, sed principium numeri. Quasi principia rerum, non sint ipsarum rerum partes, & ex consequenti ipsae res: qui legit principium libri, librum legit: qui tangit caput hominis, hominem tangit: qui videt initium stagni, stagnum videt: qui audit exordium orationis, orationem audit. Quae talia non sunt ad calumniam sophistarum referenda: sed ad hominum usum, qui verborum est autor. Omnes dicunt numerum singularem & pluralem, & unum numero, & plura numero, quem in modum non semel ipse locutus est Aristoteles. . . . Itaque melius de intellectu verborum mulierculae nonnunquam sentiunt, quam summi philosophi. Illae enim verba ad usum trahunt: isti ad lusum. Cuiusmodi est, quod ait Aristoteles numerum numerari, seu numerabilem esse. Hoc ego cum mulierculis nego intelligere: numero quod numeratur, non ipse numerus: sic nec mensura metitur, seu mensibilis est: nec pondus appenditur, seu appensibile est: sed ipsa mensura, & ipso pondere, alia metimur atque appendimus. Verum sive veritas est proprie scientia, sive noticia cuiuscunque rei, et quasi lux animi, quae ad sensus quoque se porrigit: hanc lucem esse volo ipsius animi: quasi oculorum vim videndi & visum: non exteriorem quandam veluti solarem. Quanquam ut sol oculis colores corporum, ita deus menti rerum qualitates ostendit & exhibet. Hoc nonnihil diversae protulit Plato in libris de republica, cum ait veritatem esse veluti solem: scientiam noticiamque veluti sincerum aspectum. Sed cum in nobis falsitas sit, cur non sit & veritas? Certe cum quid falsum verumque esse affirmamus, id ad animum loquentis refertur: quod in eo veritas sit aut falsitas. Nam falsus panis, & falsum vinum, & falsus propheta, nequaquam est panis, vinum, propheta: ut nos opinamur: & verus panis, verum vinum, verus propheta, non aliud est quam panis, vinum, propheta. Itaque in nobis, id est, in animo nostro est veritas & falsitas. Nonnunquam haec non in animo notantur: sed in ore. Ideoque oratio potest esse falsa, animo non errante: cum quis aliter loquitur ac sentit: & item vera, errante animo: cum quis non alium uti superiorem sed seipsum fallit."

In transcribing Latin I have throughout expanded all contractions except the

To begin with, we should notice the rich and often abrupt mixture of tones in the passage, as Valla passes from open scorn to metaphorical earnest (truth as "the light of the mind") and ironic understatement (introducing the directly contradictory opinion of Plato as "nonnihil diversae"), from lengthy periods of narration or inference to brief ones of aphoristic summary ("non in animo . . . sed in ore"). His arguments and demonstrations are sometimes straightforward and literal, sometimes oblique and suggestive; they are never formal or syllogistic. In short, Valla exemplifies the "rhetorical" philosophy that he advocates, availing himself of all the resources and registers of language at his command. His medium is indeed his message insofar as it consistently refuses to make clear-cut distinctions between grammar, logic, epistemology, and psychology—all of which are continually linked as aspects of Valla's omnipresent point of departure and standard of judgment: the "common usage" of words.

Valla's brisk delight in repeatedly using this standard to play off the high against the low—intellectuals versus housewives and the *populus*—is not some trivial form of iconoclasm but the result of his developing more fully the implications of the standard that he found in Quintilian and Horace. For Valla, the whole thrust of the "common custom of speaking" goes far beyond the particular context of the orator's obligation to be clear and avoid affectation (which is predominant in the *Institutio Oratoria*) as it seeks to invoke the wider purpose of making semantic distinctions useful in ordinary life. If one is not a number of eggs fewer than two, a useful distinction has disappeared. Valla invokes this wider purpose more explicitly but in the same tone when he attacks the Aristotelian concept of "act" versus "potentiality." Again he begins by heaping scorn on a violation of common usage: "If a box is made from this piece of wood, shall we say that this piece of wood is a box 'in

---

ampersand and introduced the consonantal "v" according to standard lexicographical practice. All punctuation is that of the cited texts, whose oddities and confusions I attempt to clarify in the translations.

the act'? Who has ever spoken thus? Who would not laugh at anyone speaking thus?" He proceeds directly to the operative question: "Of what use is it to add 'in the act?' "[20] To the reply that "potentially" the wood may be either the box or something other than the box, Valla responds that if we say that we are certainly denying that it is a box now. In short, he argues that the Aristotelian distinction is merely self-referring, that it makes as little sense to call the wood a "potential" box as to call the manufactured box a box "in the act" because the clear distinction made in ordinary language between the product and the material is thereby destroyed. He objects at length that if the idea of "potentiality" is applied to anything that can possibly be converted into anything else, then all kinds of ordinary distinctions disappear: hot is cold, light is heavy, small is large—all, of course, *potentia*. His final point is that the Aristotelian distinction also misplaces the whole concept of action or agency, attributing it "not only to the soul and to animate creatures but also to tree trunks and stones." He concludes: "Let us therefore bid farewell to these superstitious and deceitful terms of Aristotle, by which whenever he wishes to appear acute, he appears to me rather to be accused."[21]

The standard of "common usage" is thus neither a belletristic fetish nor a canon of oratorical good taste; it is a way of asking how language in fact works and of specifying what kinds of distinctions are made in the ordinary use of words. In this respect Valla's affinity with much twentieth-century critical philosophy of language is obvious. If "the populace speaks better than the philosopher" (I.xvii; 685)—a slogan that partially suggests the spirit of the later Wittgenstein—it does so according to the criterion of semantic function, not of gram-

[20] I.xvi; 678: "Fac Aristoteles ut ex hoc ligno fiat arca, dicemus hoc lignum est arca actu? quis unquam ita loquutus est? quis non ita loquentem rideret? . . . Quid attinebit addere actu?"

[21] I.xvi; 679: "eam [i.e., actus] Aristoteles non modo animae & animatis attribuit: sed etiam trunco & lapidi. . . . Valeant igitur haec superstitiosa & calumniosa Aristotelis vocabula, in quibus cum vult videri argutus, mihi videtur potius arguendus."

matical propriety or aesthetic preference. Valla's reputation as the arbiter of classical Latin elegance should not obscure the significance of his philosophy—the extent to which he sees meaning as contingent on use. As we have seen, his ideal of elegance was grounded firmly in historical usage; where the two seem to conflict, Valla does not hesitate to choose on the basis of the semantic precision of that usage. In fact, semantic precision was just what Valla meant by "elegance." As David Marsh has shown, Valla's use of the term (*elegans*) derives from the *Rhetorica ad Herrenium*, where it is defined as that which is spoken purely and openly; his plural title, *Elegantiae*, indicates the distinctions in meaning which that book describes, and only by later Ciceronians was the term reduced to mean merely harmonious cadences.[22]

A clear example of the primacy Valla habitually gives to semantic precision and clarity occurs in the first book of his *Invective in Bartolomaeum Facium*, where the argument in dialogue form concerns terms for engines of war. Facio is made to say that it would be "much more elegant" to use the older *tormentum* than the newer *bombarda* for all machines that hurl large stones because the former is the most frequent and general term for such machines. In response Valla not only cites his authorities for the use of *bombarda*, but points out at length that a "new thing requires a new term," that the machines thus named differ in material, shape, and action—the one hurling its missiles, the other discharging them "with flame and thunder." Valla is opposing mere stylistic elegance to the kind that furnishes precise distinctions of meaning: "And surely nothing is more unjust than always to flee to inappropriate generalities, and to prefer to endure this poverty of words rather than bestow on the object its own name (when it is born, as is done among men)—nothing more unjust than to deprive an ingenious invention of the honor of its own title."[23] He concludes by quoting Horace:

[22] "Grammar, Method, and Polemic in L.V.'s *Elegantiae*," *Rinascimento* 19 (1979), 100–103.

[23] P. 504: "Et certe nihil iniquius est, quam ad generalia semper, & impro-

As woods whose change appeares
Still in their leaves, throughout the sliding yeares,
The first borne dying; so the aged state
Of words decay . . .
Much phrase that now is dead, shall be reviv'd;
And much shall dye, that now is nobly liv'd,
If Custom please.[24]

The quotation is apt, for Horace is using these resonant metaphors of mortality to defend his own and other poets' neologisms, and Valla is arguing for their acceptance on the basis of meaningful function. To argue, however, merely for "new names for new things" is to remain wholly within the traditional vocabulary of discourse that postulates preexisting objects for words to refer to. Had Valla always remained here he would be only the empiricist or nominalist protester against realistic "universals" that he has often been called.

But Valla did not rest content simply with the observations of historical change in common usage provided by Horace and Quintilian. It was his chief merit occasionally to perceive that the criterion he derived from them had cognitive consequences, and it is his development of these that offers a new conception of language. Valla tends to develop such consequences primarily in contexts like that of the long passage from the *Dialectica* quoted above: a description of usage gives way to a questioning of knowledge; a negative critique shades into a positive reformulation of the issue. In this passage the transition is abrupt enough to cause perplexity, hence (pro-

---

pria confugere, & hanc verborum inopiam pati malle, quam suum (ut quaeque res nascitur, sicut in hominibus fit) attribuere nomen, & ingeniosum inventum propriae appellationis honore fraudare."

Gerl uses this passage, somewhat mistakenly, as evidence for the view that language does not "reflect" a prior reality but creates one: *Rhetorik als Philosophie*, p. 225. Indeed, Valla arrives at this view, but not quite at this point, where he is specifically defending "nova a posterioribus excogitata nomina, novis rebus accomodata."

[24] *Ars Poetica*, ll. 60–61, 70–71. The translation is Ben Jonson's (*Complete Poetry*, ed. William B. Hunter, Jr. [New York, 1963], p. 281) and is an excellent rendition of a famous and difficult passage: cf. the commentary of C. O. Brink, *Horace on Poetry* (Cambridge, 1971), II, 146–50, 157–60.

vided we are willing to regard Valla as a serious thinker) reflection. The unsignaled shift from the final example of the common distinction between a means or standard of measurement
and the material measured ("we . . . weigh other things") to
the redefinition of truth ("The true . . . is properly knowledge") comes with startling suddenness, resulting in a natural
suspicion of irrelevance. How do we get from counting to
truth, and what is the connection between them? Valla does
not say. It is no answer to recall that he is passing from an assault on one "transcendental" term, *unum*, to another, *verum*.
The answer seems rather to be suggested by the kind of redefinition he gives of the latter. Truth is "the light of the mind"
that provides a "conception" of things. This conception, however, as his subsequent examples show, resides in the names we
give them. To call this object "bread," or that one "wine," is
implicitly to affirm a truth: our "knowledge" or "judgment"
of what the object is. A dissenting judgment will call ours
"false" by denying the name we have called the object, thus
conceiving it as something else. Hence, language becomes
knowledge, the truth of which depends on the human judgment that applies names and uses words. It is here, in Valla's
direct denial of Platonic truth that exists outside ourselves and
independently of language, that the basis of his abrupt transition is implied. Language, whose use by human beings contains both truth and falsity (as both misjudgments and deliberate lies), is the "measure" of sensible reality. Words are
concepts; they are the means by which we divide up and
"weigh" the world. And Valla insists that it is "we" who do it
and not God; the cognitive process that conceptualizes the
world in language is human. Valla's unstated transition thus
compels his readers to work out for themselves that the crucial
connection between measurement and truth lies in the operation of language itself: it is cognitive, contingent, and semantically constitutive—not communicative, apodictic, and semantically cosmetic.

The revolutionary impact of these negations on the contemporary noetic economy is well summarized by Salvatore Camporeale: " 'philosophy' stops being metaphysical speculation;

'rhetoric' passes far beyond the confines of persuasive techniques; and 'logic' is no longer autonomous analysis of the
structure of thought."[25] He also sees that Valla is doing something more than merely absorbing the other two disciplines
into "rhetoric," that he is in fact redefining it as "the comprehensive science of all the teaching and analytic study of all the
modalities of human language."[26] Indeed, the importance of
Valla's work is not to be located in the Renaissance warfare to
establish the ruling discipline of *studia humanitatis*, but rather in
the integral view of language that underlies his "comprehensive science" of rhetoric. The fullest account of this view is
presented by Gerl, whose principal thesis my analysis has
sought to confirm:

Language for Valla . . . is found only in connection with things, that
is, in the sense of a necessary mastery of things for the sake of people.
For it is not a sign or copy of preextant things, but is rather what first
raises them into existence for people at all. Language for Valla is the
second, specifically *human* creation of the world, the model of reality.
Reality is therefore no longer either purely the thing (as in nominalism) or purely the abstraction (as in realism), but the thing designated
by the word, which out of the chaotic multitude of possible significances has been fixed in its particular significance for human beings.[27]

That knowledge and truth are functions of the "common use"
of language, that language creates meaning, and that philoso-

[25] *L. V.: Umanesimo e teologia*, p. 81. Later he shows how in the *Dialectica*
Valla "veniva a negare la possibilità stessa del discorso metafisico e di tutta
l'ontologia scholastica" (p. 159), and how in the *Elegantiae* he, "postosi com-
pletamente al di fuori della semantica 'ontologica' della terminologia predica-
mentale aristotelica, ha ormai assunto gli schemi concettuali e i termine cate-
gorali di carattare storico e contigente, propri del linguaggio retorico" (p.
169). Camporeale then remarks that "nonostante la chiarezza" di Valla's position in both works, "la radicale trasposizione linguistico-concettuale, com-
piuta dal Valla, è rimasta incomprensibile" not only to contemporary but also
to most modern scholars. So it has; but the very radicalism of the effort, as I
shall argue below, involves as much difficulty as clarity.

[26] *Ibid.*, p. 80.

[27] *Rhetorik als Philosophie*, p. 65.

phy consequently becomes the study of this simultaneously linguistic/cognitive process—these are the original and strikingly modern challenges that Valla offered the thought of his time.

But, as I have also tried to suggest, he was not able to offer them without both difficulty and inconsistency. As might well be expected from one who seeks to oppose received ideas of such a fundamental kind that they are embodied in the vocabulary he himself must use, Valla could not avoid sometimes making the traditional dualistic distinctions that he was generally attempting to coalesce. His attempt was, after all, to alter the entire conceptual framework of his day by basing it not on the inherited ontology but on a view of language as a system that is at once diachronically contingent and synchronically cognitive. But Valla has not left us any concise and unambiguous exposition of such a system precisely because he himself was in the process of arriving at it, of having to build it piecemeal from the materials he could salvage from the structure he demolished. Thus it is no wonder that his writings left ample room for the polemics and "invectives" that filled his own career, as well as for subsequent misunderstanding.

It is important to appreciate the difficulty of Valla's effort in order to understand its nature, magnitude, and relevance. I mean, simply, that to try to reconceive language as a whole, in all its uses, has proved no easier in the twentieth century, when it has become an effort of many thinkers, than it was in the fifteenth century, when only Valla made it. Genuinely radical thinking is never easy, especially not when it most *seems* so: that is, when it attacks the doctrines of an esoteric specialty (the apparently sophisticated) with questions from exoteric common sense (the apparently obvious)—such "simple" questions as "of what use is it?" and "how do we know?" In its subject, aim, situation, and strategy, Valla's effort is comparable to that of the most radical reconceiver of language in our time, the later Wittgenstein.[28] Both begin by criticizing the reigning,

---

[28] A virtual summary of Valla's main themes and attitudes may be found in

academically specialized concepts of language of their day
(Wittgenstein's critique includes his own earlier *Tractatus*,
which helped to establish the positivist conception). Both
make the criticism on the basis of everyday linguistic use, aggressively protesting that scholastic or positivist formulations
are irrelevant to life and falsify the nature of language. Both are
led to consider language as epistemology, the use of words as
the formation of concepts. And both extend this consideration
far into psychology (Valla by taking over large chunks of
Quintilian's analysis of kinds of argumentation; Wittgenstein
by developing the famous problems of "sensation" and "other
minds"). Finally, both, though they ask "obvious" questions,
do not give obvious answers. The difficulty of Wittgenstein,
whose historical position made him more aware than Valla of
the ways in which words "bewitch" the intelligence, is deliberate and notorious.[29] That both writers leave plenty of work
for the reader, and hence wide latitude for misconstruction, is
a natural consequence of their common aim and situation: they
must use a language that already contains the categories they
are rejecting. But to shrink Valla into a "nominalist" or Wittgenstein into a "behaviorist" is to refuse the work, to decline
the immensely difficult labor of reconceiving language, of
reordering the categories of our own perceptions, that these
philosophers require us to share.

The particular difficulty of Valla may be further illustrated
by a crucial passage in which he attacks perhaps the most basic

---

sections 114–33 of *Philosophical Investigations*, 3d ed., tr. G.E.M. Anscombe
(Oxford, 1968): the aim "to bring words back from their metaphysical to their
everyday use" (116); the situation of having to uncover "one or another piece
of plain nonsense" (119); the strategy of investigating the cognitive functions
of actual usage (122) by describing, not prescribing, the rules of that use (124);
the whole idea that this use is "a measuring-rod" or "model" of reality (131);
and the whole refusal to divide grammar from semantics, logic from epistemology (passim).

[29] For a demonstration of the perils of ignoring the difficulties that Wittgenstein was careful to emphasize, see Stanley Cavell, "The Availability of Wittgenstein's Later Philosophy," in *Must We Mean What We Say?* (Cambridge,
1969).

and unavoidable distinction of all, that between words and things.[30] The attack concludes a chapter "on qualities that are known by sense," and its general point is to criticize the confusion between the powers of sense and the qualities of their objects. He approaches the epistemological problem, as usual, in terms of grammar and common usage. And what is implicit in this procedure—that language constitutes how we know the world—here receives as explicit a statement as Valla was ever able to give it:

Words uttered by men are indeed natural, but their meaning is determined by convention; for men devised words which they might adjust to things known (of whom Adam was the first, at God's command) and they taught words together with their meanings to posterity. Sounds indeed exist in nature, but words and meanings are fashioned. Sounds are perceived by the ears, meanings by the mind, words by both. Afterwards letters were invented: mute words, one might say, or images of words, just as words themselves are images of meanings, which constitute "terms" in the strict sense. Hence, "this" is whatever we say; it is in fact substance, quality, action; and therefore it is a "thing." For just as the name "wood" belongs to wood, and "stone" to stone, and "iron" to iron, likewise in the case of incorporeal things, the name "knowledge" belongs to knowledge, "virtue" to virtue, "genus" to genus, "species" to species, "substance" to substance, "quality" to quality, "action" to action, and finally "thing" to thing. And thus "thing" signifies a thing: the latter is signified, the former is its sign; one is not a word, the other is a word and is therefore defined thus: "thing" is a word or term embracing in its meaning all terms. Therefore, you will say, the term is above the thing because "thing" is also a term; but what is signified by "thing" is more than what is signified by "term": hence the term is a thing and a single thing only. This word, however, signifies all things, just as the word "god" is below many others (for "spirit" transcends it, "substance" and "essence" transcend it, "anything" and "thing" tran-

[30] The significance of the passage is well analyzed by Gerl, pp. 217–24. But she does not quote it *in extenso*, and thus leaves a somewhat misleading impression of its tidiness. Indeed, the admirable lucidity of her whole interpretation makes Valla appear less tenuous and more systematic than it was possible, in my opinion, for him to be.

scend it), yet transcends all others in the dignity of its meaning, since he is the very creator of other things. Consequently, it makes no difference whether we say, what *is* wood, what is stone, what iron, what man, or, what *does* "wood," "stone," "iron," "man," *signify*. Neither of these can be said of "thing"—what the thing is and what "thing" signifies—since "what" analyzes into "which thing." But if I ask, which *word* is "thing," you will respond rightly: It is a word signifying the meaning or sense of all other words. But "which" now signifies almost the same as "what kind of."[31]

The very beginning of the passage is another of Valla's unannounced transitions from the previous argument, which here

[31] *Dialectica* I.xiv; 676–77: "Vox humana naturalis illa quidem est, sed eius significatio ab institutione descendit: homines enim rebus cognitis, voces quas adaptarent invenerunt. Quorum primus fuit Adam deo autore: easque cum suis significationibus posteros docuerunt. Ut soni quidem sint a natura, voces autem & significationes ab artifice: quorum sonos auris, significationes animus, voces ambo percipiunt. Postremo inventae sunt literae quasi mutae voces, sive vocum imagines: ut ipse [sic] voces sunt quasi imagines significationum quae iam proprie dicuntur vocabula. Atque hoc est quicquid loquimur: etiam ipsum substantia, qualitas, actio: atque adeo ipsum [sic] res. Nam sicuti ligno nomen lignum est, & lapidi lapis, & ferro ferrum. Item rerum incorporalium ut scientiae est nomen scientia: virtuti virtus, generi genus, speciei species, ita substantiae substantia, ita qualitati qualitas, ita actioni actio: denique ita rei res, itaque res significat rem: hoc significatur, illus huius est signum: illud non vox, hoc vox est: ideoque definitur, Res est vox, sive vocabulum omnium vocabulorum significatu suo complectens, ergo vocabulum inquies est supra res, quia res vocabulum est etiam, sed significatum rei supra significatum vocabuli est: & ideo vocabulum res est: & una res duntaxat. Illa autem vox omnes res significat: quemadmodum haec vox deus, infra multas alias est: nam illam transcendit spiritus, transcendit substantia, transcendit essentia, transcendit aliquid & res, significationis autem dignitate cuncta alia transcendit, cum sit ipse caeterarum rerum autor. Quapropter nihil interest utrum dicamus, quid est lignum, quid est lapis, quid ferrum, quid homo, an quid significat, lignum, lapis, ferrum, homo, quorum nihil de res dici potest: quid est res, & quid res significat, quoniam quid, solvitur in quae res. At si interrogavero quae vox est res, recte respondebis: est vox significans omnium aliarum vocum intellectum sive sensum: sed quae idem pene nunc quod qualis significat."

The repunctuation of this passage made by Zippel (*Repastinatio*, 1, 122–24) is helpful, but departs in important instances from that of both Basle and the final manuscript version.

has been to discriminate between the two principal powers of sensory perception (sight and hearing) and the qualities of objects they perceive. (Valla has been both borrowing and criticizing what Aristotle says of these matters in *De Anima* II, 7–8, and he here follows Aristotle's own transition between topics [at 420b.5], from sound in general to voice.) Again, the reader must infer the grounds of the transition from the whole context, which suggests an implicit analogy between sensory capacity/its object and sensory capacity/its product. As Valla's main concern in the chapter has been carefully to distinguish between the former, he begins this discussion of words by distinguishing between the latter. The importance of this distinction soon becomes apparent, and accords perfectly with Valla's earlier rejection of any special ontological status for truth and any divine sanction for cognition. Language itself is not given either by God or nature. The capacity to produce sounds is "natural," but the use of the sounds produced as words and meanings is "artificial." Significance is a matter of instruction; meaning is made—by Adam and his descendants—not born. The creative activity of God is of course allowed for, but he is not permitted to function as a guarantor of either knowledge or meaning. God's role does not extend beyond making perception and speech possible: earlier he was evoked in the metaphor of light, here in the rather vague ablative of accompaniment (*deo autore*). The distinction between capacity and product thus serves to insist once again that language and meaning are contingent on human purposes.

Valla is now ready to consider how words fulfill these purposes in relation to objects of perception and thought. His key observation is that when words are written, they themselves become such objects. Seen as silent "images of meaning," words acquire a kind of permanent and distanced physical presence that they lack as sounds. They become a class of "things." Valla develops this observation directly into the apparent collapse of the venerable dichotomies between word and thing, sign and signified. His tautological list would seem to insist that words can only "signify" that class of "things" called words. And yet the force of his final inference here remains, it seems to me, ambiguous: if we can write, *res significat rem*, is the statement, *illud non vox, hoc vox est*, to be taken as a simple statement of fact, a paradox (even a joke?), or a genuine contradiction? On the basis of the preceding identification of "terms" and "things," the last possibility is attractive and is ably urged by Gerl:

Here Valla pushes against the limits of the representational power of language, for here is the place where he can no longer maintain linguistically, and therefore logically, the separation of word and not-word and also of thing and not-thing. For the sign and the signified are on both occasions *res*, that is, word and not-word are likewise *res*; and on the other hand, in order to bring the not-word (*res*) into consciousness at all, one must make use of the word, the word *res*.[32]

This interpretation acutely describes Valla's dilemma, but the solution it suggests contains, I think, two problems. The lesser of these is that Valla nowhere in this passage explicitly makes the epistemological point that words are necessary to bring objects into consciousness. His discussion may imply this; earlier portions of the *Dialectica* have indeed implied it, as we have seen. The question is how consistently Valla remained aware of this implication, and it leads directly to the greater problem. If Valla assumed the epistemological identity of words and things in his specific statement of their linguistic identity, and therefore collapsed all distinction between "sign" and "signified" in a deliberate contradiction designed to reveal the absurdity of such a distinction, why, in the remainder of the passage, does he continue to employ it? And why, to begin with, does he not somehow emphasize that he is destroying such a ripely traditional shibboleth as the dualism of sign/ thing? It was not Valla's habit to fight shy of contradiction; usually he paraded it to the drums and trumpets of irony or contempt. But the tone here seems utterly bland; the statement that "one is a word and the other not" is embedded in a lengthy

[32] *Rhetorik als Philosophie*, p. 221.

period that culminates in a discrimination between "thing" and "term" based precisely on the generality of what they "signify." That is, even though Valla has linguistically identified sign/thing/term/object, the *process* of signification or representation remains. The relation of "standing for" continues to be posited between classes of things to which it would be inappropriate if they were identical. Nothing in the subsequent treatment would prevent the apparent contradiction from being at most a paradox, since Valla continues to discriminate between terms as signifying things of greater or lesser inclusiveness and "dignity," like "thing" itself and "god." In short, Valla has here discovered a problem, not solved one. He employs the process that his linguistic identification denies for the good reason that there was none other available.

But he does not employ it without serious modification. If we may question the extent to which Valla remained aware of and consciously developed the epistemological implications of his brilliant insight that words and things are somehow identical, there is no question that he developed the ontological and semantic ones. The equation of "being" and "signifying" is clear. As Gerl says, "Being and meaning, the thing and the word, are in the world of human beings not to be separated."[33] What the thing is is what the word means. This equation is Valla's most profound critique of all the assumptions about the relation of word/object/meaning contained in the traditional process of signification or representation. It denies both the correspondence theory of truth and the referential theory of meaning, which is no longer to be sought in objects, but rather in the words that name and categorize them.[34] That is, lan-

---

[33] *Ibid.*, p. 223.

[34] This point receives further stress in the added conclusion to this chapter (I.xiv) in the final manuscript version of the *Dialectica* (Vatican Library, Ottob. Lat. 2075, fol. 40): "Sed quae idem pene nunc, quod qualis significat. Denique significatio est vocis: quae sub praedicamentum venit: quia praedicamentum idem est, quod vox, universaliter significans. Res significata sub praedicamentum non venit: ut significato vocis, homo, sub praedicamento est: ipse autem

guage and the people who use it do not "represent" a reality but constitute one. This new conception of Valla's logically requires a different process than that of "signifying" to describe the newly constitutive role of language in the commerce between word, world, and speaker. That he could not supply it is hardly surprising, since it remains today a matter of vivid debate among philosophers and linguists. But he could at least push the old process about as far as it could go in the new direction. When he conflates the old questions, "What is x?" and "What does the word x signify?" (which presume an ontology independent of language and demand to be answered by a "thing"), and replaces them with the new question, "Which word is x?" (that is, what kind of word is x and how does it function in the language?), he is proposing a new kind of definition in a new semantics, one which requires in response not a prior "thing" but a statement of the work the word does, the categories into which it divides the world—in short, its "common usage."

Thus Valla concludes his own examination of the use of the word "thing" by saying (rather, by making the reader say) that it finally signifies not another "thing" but a "meaning." Words, that is, can indeed "signify" only themselves; their meaning is their use by human beings in a given context. The old process of signification, which located the meaning of words in the objects (whether perceivable by the senses or laid up in a Platonic or Christian heaven) that they were said to "represent," has been modified almost out of existence by being reduced to tautology. Almost, but not quite, for Valla continued to use the vocabulary of the old process (What is signified by x," "X signifies all things") in ways not incompatible with the presupposition that meaning was an object of reference instead of a function of use. He had no choice, for that very presupposition was in his Latin (and remains in our vernaculars) part of what "meaning" meant: it was *significatio*.

---

homo, qui significat, sub tecto est, aut sub caelo, non sub praedicamento: nec aliud est, quum dicis, homo est animal, quia hac appellatione homo, subauditur animal, sive subintelligitur significatio animalis."

By examining the "common usage" of words, therefore, Valla has indeed arrived at the limits of language—the vertiginous point at which the perceptual and conceptual categories imposed by that usage must themselves be called into question. The difficulty of attempting a radical reorientation of such categories is perhaps equalled only by that of accepting it.[35] No one else in the fifteenth century seemed prepared to reconceive of language as constituting both the meaning and being of the world.

Thinkers contemporary with Valla, whether they were dialecticians, jurists, or theologians, who in his eyes had abandoned the realm of common sense and of common speech, . . . did not understand at all the function of the word as the expression of the human dimension of a thing. Indeed, their theories even carried on the explicit separation of the thing-in-itself from its human meaning and disregarded the creative judgment of the community in favor of a purely external "scientific" explanation. By thus deserting language they missed the *thing* at the same time and emptied the word itself of its role in the construction of reality, making it into an exchangeable, negligible vessel for a fixed content indifferent to human beings.[36]

And it would have been astonishing, had "they" done otherwise. For the challenge Valla offered, besides being a direct threat to the vested interests of separate academic specialties, was the profoundly disturbing demand for the literal re-vision not merely of what we think but of how we are able to think anything at all. Valla proposed the first explicit alternative to the dominant matrix of Western assumptions about language and its relation to meaning, the world, and its users, since Plato's victory over the Sophists. Valla attempted to conceive of *significatio* as different from, other than, the *res significata* whether in the world or in the mind: as a function of words and

[35] On the emotional distress that results from the violation of purely perceptual categories, see the fascinating summaries of psychological research given by Thomas S. Kuhn, *The Structure of Scientific Revolutions*, 2d ed. (Chicago, 1970), pp. 62–64, and Jan B. Deregowski, "Illusion and Culture," in *Illusion in Nature and Art*, ed. R. L. Gregory and E. H. Gombrich (London, 1973), pp. 168–69.

[36] Gerl, *Rhetorik als Philosophie*, pp. 227–28.

their use, not as their objects of reference. For him, words had cognitive force, and meaning was an activity multiply determined by grammatical relationships and historical contexts. It is far less remarkable that his alternative should not have found acceptance five centuries ago than that it should remain a cogent alternative today.

Because it so remains, we should be encouraged to trace its effects in the widely diffused influence and prestige that Valla's work enjoyed among subsequent humanists. Most of them, of course, shared his stylistic prejudices and took over his methods of textual analysis while ignoring their basis in his new language-centered philosophy. To what extent, therefore, did the whole subsequent development of Renaissance hermeneutics, both secular and spiritual, assimilate in practice what it could not confront in theory? And to what extent did this assimilation preserve Valla's challenge sub rosa, resulting in the tension between treating language as constituting meaning while still conceiving it as cosmetic to it? Suffice it for the moment to recall three well-known, though by no means thoroughly studied, dimensions of Valla's influence: Luther's admiration of his theology and the general adventitious utility of parts of his work for Protestantism; the textual discipleship of Erasmus; and the rapid expansion of the domain of rhetoric under the dual aegis of Cicero and Quintilian.[37] The shadow of Valla falls repeatedly across the major arguments about language that were carried on during the entire period. If indeed "Erasmus learned . . . from Valla the role of eloquence, the meaning of words, and the sense of history,"[38] just what did he

---

[37] Luther's praises are cited by Fois, *Il pensiero cristiano di L. V.*, pp. 192, 637. The crucial importance of Quintilian for the expansion of rhetoric in the Renaissance is outlined by James J. Murphy, *Rhetoric in the Middle Ages* (Berkeley, 1974), pp. 357–62. It is nicely ironic that the whole text of the *Institutio Oratoria* was first discovered in Switzerland by Poggio, who so bitterly opposed what Valla did with it.

[38] Roland H. Bainton, *Erasmus of Christendom* (New York, 1969), p. 25. This kind of general assessment of Erasmus' debt to Valla has been taken for granted for years. The facts that permit the assessment are chronicled by Augustin Renaudet, *Erasme et l'Italie* (Geneva, 1954), pp. 14–16, 39. Camporeale

learn about these matters? Did he, or did the rhetoricians whom Valla sent scurrying to Quintilian, begin to see language both systematically and historically more as creating meaning than as containing it?

These are the questions posed by the fact of Valla's influence seen in the light of the nature of his achievement. Each deserves more detailed answers than I shall be able to supply. All suggest the possibility, even the likelihood, that a great deal of the linguistic pedagogy and argument (from the teaching of Latin to the interpretation of Scripture) that continued to preoccupy the Renaissance would proceed according to working assumptions about the operation of language that were at odds with, or subversive of, theoretical conceptions of that operation. And, since students are likelier to absorb and retain the methods and procedures than the precepts of their instruction, this situation would seem to provide one basis for a generally altered consciousness of language during the period— for the kind of attitudinal shift we observed in poets between Dante and Pope. Valla's new idea that words constitute meanings, however tenuously arrived at and badly understood as such, nonetheless helped to make possible, by being exemplified in his actual practice of dealing with a text, the constitution of new kinds of meaning in religion and in literature.

ii. Juan Luis Vives

The notion of pure thought in abstraction from   —J. R. FIRTH
its expression is not one of the most useful fig-
ments of the learned world.

The most immediate and hitherto the best documented area of Valla's influence is the pedagogical revolution in the teaching

---

laments the lack of any full analytic study of Valla's relation to Erasmus, p. 435. With respect exclusively to N.T. scholarship, the lack has recently been well filled by Jerry H. Bentley, *Humanists and Holy Writ* (Princeton, 1983), who stresses their common interest in the semantic nuances of historical context.

of dialectics—so diffuse as to be often synonymous with humanism itself—achieved by the inspiration of his *Dialecticae disputationes* and the agency, primarily in Northern Europe, of Rudolf Agricola's textbook, *De inventione dialectica* (1483).[39] The displacement of the narrowly syllogistic procedures of medieval logic by the Ciceronian topics and the vastly more flexible argumentative strategies of Quintilian is indeed one of the hallmarks of humanism, and one that has not until recently been regarded with much favor by historians of philosophy. One of them, however, argues convincingly that this change has both philosophical validity and significance, that it "is not a shift from respectable dialectic to the 'soft option' of rhetoric, but a shift from certainty to probability as the focus of intellectual attention."[40] Such a shift is certainly consistent with Valla's new conception of semantically constitutive language and his general attempt to derive first principles not from a priori postulates but from an examination of ordinary usage in natural language.

In the sphere of philosophy proper, another major Renaissance figure to continue this effort was the Spanish humanist, Juan Luis Vives. His work provides the fullest example of the potent influence of Valla's insights, the tensions they caused, and the attitudes that prevented their conscious acceptance while preserving their implicit challenge to traditional assumptions. The testimony that Vives's effort to reorganize the noetic economy gives to the depth and extent of Valla's influence is the more persuasive because it is the testimony of a hostile witness. Like many of Valla's Italian contemporaries, he explicitly repudiated Valla's view of language and dialectics. Unlike them, however, he sensed the philosophical importance of Valla's historical and systematic investigation of linguistic usage, and so undertook to do something similar in his own way.

Like Valla, only with greater justification, Vives has been

---

[39] See Jardine, *J. Hist. Phil.* 15, 147–48, and the material there cited.

[40] *Ibid.*, 164. A wider-ranging view of the philosophical and linguistic importance of Cicero's topics in humanism is offered by Apel, *Die Idee der Sprache* (Bonn, 1963), pp. 143–54.

better known to posterity as a polemicist, pedagogue, and scholar than as a philosopher per se. His reputation as "the father of modern psychology" and the chief precursor of Francis Bacon dates from around the turn of this century and continues, with some qualification, to prevail today.[41] In his own time, his widest fame was secured by his straightforward popular and didactic tracts on wisdom and the duties of Christian marriage.[42] Warmly admired by Erasmus, Vives spent almost all of his working life in the Low Countries, except for a rather uneasy sojourn in England, at Oxford and at court, where he became a close friend of Thomas More and was briefly thrown in jail by Henry VIII for objecting to the divorce from Catherine of Aragon. The large and enduring influence of Vives on education in Northern Europe was exercised not professionally—he hated teaching and avoided it as much as possible—but through his voluminous writings on theoretical and philosophical as well as practical questions.

His major work, literally a kind of new organon that aims to rearrange the categories of all knowledge (a less radical but still Vallesque ambition), is *De disciplinis libri xx.*[43] The order and

[41] See the bibliography in M. Sancipriano, *Il pensiero psicologico e morale di G. L. Vives* (Florence, n.d.), pp. xiv–xviii. The quoted phrase is the title of an article by Foster Watson (not listed in Sancipriano), *The Psychological Review* 22 (1915), 333–53. The extreme development of nineteenth-century positivistic enthusiasm is Vasoli's *La dialettica e la retorica dell'Umanesimo*, whose thesis is that Valla's philology, Vives's psychology, and Ramus's logic are all linked and originating steps in the triumphal march of modern empirical science. The difficulty of believing this is exceeded only by his difficulty and diffidence in asserting it: e.g., p. 635. Some essential qualifications are presented by Vives's latest biographer, Carlos G. Noreña, *J.L.V.* (The Hague, 1970), p. 242.

[42] In England, for example, these were the only works of his to be translated. *An Introduction to wysdome*, tr. Richard Moryson, which defines it for the vulgar in purely Platonic/Augustinian ethical terms, went through five editions between Vives's death in 1540 and 1564.

[43] 1st ed. Antwerp, 1531. It is included whole in his *Opera*, 2 vols. (Basle, 1555) and its contents are scattered throughout the *Opera Omnia*, ed. G. Mayans, 8 vols. (Valencia, 1782–90). In the absence of any definitive edition, and because it is most readily accessible (in a modern facsimile reprint), I shall cite Mayans (hereafter M) but shall give an occasional reference to Basle (hereafter B). Since Mayans separates the integrated contents of single works according

division of the twenty books suggest the nature of his procedure: *de causis corruptarum artium* (7), *de tradendis disciplinis* ("sive de doctrina Christiana" [5]), *de prima philosophia* (3), *de explanatione essentiarum* (1), *de censura veri* (2), *de instrumento probabilitatis* (1), *de disputatione* (1). Like Valla, he begins critically, with a detailed attack on the conceptual failings of scholasticism in the trivium, in natural and moral philosophy, and in civil law. He next presents both the principles and the kinds of practice that should govern the communication and acquisition of learning, emphasizing its primarily ethical importance in Christian life. Only then does he explore the substance of metaphysics, logic, and rhetoric, dealing freely in all these areas with matters of epistemology and psychology. Not only does this scheme display the typically pragmatic humanist bias of ordering knowledge for the use of life, but in so doing it deliberately refuses to separate speculation from implementation and to accept the received compartmentalization of disciplines. These refusals, however, are not made on the basis of any clearly articulated alternative scheme, but as a consequence of the reluctant awareness that all categories of thought are given by language. At every stage in the inquiry Vives finds himself having to interrogate words, their usage, and their ever-problematic relation to experience. He does not like this situation and is not comfortable with this awareness. Again and again he insists that a philosopher (or a teacher) must pay the closest attention to the fullest range of nuances in the common use of words, only to say in the next breath that of course he mustn't do too much of this, since his real business is with "things." Vives is thus led into many confusions, contradictions, and evasions, which have the collective result of making the exact contours of his new noetic map very difficult to identify.[44]

---

to his own notion of their subjects, divides them into chapters, and completely repunctuates and reparagraphs the text, any sixteenth-century edition is preferable as an indication of how Vives actually thought and wrote.

[44] Eugenio Coseriu, "Zur Sprachphilosophie von J.L.V.," in *Aus der Französischen Kultur- und Geistesgeschichte*, ed. W. Dierlamm and W. Drost (Heidelberg, 1971), pp. 234–55, finds it both "original" and "unified." It is neither.

So it is that the question of the relation of this map to those of Plato and Aristotle has been, with almost equal plausibility, so variously answered. The modern scholarly consensus that finds in Vives a solid Aristotelian who opened all experience to empirical investigation is not unanimous; for some he is quite capable of remaining a Platonist "par excellence."[45] Nor can this variance be resolved by appealing to the traditional distinctions between disciplines (so that Vives might be Platonic in his ethics and Aristotelian in his logic), since it is precisely these distinctions that the whole procedure of his thinking denies. His intellectual ambivalence is deep, fundamental, and pervasive; it is in a sense the motivation of his entire program. And it proceeds, as I hope to show, from his attempt to follow in Valla's footsteps and his unwillingness or inability to follow them far enough.

This ambivalence, specifically toward Aristotle and Valla, is evident in his treatment of dialectics in the third book of *de causis corruptarum artium*. His general aim here is clear enough: to dethrone dialectics from its self-contained pinnacle in the late medieval trivium and make it instrumental to other "arts." For this purpose the Ciceronian topics are much more suitable than Aristotle's ten "predicaments." But Vives cannot simply reject the latter as Valla does; instead he must worry over their ontological status, which he both denies and wishes somehow to reconstruct. Aristotle, he says,

created ten classes of things . . . yet this is not the order of the essences of things themselves, which no one can perceive or grasp, since the essences of things—as even Aristotle himself admits—are wholly

---

All of the attitudes toward language that Coseriu singles out as original—the description of common usage and its historical differences, using such description to criticize rhetoric and logic, seeing languages as the contingent creation of societies—were fully deployed in theory and practice by Valla. Coseriu completely overlooks the contradiction in Vives between the traditional dualism of *res/verba* and the sociohistorical linguistic perspective, the significance of which is my present subject.

[45] This is the view of Eugenio d'Ors, "Le style de la philosophie de Vivès," in *Vivès: Humaniste Espagnol* (Paris, 1941), p. 28.

concealed and far distant from the cognitive powers of the human mind. For even now, it is still disputed among those who devote any work to studies of philosophy, which things are inherent in the substances to which they belong—not in mind and thought but in the particular thing itself (though not by virtue of placement or location)—and which are not. He did not establish his doctrine on the basis of our sensation or cognition. Otherwise we would have no problem in considering essences as inherent in things, and things which he connected would have been disjoined; others united, which he separated. That is, things would have been classified according to which and how many senses they are perceived by. For indeed in nature first come causes, beginnings, unmixed elements, then acting and suffering, last of all compound things. Quantity of number and quantity of mass are not coextensive, since the former arises from the latter. And quality is prior to relation, and relation is not in nature but is an acquired condition. For as Aristotle himself wisely says in the *Metaphysics*: our mind is to the most palpable things of nature just as the eye of the night owl is to the light of the sun.[46]

Vives is unable to regard the ten logical categories as merely heuristic (and so easily replaceable by another set); he thinks they should correspond to the structure of the natural, or at least the psychological, universe. Finding that they don't, he is

---

[46] M VI, 114–15: "Decem fecit rerum genera . . . neque enim ordinem essentiae ipsarum rerum, quem nemo percipere, et tenere potest, quum sint rerum essentiae, vel ipso Aristotele teste, obscurissimae, et procul a cognitione mentis humanae remotae; adhuc enim inter eos, qui operam aliquam in studiis philosophiae ponunt, ambigitur, quae vera sint inhaerentia, a substantiis illis, quibus adhaerent, non mente, et cogitatione, sed re vera distincta, tametsi non sede, aut loco, quae contra; sensuum vero, et cognitionis nostrae ordinem, non est secutus, alioqui primas obtinuissent partes inhaerentia, et alia essent disjuncta, quae connexuit, alia copulasset, quae disgregavit, nempe quae sub eundem sensum caderent, aut diversos, tam internos quam externos: at vero in natura, prima sunt causae, principia, elementa simplicia, tum agere et pati, postrema omnium, composita; nec simul sunt quantitas numeri, et quantitas molis, quum ex hac nascitur illa; et prior qualitas, quam ad aliquid; nec ad aliquid naturae est, sed artis, ut habitus: adde quod, sicut ipse idem Aristoteles in prima philosophia sapienter dicit, Mens nostra non aliter se ad naturae manifestissima habet, quam noctuae oculus ad lumen solis."

In quoting from Mayans I have omitted his copious italics and uniquely Spanish punctuation marks.

equally unable to accept the formally skeptical conclusions that he is at pains to draw from the philosopher himself. If "essences," even palpable ones, are wholly beyond our grasp, then there is no reason why any set of categories must be preferred to another. But Vives wants there to be such a reason, and he wants to find it in those "first" things that are "indeed in nature." Provisionally, he will go on to make do with the Ciceronian categories; but he will return (in *de prima philosophia*) to the vexing, and for him insoluble, question of how we are to discover these first things. Vives sees that our notions of quantity and quality do not inhere in the natural order, that they are produced by "art": he simply cannot accept the consequences of this perception. He uses it, and will continue to use it, in order to reject what he wishes to replace, without ever seeming aware that it can, with equal justice, reject his replacement too.

Given his nostalgic yearning for apodictic truth even while he is recommending the probabilistic procedures of Ciceronian dialectics, it is easy to see that the language-centered ontology of Valla—the radical insistence that "being" is "meaning"—would be anathema to Vives. Equally antipathetic to him, for the same reason, are the ultimate consequences of the Ciceronian practice itself: the disconcerting ability of the dialectician thus trained to argue *in utramque partem*. So Vives concludes book three of *de causis corruptarum artium* with a lengthy diatribe against the "sophistic" habit of arguing on both sides of an issue (which he attributes to Thomists, Scotists, Albertists, Ockhamists, et al.). Even though this may be done clearly and in ordinary language—both prime desiderata in Vives's own humanist proposals for reform—it cannot arrive at the "truth": the conclusions such a method may urge can always be opposed by others equally drawn from common life. At this point Vives delivers his almost all-inclusive indictment of Valla, which ends the book:

Lorenzo Valla tried to revise dialectics, and produced a new version, dissenting from Aristotle and from the peripatetics both old and new. His teaching is by no means bad in some places, though these are very few; mostly he is mistaken, since he was a vehement man and hasty in making judgments. Not only is he wrong in dialectics, but in philosophy (for he dealt with that, too), and what is more to be wondered at, in his precepts of the Latin language. But he went astray in his criticism there no less than in his *Elegantiae* and *Invectivae*. The errors in his *Dialectica*, which are very many, we shall either omit entirely or save for some other occasion, since to undertake a dispute with him would be too lengthy an affair, and not at all necessary at present, for his arguments do not depend on weighty reasons, and therefore are not accepted by anyone as the firm rules of this art.[47]

The shabby evasions and the disingenuous revelation of bad conscience in this blanket and unspecific attack do not seem to require comment: what is being evaded is the point. And this is nothing more nor less than the logical conclusions of Vives's *own* treatment of dialectics. By fathering these on his *bête noire*, scholasticism in general, they are tarred with the same brush he has used all along and now applies to Valla. It is appropriate and significant that Valla should be excoriated at just the moment when Vives must firmly close the door on the plurality of acceptable opinions ("tanta est opinionum inter illos etiam probatarum varietas") sanctioned by a rhetorical dialectic. Indeed, this context is all that reveals what in fact Vives is objecting to in Valla, since he doesn't condescend to state it. The dispute he here postpones (forever, so far as I know) would no doubt be lengthy, as it would force him to confront his own

[47] M VI, 151: "Laurentius Valla aggressus est reconcinnationem facere dialecticae, in qua dissentit ab Aristotele, et Peripateticis veteribus, ac novis; monet in quibusdam neutiquam prave, etsi ea sunt perpauca; in plerisque labitur, ut fuit vir ille vehemens, et ad faciendum judicium praecipitatus; nec solum in re dialectica falsus est, sed in philosophia nam hanc quoque attingit, et quod magis mirere, in praeceptis Latinae linguae; sed non minus illic improbando aberravit, quam in elegantiis, et invectivis: ceterum dialecticae illius errores, qui sunt sane multi, nos vel omittemus prorsus, vel in aliud tempus, si videbitur, reservabimus, nam suscipere cum eo disputationem, res esset nimium prolixa, minimeque in praesens necessaria, quod illius argumenta nec magnis rationibus nituntur, nec proinde sunt ab ullo recepta tamquam dogmata artis huius."

ambivalence by dealing with Valla's radical linguistic critique of the metaphysical notions that Vives himself cannot fully accept, but nevertheless still wishes to salvage.

Valla certainly criticized more than Vives, or anyone else, could tolerate; but when Vives is occupied with rejecting some of the same things he can be both more generous to and more accurate about his great predecessor.[48] Regardless, however, of whether or how Vives acknowledged it, the influence of Valla is manifest throughout his career. One of his earlier works, *In pseudo-dialecticos* (1520), shows how thoroughly he has absorbed the negatively critical perspective of Valla's view of language. This treatise, in the form of a letter to Johann Fortis, is a direct denunciation of the scholastic treatment of the trivium at the University of Paris, which Vives describes as "Cimmerian darkness." The grounds of the attack are that the three arts of speech should be descriptive, not prescriptive. It is usage— ancient, of course, not medieval—that determines precept, not vice versa. Scholastic textbooks are thus as wrong in theory (Peter of Spain is Vives's favorite source of horrible examples) as their Latin is bad in practice: Cicero could never understand it. "We do not speak Latin in a certain way because Latin grammar commands it; rather the contrary: grammar commands it because that is how the Latins speak." The same is true of rhetoric and dialectics, both of which must simply derive their precepts from the observation of common usage in already extant speech.[49]

---

[48] Later in *de causis corruptarum artium* (bk. IV) Valla is praised along with Aretino, Filelfo, Perotti, et al., for having revived the study of ancient languages: M VI, 171. In an earlier work (Preface, *Declamatio . . . pro noverca*, 1521) Vives singles out Valla and Agricola as "diligent readers" of Quintilian, who are "not unworthy of either his wit or eloquence": M II, 486.

[49] M III, 41–42: "sunt enim hae tres artes de sermone, quem a populo accipiunt, non ipsae tradunt; nam prius fuit sermo latinus, prius graecus, deinde in his formualae grammaticae, formulae rhetoricae, formulae dialectices observatae sunt, nec ad illas detortus est sermo, sed illae potius sermonem sunt secutae, et ad eum se se accommodarunt, neque enim loquimur ad hunc modum latine, quia grammatica latine ita jubet loqui, quin potius e contrario, ita jubet grammatica loqui, quoniam sic Latini loquuntur. . . . illam orati-

Vives does not merely take over the negative employment of Valla's method of examining actual usage; he also, in the course of his major philosophical work, develops some of its positive implications. How these tend, for Vives no less than for Valla, to unify epistemology and semantics is most apparent in the two small books of *de disciplinis* called *de censura veri*. Here Vives begins by insisting that the same "tool" or method is to be used in judging what is true in all subjects.[50] The truth, moreover, is a matter of relative probability; the method inquires where truth may be "properly" expressed and where only approximated. The method consists in weighing or assessing "whole words, which are established in order to signify something" (voces integrae, quae ad aliquid significandum sunt institutae). It requires distinguishing sign from signified and discriminating the many ways in which signifying may be accomplished—from simple predication to complex trope. The two books proceed to specify these ways, offering in effect a brief, simultaneous compendium of traditional logic and rhetoric. What is interesting here is that Vives's universally applicable "tool" for discerning truth is the semantic analysis of language.

Even more interesting is that the meaning this analysis arrives at is first located not in objects, either eternal or transitory, but in the sociohistorical context of a consensus of speakers. Vives articulates this by drawing a new and Vallesque conclusion from an ancient cliché: "Let us therefore define the signifying word as follows: a public token by which people ex-

---

onem populus Romanus . . . latinam judicavit. . . . idcirco rhetorica diligentia ea observata tradidit: ad eundem modum in dialectica usu venit . . . nam antequam ulla dialectica inveniretur, ea erant, ut dialecticus esse docet, quae idcirco docet, quoniam loquentium sive Latine sive Graece consensus approbat, quapropter praecepta dialectices non minus, quam grammatices atque rhetorices, ad usum loquendi communem aptanda sunt." This text, along with parts of *de causis* III, has been recently translated by Rita Guerlac, *J. L. V. Against the Pseudodialecticians.*

[50] M III, 142: "Instrumentum examinandae veritatis singulis disciplinarum atque artium idem accommodatur, nec ullam habet certam materiam rerum, in qua versetur, sicut nec illud alterum de quaerenda probabilitate."

hibit to others their notions (that is, what they conceive in their minds): and so usage is the ruler of what is signified."[51] The definition is that of language given by Aristotle and repeated by Cicero; the inference is that drawn by Horace and exploited by Valla. Vives now exploits it to a lesser extent, giving as examples of disused words that therefore no longer signify the early Latin inscriptions that Cicero could not read.[52] This historical reflection leads Vives directly to conclude that

Therefore the significance of words, that is, meaning, regards the mind, not the thing; for "Hector," "the chimera," "the Punic War," etc., of which the things signified nowhere exist, still signify something, i.e., are the token of some thing to the mind. Although the thing itself is no longer to be found in nature, still it now survives in the mind and lives as long as it is comprehended by the intellect.[53]

From truth as relative probability—implicitly a quality of propositions and not of objects—to meaning as not objectively referential but socially and historically constituted: so far and no farther is Vives willing to travel along Valla's path toward Valla's view of the cognitively constitutive function of language. So far does he preserve and transmit Valla's challenge to orthodox referential semantics.

But he immediately deflects the challenge by redirecting the process of reference. Taking his cue from the terms of the venerable definition of language as merely the means for express-

---

[51] M III, 143: "Sic ergo diffiniamus vocem significantem, ut sit: Communis nota, qua inter se aliqui aliis notiones suas explicant, id est, quae mente concipiunt: itaque usus est dominus significatuum."

[52] The same examples, indeed the whole aim of rescuing the classical arts of discourse from degeneration by reintegrating them according to the Vallesque observation of actual historical usage, are repeated in *de ratione dicendi* (1532), a similarly compendious treatise of a less theoretical and more pedagogical kind: M II, 95ff.

[53] M III, 143–144: "Quocirca vocum significatio, hoc est, notatio, animum spectat, non res, nam *Hector, chimaera, bellum Punicum*, et cetera, quorum res nusquam sunt, aliquid tamen significant, id est, animo sunt alicuius rei nota, quae res etsi ex natura sit sublata, animo tamen superest etiamnum, et tamquam vivit, dum intelligentia comprehenditur."

ing what is already in the mind, Vives goes on to locate meaning as the "image of some thing" (rei alcuius imaginem) in the mind. Moreover, he sees his example of fictional creatures and past events as but a special case: those words signify something that is *only* in the mind; but most words signify (i.e., produce a mental image of) things that exist in nature. Not all of them do, though; and Vives draws the distinction (common in late medieval nominalism) between "significative" words that so signify and "consignificative" (i.e., "syncategorematic") ones that do not. Still, meaning, which had almost become a function of whole utterances in social contexts, is returned to individual words, which, though they can no longer be said to possess it by referring unequivocally to objects, now refer to mental images.

Before leaving the subject, however, Vives makes one more observation from the sociohistorical perspective, which, like the many others thus generated, is not explicable by his theory.

Someone may ask whether words signifying the same thing in diverse languages, like *homo* and *anthropos*, may be called synonyms. It seems not, for they do not signify the same thing to each nation, except where a nation uses both its own and the loan-word, for example, Zephyrus and Favonius, phlegm and catarrh, Pallas and Minerva. For we have said that "to signify" is not simply what is spoken, but what is spoken with respect to something.[54]

If apparent synonyms do not "signify the same thing" because they are *used* differently by different nations, a functional criterion of meaning is being invoked that is incompatible with both the mentalistic criterion Vives has stated and the whole process of reference by which it is said to operate. Vives never questions this process by inquiring into the referential status of his own examples: by asking, for instance, just what different

[54] M III, 145: "Quaerat aliquis an voces in diversis linguis idem significantes, ut, *homo* et *anthropos*, synonymae sint dicendae? Non videtur; nam non idem utrique genti significant, nisi forte apud quam in usum sunt receptae ambae, sicut, Zephyris et Favonius, phlegma et pituita, Pallas et Minerva, diximus enim significare non simpliciter dici, sed secundum respectum."

pictures of "man" there are in the heads of Romans and Greeks and how we might perceive them, or just what form the "image" of the Punic War might take in our minds. He presumes the process; but he explicitly and often, as here, employs at the same time criteria of meaning whose mutual incompatibility he seems scarcely aware of.

This situation illustrates in little the virtually subterranean way in which attitudes toward the relation between language and meaning were shifting at large during the Renaissance. The treatment of sociohistorical usage as a determinant of meaning, the revival of the "probable" dialectics of Cicero and Quintilian, the insistence on a unified perspective from which to regard both the arts of discourse and the discourse they produce, and the pursuit of the cognitive consequences of these new forms of linguistic attention—all initiated by Valla—generated an implicitly revolutionary semantics that was not always perceived to contradict received theory and so became embedded and transmitted therein. One set of assumptions about meaning could thus be used in the actual analytic investigation of discourse, or be recommended for the actual teaching of the traditional "arts," that was basically subversive of another set derived from the current concept of language. The tension between language *treated* as creating meaning and *conceived* as but containing it begins to be felt as a result of the humanistic "rebirth" of classical letters in the Renaissance, and continues to find expression in both intellectual disputation and literary production at least until the eighteenth century. When Pope in the same poem has words "echoing" meaning and also creating "new worlds," he is doing exactly what Vives is doing when in the same sentence he appeals to notions of meaning as "signifying" and as use. Both the philosopher and the poet are enmeshed in the same contradiction because they both find themselves in a linguistic field whose energy they admire, hence wish to promote, and fear, hence wish to control.

This admiration and fear are manifest when Vives returns, in Book One of *de prima philosophia*, to the investigation of "first things," which involves the cognitive functioning of language with which Valla had replaced traditional metaphysics altogether. Vives of course wants to reinstate it; but he cannot do so without first at least acknowledging the epistemological problems posed by the new forms of linguistic awareness initiated by Valla. Vives begins by setting the inquiry in a theological frame: he declares the glory of God, the ultimate cause and origin of all things, who gave us the capacity to learn, which original sin has considerably damaged, though by no means wholly destroyed. Our debilitated mind makes learning difficult and strenuous, so that if we cannot penetrate what seems to us the secret workings of nature, the "darkness" is in our mind and not in "things."[55] By thus invoking the Edenic cognitive state when there was perfect and effortless congruity between perception and reality, Vives makes two points. The first, explicit, is that it is not impious to inquire, so far as we can, into first principles. The second, implicit, is that the natural order of things is in itself transparent and, in theory anyway, knowable. The theological frame allows Vives to deny by implication at the outset the most radical conclusion of the new linguistic awareness: that human knowledge is irrevocably mediated by and contingent upon forms of speech. Nevertheless, the latter become the primary focus as Vives proceeds to unfold the scope, purpose, and method of the discipline of metaphysics, which is fundamental to all others:

Moreover, the power of almost all knowing and understanding is located in words; for in words are perceptions registered, and all that takes place in the mind and in thought is expressed in words which are made to conform, as far as possible, to the real description of the nature of each thing. Hence the common use of words must be diligently observed. It is responsible for both the emergence and the disappearance of most problems in all disciplines, as is seen in Aristotle, Plato, and others. Yet we shall, I hope, discuss elsewhere the concessions that a philosopher should make to general usage. He should certainly be aware of the common meaning of words, but moderate in his discussion of it, lest he appear occupied not so much with things as with words, which is alien to his profession. Like anyone else, he

[55] M III, 190.

should describe things, as far as he can, in common language and should speak plainly in words taken from the people. For this reason, common speech must be accurately known by him who collects any riches from a bunch of tiny coins, like water from droplets. Therefore this discipline that we are establishing at present is applicable to the principles of all arts. For the causes and origins of things, which others accept as unexplored beginnings (for nothing is prior to a beginning), this discipline surveys and explores. Common use, then, gets out the kernel of words that others accept in good faith like coverings of bark, fearing no deceit; indeed, this discipline, which scrutinizes each single word, if deceit lay hidden in any way, uncovers it. Thus other disciplines here borrow the first foundation, so to speak, of their edifice. It is moreover designed for the practice of life and for well perceiving and judging those meanings that dwell in the common use of men.[56]

The general thrust of Vives's program, if not very cogent, is clear enough: his metaphysics, in implied contrast to the hairsplitting terminology-mongering of the scholastics, will be

---

[56] M III, 193: "Ad hoc vis prope omnis sciendi atque intelligendi in verbis est sita, nam verbis sensa consignantur, et quae quisque mente ac cogitatione assequitur, verbis exprimit, iisque, quantum facere potest, conjunctis cum explicatione naturae rei cuiusque; itaque diligenter communis verborum usus est animadvertendus, ex quo plurimae in omnibus disciplinis et existunt quaestiones, et profligantur, quod est videre apud Aristotelem, Platonem, et alios; quanquam quid Philosopho tribuendum sit consensui loquentium, alias dicemus, ut spero: teneat philosophus sensum communem in verbis, sed de illo disserendo adsit modus, ne non tam in rebus videatur esse occupatus, quam in vocibus, quod alienum est ab eius professione; tum ipse, ut quivis alius, quae dicat, ea, quoad eius facere poterit, lingua et verbis de vulgo sumtis eloquatur, quocirca communis sermo exacte cognoscendus est ei, qui ex collatione minutorum assium aliquas divitias corrogat qualescunque, id est, aquam ex stillicidiis; ideo disciplina haec, quae a nobis in praesentia instituitur, accommoda est principiis omnium artium, nam causas et origines rerum, quae aliae tamquam principia inexplorata accipiunt, principio enim nihil est prius, haec contemplatur, et explorat; tum verba communis usus enucleat, quae ceterae velut tecta cortice accipiunt bona fide, nihil metuentes fraudis, haec enim fraudem, si qua delitescebat, retegit, quae singula scrutatur; ita aliae hinc mutuantur illa prima, et quasi fundamenta sui aedificii; est etiam ad usum vitae apta, et ad bene sentiendum judicandumque intellectiis iis quae versantur in usu commumi hominum." (The sentence divisions in the translation conform more closely to those of B I, 532.)

practically useful both by employing and interrogating the common meanings of words. His fear is that this activity, however necessary, may overshadow the real objective of the discipline, which is to fathom the origins of things. On the other hand, one can only penetrate to these origins by cracking the semantic nut of individual words. Vives is in a bind: words are all we have to work with, but they are not, somehow, enough. To ground metaphysics in semantic analysis is a potentially revolutionary step; but Vives cannot complete it, cannot go on to regard the categories of our perception and knowledge as constituted by language. The "power of understanding" that he locates in words is not, finally, a constitutive power, but remains a traditionally expressive one. This ambivalence—between granting and denying a primary cognitive role to language—becomes acute as Vives attacks next the crucial question of epistemology per se:

We enter upon the cognition of things by the passages of the senses, nor have we other means, enclosed in this body. As those in a room who have but one window, by which light is admitted and through which they see outside, see nothing but what the window allows them to see, so we see only as much as is permitted by the senses, although we glimpse outside, and the mind gathers something beyond what the senses have presented—but only as far as is granted by them. The mind certainly mounts above them, but is still supported by them; they open the way, and no other way is open to the mind. Indeed it decides that other things exist, yet it does not observe those things. Therefore when we say that such-and-such things exist or do not exist, or are these and those, of such or of a different kind, we reckon on the basis of our belief, not of the things themselves. It is not they that constitute their measure for us, but our mind. For when we call things good, bad, useful, useless, we are not speaking according to things, but according to ourselves. And sometimes we follow the lead of the senses to the point that just as things appear, so do we openly report them, although the mind may determine to the contrary. Hence Cicero may say those things do not exist that cannot be touched or perceived; nonetheless they are comprehended by the mind and the intelligence. Therefore things must be assessed by us not by their own characteristics but by our estimation and judgment.

But neither do we immediately agree with the opinion of Protagoras of Abdera, who said that all things were such as they were judged by anyone to be, on which he is rightfully refuted by Plato and Aristotle. For we do not say that, in determining of things on the basis of our judgment, we distort the truth of those things according to our judgment. We have therefore cognition and judgment of the senses, of the imagination, and of the mind.[57]

Having triumphantly, if not very logically, asserted these three kinds of cognition, Vives spends the rest of the treatise discriminating their means and objects, beginning with the five physical senses and ascending to the knowledge of angelic substance possible only to the mind. He is also careful to remind us, at the end of each of the three books, of the limiting theological frame in which the whole enterprise takes place: the ultimate cause remains hidden in eternity, and the greatest obstacle to earthly knowledge, as St. Paul taught, is self-love. Within the frame, however, Vives moves back and forth with clocklike regularity between saying, in several different ways, that our cognition is contingent, and then saying that it isn't.

---

[57] M III, 193–94 (B I, 532–33): "ingredimur ad cognitionem rerum ianuis sensuum, nec alias habemus clausi hoc corpore; ut qui in cubiculo tantum habent speculare unum, qua lux admittitur, et qua foras prospiciunt, nihil cernunt, nisi quantum speculare illud sinit, ita nec nos videmus, nisi quantum licet per sensus, tametsi foras promicamus, et aliquid ulterius colligit mens, quam sensus ostenderunt, sed quatenus per eos conceditur; assurgit quidem supra illos, verum illis innixa; illi ei aperiunt viam, nec alia egreditur; alia quidem esse judicat, non tamen alia intuetur: ergo nos quae dicimus, esse aut non esse, haec aut illa, talia non talia, ex sententia animi nostri censemus, non ex rebus ipsis, illae enim non sunt nobis sui mensura, sed mens nostra, nam quum dicimus bona, mala, utilia, inutilia, non re dicimus, sed nobis, et sensus interdum adeo sequimur duces, ut quomodo illis videantur ita etiam pronuntiemus vulgo, quam libet mens contrarium statuat, ut non esse dicat ea Cicero, quae tangi aut cerni non queant, animo tamen atque intelligentia comprehendantur: quocirca censendae sunt nobis res non sua ipsarum nota, sed nostra aestimatione, ac judicio: nec protinus sententiae accedimus Protagorae Abderitae, qui talia esse dicebat quaeque, qualia a quoque judicarentur, de quo a Platone et Aristotele jure reprehenditur, neque enim qui dicimus ex judicio nos nostro de rebus statuere, iidem et veritatem rerum ad nostrum judicium detorquemus: nos ergo cognitionem, seu judicium habemus sensuum, phantasiae, mentis."

In this passage, the image of the enclosed room produces the kind of Vallesque inference that associates perception with language by denying that either process is objectively referential. What we "see" we partly construct; what we "say" refers to our construction. Our "judgment" and the language that declares it constitute our picture of the world. But no sooner has the *ding an sich* disappeared in this analysis than it is baldly reasserted by the same means that Vives employed to dispose of his earlier examples of nonreferentiality, the chimera and the Punic War. The creatively cognitive processes of perception and language, hitherto unqualified, are suddenly said to be but a special case, a minority opinion already confuted by greater authorities. Man is not the measure of *all* things, merely of some. So no argument need be offered for the final denial of the purport of the whole preceding discussion: we are comfortably assured that our inward "determination" entails no outward "distortion." Objective "truth" is still out there, and we can know it.

In conclusions like these one can easily find a blueprint for empiricism, if one is looking for that—but only by ignoring the context from which such conclusions conspicuously do *not* follow.[58] There, one finds as easily an even more detailed blueprint for the critique of empiricism. The typically pendular motion of Vives's thought, along with its rather timorous eclecticism—characteristics that it shares with a great deal of Renaissance humanism—are precisely what make efforts to see it as ancestral to some single, favored modern development so pointless. More important, and more damaging, such efforts wholly obscure its most salient feature: the rich mix of confusion that recommends one theory and proceeds according to another, that seeks to preserve certainty while having to make do with probability, that claims to arrive at "things" and

---

[58] One scholar, however, who presents Vives as a founding father of empirical science, is also aware of his difficulties and ambivalence, specifically on the question of "essences," which Vives, typically, regards sometimes as a function of language and sometimes as inherent in the nature of things: Angelo Crescini, *Le origini del metodo analitico: il cinquecento* (Udine, 1965), pp. 77–78.

yet remains continually obsessed with the sprawling energy and recalcitrant opacity of words. It is less the programmatic attempt to restructure all knowledge than the confusions and tensions produced in the attempt that provide the real medium and agency of cultural change.

Valla's attempt, as we saw, was genuinely to reorder our conceptual/perceptual categories by examining their basis in the common use of words—an attempt of such radical difficulty as not to be sharable. Vives's attempt is merely to rearrange these categories within the given conceptual frame; but in making it he cannot avoid the Vallesque interrogation of language that threatens, again and again, to call that frame into question. Vives must repeatedly sidestep this threat because he himself repeatedly raises it, drawn evidently against his will by both the analytic power and the polemic utility of Valla's unitary, language-based philosophical perspective. Like a moth to a candle flame, Vives constantly returns to the linguistic ideas whose consequences he must escape, whether in dialectics, metaphysics, or epistemology. He does so again in psychology, when he deals with the subjects of speech and cognition in Book Two of *de anima et vita* (1538). Here speech is hailed as being born from reason—the conventional lineage that usually assures the objective universality of both its operation and referents. But not so: the universality of speech is straightaway confined to the human capacity to produce it; its uses and usages are neither fixed nor given by "nature" but are rather of human manufacture. Though words are indeed "signs," they are not signs of external objects but of the internal apparatus, collective and individual, that produces them: of emotion, intelligence, and will.[59] This whole apparatus in turn is active in the process of sensory perception and cognition. The mind casts its own light; it is neither a passive recorder nor a faithful

---

[59] M III, 371–72: "At quandoquidem sermo ex ratione oritur, tam naturalis est homini sermo, quam ratio, ubicunque enim est fons, ibi et rivus; nullus tamen certus est, ac naturalis, omnes sunt ex arte, unde distinctae sunt linguae. . . . voces in homine signa sunt animi universi, et phantasiae, et affectuum, et intelligentiae, et voluntatis."

reflector of external objects. "Thus the measure of cognition and of light in apprehending truth belongs to our minds, not to things."[60] As usual, the context in which these remarks are made, here didactic and hortatory, ignores their implications; it merely urges the reader to appreciate the wonder of writing systems and to cultivate his own intelligence by hard work. Again, Vives makes anti-referential observations while maintaining a traditionally referential position.

★

The net result of the abortive intellectual revolution I have been describing in these two mainstream humanist thinkers is to have rendered problematic traditional assumptions about how language means. Just the kind of "correspondence" between word/fact/meaning that Dante took for granted, in theory, is no longer sustainable without question. The observation of historical semantic change, obvious to Dante, and the recognition that conceptual categories are contingent on human purposes, obvious to some ancient thinkers, have for the first time in the modern West been incorporated into theoretical reflection about language itself. It was Valla who put them there, where, widely diffused in the central humanist effort to revive classical eloquence and reform the trivium, they both delighted and disturbed subsequent generations. The disturbance, to which Vives is an eloquent witness, maintained the continuous if sometimes inadvertent possibility of regarding language not as the cosmetic vehicle of a single cosmic order, but as creating new, perhaps even plural and competing orders of experience. The intoxicating and terrifying possibility of *making* meaning, reacted to and against in a bewildering variety of ways, is, I believe, one of the principal defining energies of the entire Renaissance.

This possibility, initiated and kept alive in great part by the

---

[60] M III, 378–79: "et quemadmodum oculi corporis indigent lumine exteriore ad cernendum, ita oculus mentis lumine interiore ad intelligendum et cognoscendum. . . . itaque modus cognitionis, lucisque, in assequenda veritate, nostrarum est mentium, non rerum."

potent stress on the human agency of communal use as a semantic determinant, had one immediate and obvious application that neither Valla nor Vives was anxious to encourage.
This was nothing less than the shift of attention from past to
present communities of speakers. The humanist movement,
focused on recapturing the various riches of antiquity, derived
the criterion of common usage from a linguistic community
that was dead and applied it in order to revive that usage and
that language in the present. Vives defended the primary concentration on Latin with the rather modest argument that it
was good to have a separate language of and for the learned;
Valla defended it with the much more ambitious contention
that Latin was intrinsically superior for all learned, civic, and
ethical purposes.[61] Despite their linguistic elitism, however,
the very *idea* of a speech community—and the importance they
gave it—could hardly be confined to speech hearable only in
the classroom or from the pulpit, when what it urged attention
to was everywhere available in spoken vernaculars. It was an
idea whose time, early in the sixteenth century, had finally
come; that is, a context was now established in which vernacular languages could become the objects of serious study.
Hence Trissino's translation and revival in the 1520s of Dante's
proposals for an "illustrious" vernacular, which had been ignored for two centuries. Principles and procedures developed
in Latin for the use of Latin provided the means and part of the
motive to examine, systematize, and legitimize living languages. This genuine revolution was thus inspired by the humanist lover of Latin who, willy-nilly, had made it possible to
conceptualize the most important fact about language—its
meaning—not as a static object of reference but as a dynamic
function of use.

[61] Vives's comments are found in book three of *de tradendis disciplinis*, one of
the few portions of his major work that has been translated into English: Foster Watson, *Vives on Education* (Cambridge, 1913), p. 93. Valla's views on the
preeminence of Latin are described and analyzed by Gerl, pp. 231–50.

4

THE CHALLENGE FROM

VERNACULARS

> When thou didst not, savage,   *—The Tempest*
> Know thine own meaning, but wouldst gabble like
> A thing most brutish, I endowed thy purposes
> With words that made them known.

When Thomas More in 1516 contrived his fable of *Utopia* as the response of his humanist erudition to political and moral issues of the day, he of course published it in Latin. A century later, in 1620, Robert Burton complained that he could not find a publisher willing to print in Latin his encyclopedic investigation of "abnormal" psychology, *The Anatomy of Melancholy.* In 1534 the first arguably "modern" history of England appeared. *Anglicae historiae libri XXVI* was written by Polydore Vergil, a naturalized Italian humanist who enjoyed the patronage of the first two Tudor monarchs. In 1614 Sir Walter Raleigh presented to the public the more ambitious product of his imprisoned leisure, *The History of the World.*

These facts illustrate in the marketplace the well-known displacement of Latin by vernaculars that occurred during the sixteenth century in the main areas of humane letters: the conscious development of native national literatures, including history, in Italy, France, and England, together with the concurrent explosion of biblical translations and theological controversies set off in Germany by Martin Luther. Facilitated by the agency of the printing press, stimulated by the humanist demand for "useful" knowledge, the Protestant demand for widespread literacy, and the rising sentiment of membership in nation-states, vernacular languages had effectively replaced

Latin, even for many educated purposes, by the early seventeenth century. Though Latin continued, for the following century or two, to be the language of publication in the increasingly abstruse reaches of philosophy, science, and theology, and while Latin instruction remained the basis of education until this century, by the end of the sixteenth century the language had ceased to dominate the field of discourse in much of Europe.[1]

Mikhail Bakhtin describes the general result of this process of displacement during the sixteenth century as a newly acute awareness of the boundaries of both time and space, a "new consciousness . . . born at the intersection of many languages and at the point of their most intense interorientation and struggle," that produced "the ability to see one's own media from the outside . . . through the eyes of other idioms" and led to "exceptional linguistic freedom." Though Bakhtin overestimates the extent to which this freedom overthrew all old forms of "dogmatism," he is right to emphasize its importance, since "languages are . . . concrete, social philosophies, penetrated by a system of values inseparable from living practice."[2] It was precisely to such "practice" that the humanist mode of observing the historical usage of Latin, most fully developed by Valla, directed attention. To transfer that kind of descriptive, not prescriptive, attention to "living" practice—indeed, so to distinguish for the first time the difference between "dead" Latin and "living" vulgar languages—[3] was nec-

[1] The basic accounts of the sixteenth-century development are Bruno Migliorini, *Storia della lingua italiana*, 3d ed. (Florence, 1961), esp. pp. 311–28; Ferdinand Brunot, *Histoire de la langue française*, vol. II (Paris, 1906); and R. F. Jones, *The Triumph of the English Language* (Stanford, 1953). Cf. Father Ong's brilliant analysis of "Latin Language Study as a Renaissance Puberty Rite," in *Rhetoric, Romance, and Techology* (Ithaca, 1971), pp. 113–41.

[2] *Rabelais and His World*, tr. Hélène Iswolsky (Cambridge, Mass., 1968), pp. 467–71.

[3] K.-O. Apel, *Die Idee der Sprache* (Bonn, 1963), p. 213, notes that Benedetto Varchi in 1570 first used as a principle of classification the living/dead contrast made earlier by Speroni and Bembo; its development is traced by Hans Wilhelm Klein, *Latein und Volgare in Italien* (Munich, 1957), pp. 91–95.

essarily to call in question the unique cultural privilege of Latin and at the same time implicitly to regard the meaning of language not as a fixed correspondence with things, but as contingent on the purposes of a human community.

The Renaissance debates that sought consciously to establish the worth of vernacular tongues did not take place on the summits, or even the foothills, of philosophy. Instead, they were the more casual products of men with more active interests in society, politics, literature, and science (as well as in historical philology). For this reason, they are good evidence for the general diffusion of contradictory assumptions about how language means. Their significance in this respect is exactly analogous to that of the widespread pedagogical influence of Vives: in practice, they often treat meaning as inextricably connected with and created by words; in theoretical pronouncement, they continue to see language as a mere semantic vehicle, a telegraph wire for "conceits" that come from somewhere else. The pressure to retain this old form of "dogmatism" was well-nigh insurmountable, resulting from the constraints imposed by the very necessity to present vernaculars as "equaling" Latin.[4] One had to show that a vulgar was capable of doing all, or almost all, that Latin could do. For this purpose, the handiest theory was the traditional one of language as a channel of communication. The strategy became simply to demonstrate that vernaculars were as efficient a means of transmission as Latin. The tactics, of course, were to encourage the importation of neologisms, the production of both native literature and translations, and the "reduction" of vulgar tongues to the rules of grammar.

Thus began the long process by which the modern European languages were assimilated into the canons of description and analysis—grammatical, syntactic, rhetorical, and prosodic—developed in and for Latin. In the long term, this cul-

---

[4] The only sixteenth-century writer concerned with vernaculars who vehemently refuses this constraint—noted as exceptional by Brunot, *Histoire*, II, 132—is Charles de Bovelles, who will be discussed below.

tural hegemony is analogous to that of Rome conquering Greece and then being conquered by its culture: vernaculars overthrew the dominance of Latin only by subjugating themselves to its terms. The semantic portion of those terms—the traditional, ontologically bound dualism of sign/thing and the concomitant view of language as cosmetic—thus continued to prevail in theory even while many of the controversial points were made on contradictory grounds.

★

How the effort to legitimize vernaculars thus preserved the implicit challenge to its own accepted theory may be seen by examining the principal and recurrent topoi (in the sense of both images and arguments) employed. These were first developed in Italy and later bequeathed, without much modification, to France and then to England. The English examples I cited above were but the last stage in the process that was well under way in Italy almost a century earlier. Machiavelli and Guicciardini were already using the vernacular for the kind of political and historical writing that their humanist predecessors of the fifteenth century had done in Latin. It was, however, this earlier generation of humanists who had made the first efforts to put the vernacular, at least potentially, on a par with Latin. Although they initiated the basic moves in the argument, they lacked the catalytic idea that would firmly establish vernaculars only in the next century.

While Valla was formulating this idea—that of the speech community and its semantic importance—in the second quarter of the fifteenth century, his contemporaries in Florence, Leonardo Bruni and Leon Battista Alberti, were extending the metaphor of organic growth, derived from the fundamental humanist perception of maturity and decline in the historical use of Latin, to include all languages.[5] If Latin had its

---

[5] That Latin itself was not only subject to change but also contained differing levels of usage even in antiquity, was argued by Flavio Biondo, *de locutione romana* (1435). See the discussion by Cecil Grayson, *A Renaissance Controversy: Latin or Italian?* (Oxford, 1960), pp. 11–13, who observes that the ensuing con-

"natural" cycle of flourishing and decay, Bruni saw no reason why other languages could not so develop. Alberti urged further that all languages could thus arrive in time at periods of supremacy and encouraged the learned to hasten this arrival for Italian by improving and using it. It was most likely Alberti who also produced the first vulgar grammar, which applies Priscian's categories to Tuscan speech and argues that it is as fit to be described by "art" as Greek or Latin.[6] Later in the century, Lorenzo de' Medici offered his own sonnets as evidence of the continued natural growth of the Florentine tongue from its great "youth" in the works of Dante, Petrarch, and Boccaccio. Defending these and other native authors, Cristoforo Landino claimed equal power for the vulgar and harmoniously reconciled its cultivation with classical learning by linking good vernacular writing to good Latin training: as Latin literature was improved by digesting the Greek, so is the vernacular by Latin.[7]

These Quattrocento writers were thus seeking at least to modify the earlier and continuing humanist attitude (shared by Dante and Petrarch) that Roman antiquity and its language were intrinsically and irremediably superior to the present world and its spoken idioms. In addition to the basic strategy

troversy over Latin—to freeze it at Cicero or to admit later usages—was simply transferred to the vernacular—to freeze it at Petrarch or to admit current speech. The importance of the fifteenth-century debate about Latin as discovering history is well presented by Riccardo Fubini, "La coscienza del Latino negli umanisti," *Studi Medievali* series 3, 2 (1961), 505–50.

[6] The attribution of authorship, a long-vexed question, is persuasively made in the Introduction of Cecil Grayson, ed., to Leon Battista Alberti, *La prima grammatica della lingua volgare* (Bologna, 1964). Grayson gives an English summary of the evidence in "Leon Battista Alberti and the Beginnings of Italian Grammar," *Proceedings of the British Academy* 49 (1963), 291–311. Alberti's grammar, however, remained in manuscript until this century; the first printed one (in 1516) is discussed by Migliorini, pp. 360–61.

[7] See the accounts of all these contested developments by Hans Baron, *The Crisis of the Early Renaissance* (Princeton, 1955), I, 308–12, and Klein, *Latein und Volgare*, pp. 50–67. Baron also observes that the one notion (later developed) not present in the early Quattrocento was that of language as taking form in "social interchange," II, 428.

of demonstrating equality and the metaphor of organic growth that provided its rationale, both of which were foundations for future debates and programs, there was the whole newly historical kind of linguistic perception that suggested that metaphor in the first place. To say that other languages could grow as Latin had done was implicitly to deprive it of its uniquely superior status. Though no one in the Quattrocento wished to enlarge on this consequence (beyond the claim of potential equality for vernaculars) as later writers did, both Alberti and Lorenzo made historical observations about the use and dominance of Latin quite subversive of its long-assumed superiority. The former argued that the Romans did not write in some esoteric, purely literary idiom, but in the currently spoken language of their day; the latter pointed out that the universality of Latin was not due to its innate superiority but to its empire, and that Latin had once been simply the spoken dialect of a single region. The context and tone of these observations is not competitive, but assimilative: the changes perceived in the literary and political development of ancient Rome are presented as spurs to achieving similar glory for modern Florence.

Such a desire to assimilate, to remain loyal to a venerable past while honoring the vitality of the present—indeed, to see a devotion to past ideals as a way of improving the present— was, as Hans Baron says, "a prototype of the relationship to antiquity known in the sixteenth and seventeenth centuries."[8] In a wider context, it is the Renaissance phase of the whole *translatio studii et imperii* traced by Frank Kermode, the current phase of which he identifies as the "secularization" or demystification of the "classic" "by a process which recognizes its status as a literary text."[9] Perhaps prior to this process—which is itself at least as old as Rabelais, Montaigne, or Cervantes— is an analogous demystification of language, which recognizes

---

[8] *The Crisis of the Early Renaissance*, I, 312.
[9] *The Classic* (London, 1975), p. 139. Kermode is referring here to contemporary criticism.

its contingent, as opposed to God-given, status, and which begins to be widely felt in the Renaissance campaign to legitimize vernaculars. Language becomes subject to, and will soon be regarded as originating in, human will and judgment. The production of self-aware and self-questioning literary texts seems to coincide with the linguistic struggle and "freedom" remarked by Bakhtin, and with the nascent awareness that meaning is manufactured, not merely transmitted, encoded, or enshrined.[10]

To see oneself as able to reenact the literary or imperial achievements of Rome, to take it as a model for "imitation," was not (as it later became) to impose limits but to expand possibilities. It was to assert the eventual equality required in adopting a role-model relationship, such as that of fathers and sons. We must feel ourselves, though immature, enough *like* them to believe that someday we can and will do what they have done, that their power will be ours. Imitation of this kind depends on action; it is neither passive reception of a heritage nor passive worship in a temple, but rather energetic effort to create oneself, one's country, or one's language in a favored image. The enormous enthusiasm with which the Renaissance preached, practiced, and argued about the doctrine of imitation has sometimes puzzled or irritated later observers. But its satisfactions as well as the energies it released should be apparent: imitation was the Renaissance mode of self-fulfillment, a striving to become what one admired, a personal realization of a possible ideal—not deference, but performance.[11]

[10] That Renaissance literary texts typically call into question their claims to authority and truth has been recently demonstrated by David Quint, who attributes this activity to the humanists' having "made meaning itself into a historical problem": *Origin and Originality in Renaissance Literature* (New Haven, 1983), p. 7.

[11] The ambiguities and tensions in conceiving of imitation as following, transforming, and surpassing the model are well discriminated by G. W. Pigman, III, "Versions of Imitation in the Renaissance," *Renaissance Quarterly* 33 (1980), 1–32. The tensions are more fully classified and brilliantly analyzed by Thomas M. Greene, *The Light in Troy: Imitation and Discovery in Renaissance Poetry* (New Haven, 1982), who sees them as proceeding from the historical self-consciousness of the text that constitutes the Renaissance as a period.

The localized patriotism this attitude engendered in Italy, intensified by the rivalry among the numerous city-states and principalities, would provide the motive and the explicit issues of subsequent discussions of the vernacular, which tended to focus on the "name" it should bear.[12] Of the main documents in the controversy I shall discuss those that are most interesting, influential, and representative of the various positions.[13] Whether to label the vulgar "Florentine," "Tuscan," "courtly," or, as Dante had proposed, an "illustrious" composite "Italian" was the immediate occasion of debate in Italy and, as such, was not exportable. Though sixteenth-century Englishmen and Frenchmen concerned with their own vernaculars could observe great geographical diversity of dialects, none of these presented itself as a serious rival to the language of the centralized capitals and courts of London and Paris. Owing to their different political organization, the French and English did not have to adjudicate, as the Italians did, between versions of the vernacular, and could proceed more directly to the business of defending it, embellishing it, and reducing it to rule. Perhaps this difference in national situation also accounts for the difference in the form of their arguments. To defend their vernacular, the French produce univocal treatises; the English make remarks by the way in other contexts; the Italians compose dialogues.[14]

[12] This was in effect *La Questione della lingua*, most recently surveyed by Maurizio Vitale (Palermo, 1967). His account of sixteenth-century texts (pp. 22–63) is supplemented by those of Migliorini, pp. 339–61, and Bortolo Tommaso Sozzi, ed. Niccolò Machiavelli, *Discorso o dialogo intorno alla nostra lingua* (Turin, 1976).

[13] These are: Pietro Bembo, *Prose . . . nella quale si ragiona della volgar lingua* (Venice, 1525); Giovan Giorgio Trissino, *Il Castellano: dialogo . . . della lingua italiana* [1529] (Milan, 1864); Sperone Speroni, "dialogo delle lingue" in *I dialogi* (Venice, 1542); Claudio Tolomei, *Il Cesano . . . nel quale da piu dotti huomini si disputa del noma . . . si dee . . . chiamare la volgar lingua* (Venice, 1555); Benedetto Varchi, *L'Hercolano: Dialogo . . . nel qual si ragiona generalmente delle lingue* (Venice, 1570).

[14] The importance of the earlier humanist revival of this form as a philosophical alternative to scholastic dialectic is well argued by David Marsh, *The Quattrocento Dialogue* (Cambridge, Mass., 1980). What he finds crucial about the Latin dialogue—its assumption "that knowledge is not fixed eternally: his-

To advocate and defend the spoken language in dramatized verbal encounters (in which the real speakers outnumber the fictional ones) is not just highly appropriate—a nice observance of decorum—it is also a way of acknowledging and confronting the multiple claimants in the case. The popularity of the dialogue in Italy owes much to the great prestige of Plato, and the form is handled with as great variety as his. It can be merely an excuse for long set speeches offering various points of view, which are then summarized and refuted in an even longer speech advocating the writer's own conclusions (Tolomei). It can be a genuine give-and-take that allows several participants to employ irony and mockery at each other's expense and leads to no dogmatic conclusion at all (Speroni). Or it can be totally one-sided, with the titular hero relentlessly and logically exploding the feeble objections of a Socratic stooge (Trissino). But however handled, these sixteenth-century dialogues enact an awareness of language as the possession of a community of speakers that includes, as norm, the great literature of the Trecento; that practices, as method, rational argumentation between present users; that postulates, as necessary condition, the fact of historical change; and that assumes, as goal, the community's conscious ability to mold its common possession into various and competing desired shapes. In short, the diachronic contingency of language has become not only respectable but exhilarating. The principle that enabled it to become so—the idea that catalyzed the flow of sixteenth-century vernacular debates from the trickle of fifteenth-century observations—is apparent from the form those debates took. The way in which the dialogue itself was used reflects the powerful new concept of the speech community and the descriptive approach to "common usage" pioneered by Lorenzo Valla.

The kinds of usage, however, really at issue in the dialogues

torical context and the fluidity of debate both play a role in the search for truth" (p. 34)—also characterizes its vernacular descendents in the next century.

are for the most part less "common" than Valla may have had in mind. Actual contemporary speech is only occasionally appealed to; attention is focused primarily on the norm of literary usage, what it was, how it developed, what it should be. The constraint of the Latin model largely, though not entirely, restricts the field of application of the new perspective. The same constraint, of course, also prevents pursuing the new perspective as far as Valla did. No matter how much the dialogues may conceive of language as a social product, they never explicitly draw the inference of its cognitive function to make the Vallesque connection between usage, meaning, and epistemology. The ultimate result of the constrained strategy was that models became idols, "and Italians became accustomed to learning how to write their language as though it were Latin or Greek."[15] In the process, however, they investigated those models with some linguistic assumptions not always consistent with the special status the models acquired. Again, there is the tension between procedure and aim: the descriptive mode of the former is almost always in the service of the prescriptive desire of the latter.

This tension is implanted in the debate at the outset by the great cultural authority of the platonizing future Cardinal Bembo—who recurs as a major speaker in the dialogues of Speroni and Tolomei and is copiously cited by Varchi. His *Prose* is an epistolary account of a conversation between "illustri gentili" addressed to Giulio de' Medici, and its purpose is, naturally, to establish Tuscan as the noblest vernacular. Bembo begins with the standard, but later contested, assumption that the dialects of Italy are the historical result of the "corruption" of classical Latin by the invading barbarian tongues. Of the ensuing mélange of vulgars, the first to create a noble

---

[15] Francesco de Sanctis, *History of Italian Literature*, tr. Joan Redfern (New York, 1931), II, 629. He goes on to heap contempt on the whole practice, to which his hatred of verbal artifice and his *Risorgimento* nationalism made him implacably and not unreasonably hostile. His point, accepted by most subsequent scholars (e.g., Klein, *Latein*, pp. 98–99), is that the Accademia della Crusca, founded in 1582, made literary Italian as "dead" a language as Latin.

literature was Provençal. Bembo therefore bases his argument for the superiority of Tuscan on the fact that its literature is most indebted to, and its language has taken most from, Provençal (fols. 7ᵛ–8ᵛ). The Tuscan thus recommended is explicitly archaic; Bembo wants to fix a literary idiom that is not (though it may partly coincide with) what contemporary Tuscans speak. He justifies such an idiom by the precedent of Virgil, who, even when he wrote to instruct the peasantry, wrote in such a way that only the learned could understand him fully.[16] This way of using Latin then should be our way of using the vulgar now. Bembo concludes his version of the assimilative strategy by emphasizing, despite its partial archaism, its value as present communication: "One must say that whoever writes in Latin now is writing for the dead rather than for the living."[17]

Having thus defined the norm, Bembo proceeds to discriminate its uses in the lyric verse of Cavalcanti, Dante, Petrarch and Boccaccio: sounds of words, differences of dialect, diction, and grammar are all analyzed in detail. The attempt is to formulate precepts of style and general rules of grammar, observing at the same time that changes have occurred even in the elevated literary idiom as the language itself has altered.[18] On the one hand, both the literary norm and the language in which it is embedded are seen continually to change; on the other, the aim is to extract from this flux regulations whose application will prevent its further occurrence. This paradoxical position is that of any traditional grammarian who seeks to apply prescriptions derived from a language that has ceased to

[16] "Scrive delle bisogne del contado il Montavano Virgilio; et scrive a contadini invitandogli ad apparar le cose, di che egli ragiona loro. Tuttavia scrive in modo; che non che contadino alcuno; ma niuno huomo piu che di citta, se non dotto grandemente et letterato, puo bene et compiutamente intendere, cio che egli scrive," fols. 17ᵛ–18.

[17] "Che quale hora Latinamente scrive, a morti si debba dire che egli scriva piu che a vivi," fol. 18.

[18] E.g., "Ma passisi a dire del verbo: nel quale la licentia de poeti et la liberta medesima della lingua v'hanno piu di malagevolezza portata," fol. 50ᵛ.

change by natural usage to one that is still doing so. The paradox may seem depressingly familiar to us, after four centuries
of the pedagogy that the humanist strategy of assimilation imposed; but it passed unnoticed at the time, preserving, in the
midst of arguments to transfer the privilege of Latin to one variety of the vernacular, the potentially subversive awareness of
the social dynamism of all language.

Such awareness begins to broaden as interests and standards
other than the purely literary are brought into the debate. Trissino, for example, brings in logic, both abstract and empirical,
to demonstrate the existence of the composite "Italian" that
Dante had wished for. Trissino had earlier proposed to rationalize the vernacular by supplying it with two new vowels to indicate differences in pronunciation.[19] The stooge in his dialogue is made to object to his having in the proposal called the
language "Italian," whereupon the stooge is pulverized by a
Socratic, step-by-step demonstration of the relations between
species and genera. Only after the auditors (one of whom is the
poet Sannazaro) are thus convinced by "reasons" that "Italian"
is the legitimate genus and local dialects the species does the
hero adduce the "authority" of Dante. This is not dwelled on
but immediately gives way to a statistical review of the dialect
words in Dante and Petrarch, designed to show that only a
tenth of their vocabulary is uniquely "Tuscan." Appeal to any

---

[19] This proposal, in a letter to Clement VII, is printed along with *Il Castellano* in the ed. of Milan, 1864. Spelling reform was another popular way to
legitimize vernaculars by subjecting them to rational rules, an effort as paradoxical as the grammatical one in that it recognized the aural facts of pronunciation and disregarded the visual conventions of its representation. Again, the
assumption of the description is that language is a social product, which is denied by the giving of prescriptions for recording speech. The accurate description of a social practice cannot enforce change in a social phenomenon. Spelling reformers tend to be extreme—and in this area, mistaken—rationalists,
like G. B. Shaw; and their efforts have always been doomed. Brunot, II, 93–
123, describes the sixteenth-century French attempts to simplify orthography
made by such various eminences as Meigret, Peletier, and Ramus. In England
two different systems had been proposed before the better-known William
Bullokar offered his scheme *for the amendment of orthographie* (London, 1580).

sense of geographical/political patriotism is notably absent; the effort is strictly to establish "Italian" as both a logical and extant fact. Trissino's definition of that fact depends on the traditional assumption of universal, a priori meanings, which all men share but manifest in different words.[20] On this basis a language becomes the generic speech of a nation that used "almost all the same words in the same senses."

Both the assimilation of the Latin model, urged by Bembo, and the establishment of a common "standard" national speech, urged by Trissino, will remain basic moves in the sixteenth-century efforts to legitimize vernaculars. But both points will also be disputed from the very same grounds on which they were in part based: the awareness of language as the product of a community. The most radical inferences from this awareness, which vigorously deny any possibility of either assimilating vernaculars to Latin rules or codifying a "standard" vernacular speech, were made by the contemporary French humanist, mathematician, numerologist, and mystagogue, Charles de Bovelles.[21] Beginning with the ordinary pejorative postulate that vernaculars are the historical result of a variously contaminated Latin, Bovelles catalogues the "faults" (vitia) of word formation in French, classifying, for example, its vowels either as "barbarous" or as remaining from Latin. The body of the treatise, however, observes in great detail historical and geographical differences in spoken French. Its dialects are carefully discriminated from similar but separate languages, like Basque. Changes in the pronunciation of every letter in the alphabet are traced, one by one, as transmitted from Latin to French. The sounds themselves are clas-

[20] A language, he says, is "un parlare umano, che usa le medesime parole nel manifestare i medisimi sensi; perciò che tutti gli uomini hanno i medesimi sensi . . . ma quelli poi fanno variamente manifesti," p. 28.

[21] *Liber de differentia vulgarium linguarum* (Paris, 1533). There is a French translation, *Sur les langues vulgaires*, by Colette Dumont Demazière (Paris, 1973). On Bovelles' whole career there is now Joseph M. Victor, *C. de B. 1479–1553: An Intellectual Biography* (Geneva, 1978), who, however, somewhat misconstrues the argument of *liber de differentia*: pp. 29–30.

sified by both physical method of production and aural impression. The thoroughness of the descriptions makes the book a pioneering step toward systematic and historical phonetics as well as lexicography (it includes a small etymological dictionary of French).[22] What Bovelles has managed to describe leads him to some remarkable conclusions.

The first of these is to deny the pejorative implications of his initial assumptions and his own vocabulary. Changes in pronunciation are simply inevitable; their causes—whether by "error" or intervals of space and time—defy regulation. Even Latin words, whose exact pronunciation can be taught, will be pronounced by ordinary people according to the "custom of the country" (patriae consuetudinem). Bovelles therefore spends a whole chapter arguing that "the ignorant lips of the common man are not blamable, nor do they commit faults in any native tongue whatever." To castigate "the errors of a mother tongue" (maternae linguae vitiis) would be "immense and useless labor." Each nation speaks as it likes; vernaculars cannot be stabilized by a pure notion of total uniformity nor made to conform to exact rule. Even in Latin, what one nation says seems vicious to another. "Who therefore would wonder that faults of pronunciation occur in the language of the people and in vulgar speech, when not even the Latin language appears to be free of them?"[23]

Bovelles, finding no order or pattern in all the synchronic and diachronic changes he has detected, accepts the fact of lin-

---

[22] That Bovelles was also a pioneer collector of native proverbs is shown by Natalie Zemon Davis, *Society and Culture in Early Modern France* (Stanford, 1975), pp. 232–45. Her excellent analysis of the whole practice of proverb collection further illustrates the assimilative strategy at work: vernacular resources are being mined in the learned campaign to make French as rich as Latin.

[23] Pp. 42–43: "Incastigabilia esse imperitae plebis labia, ne in verna quavis lingua vitium patrent. . . . frustra quis tentaverit in vulgari qualibet lingua aut . . . stabilire synceram totius uniformitatis ipsius ideam, aut exactam conflare regulam. . . . Quis igitur demiretur, in plebeia lingua, & in sermone vulgi, vitia labiorum apparere, cum ne Latina quidem lingua videatur eorum esse expers?"

guistic change as entirely arbitrary. The localized speech community has become the only lawgiver, and its laws cannot be formulated. Hence he insists that any search for a "standard" or "original" vulgar speech is pointless. "In what region of France," he asks, "shall we locate the archetype of the speech of all the French?"[24] What cannot be found in the case of French, which is at least partly related to Latin, is even more elusive in the case of German and other "barbaric" tongues, whose origins are wholly uncertain and which are "utterly contrary" (prorsus dissentanea) to Latin. Bovelles ridicules the ambition of Johannes Trithemius, the German polymath, to make the language of the Germans "equal" (adaequare) to Latin by formulating rules of correctness for its cultivation and instruction. His contempt for this conventionally prescriptive humanist undertaking is tonic: "Where are you going to seize this standard of the German language, which you will supply with the ramparts and whipcords of rules by which the lips of the ignorant multitude, inclined to error, must be constrained, that they may never deviate from the ideal try-square and plumb-line of their language?" Pointing out some common differences in spelling and pronunciation between high and low German, he urges that there is no way to choose between them, that each kind of speech is correct and attractive to its users, "since each language pleases its own speakers and no one thinks he makes mistakes in his native tongue."[25]

The radical equality that Bovelles thus discovers between all languages by finding their social dynamism ungoverned and ungovernable allows him to jettison another issue cherished by

[24] P. 43: "Superfluam & cassam fore disquisitionem ideae in omni sermone vulgi. . . . Ubinam igitur, & in qua Galliae regione locabimus totim Gallici sermonis archetypum?" Bovelles' Platonic terms, *idea* and *archetypus* of course connote both "ideal" and "origin," as well as a composite "standard" form of speech.

[25] P. 45: "Ubinam . . . apprehensurus es ipsam Germanicae linguae ideam, quam succingas vallis ac loris regularum, quibus astringi oporteat, prona in vitium suum imperiti vulgi labia, ne ab amussi ab idea, & a perpendiculo suae linguae usquam titubent. . . . Quandoquidam vox utraque suo placeat vulgo: & in suo dicendi modo vitium se committere arbitretur nemo."

conventional humanism. "The controversy about the primal origin of languages," he roundly declares, "can scarcely be rightly resolved by anyone."[26] Given the great variety and chaotic development among and within spoken languages, no one can extrapolate from their present state a more correct or purer form to honor as their ideal origin. We might well expect that Bovelles' exaggerated and literal-minded adherence to description, his resolute rejection of any form of prescription in the matter of vernaculars, would produce at least a muted conservative argument in favor of Latin as the only language theoretically reducible to rules (even if these are not obeyed). But no such explicit argument is made. Instead, Bovelles concludes his treatise by transforming the arbitrariness he has described in practice into a theological principle: "As indeed the free and spontaneous origin of all substances depends on the will of God, so without doubt God willed and decreed that the origin of all names, words, and pronunciations should arise from the choice of man (namely, from the first parent)."[27] Bovelles locates the ideal, standard, or origin of all languages in the speech (carefully unspecified) of Adam and Eve, which we shall all learn, according to the prophets, only in the last days of the world. Until then, and after Babel, we must simply tolerate both the faults and the variety of all languages and dialects.

This conclusion clearly suggests where Bovelles thought real knowledge to lie: not in the competing grammars of willful human construction, but in the symbolic grammar of divine creation. He had no interest in systematizing language—indeed his whole book is a kind of demonstration that the effort is a waste of time—but preferred to systematize the cos-

---

[26] *Ibid.*: "Contentionem de primatu linguarum, vix rite a quoquam discuti posse."

[27] P. 46: 'Sicut enim ab arbitrio dei, libera & spontanea substantiarum omnium origo pependit, ita nimirum voluit sanxitque deus, omnium nominum, vocum, & appellationum originem ab hominis (nempe a primi parentis) arbitratu proficisci debere." How revolutionary this interpretation of Gen. 2:19 then was will be discussed later.

mos in terms of cabalistic numerological mysticism.[28] Given his motive, he could easily afford the sort of wholesale rejections, the attitude of laissez-faire toward language, that more secular-oriented epistemologists and literati could not. It is therefore all the more striking that he should adopt their very secular perspective on the social dimensions of language usage and push it to a virtually nihilistic conclusion. The voluntaristic principle he draws from this perspective—that the actual use of spoken language depends entirely on a collective human will—will reappear in subsequent debate as a powerful defense of the equal worth of all vernaculars. As such, the principle will serve as an added stimulus to and justification of exactly those activities that Bovelles found inadmissible: the assimilation of the power of Latin by vernaculars and the codification of standard vernacular forms.

★

The most direct kind of assimilation was of course translation. Although the most furious battles on this subject were waged in the field of Scripture, the enormous output of secular translation in the Renaissance also generated occasional reflection, usually quite practical or self-defensive, on how it should be done. Such reflection inevitably has recourse to another notion of will—individual rather than collective—as well as to a common-sense realization of the semantic importance of context. Both considerations furnish a further example of how opposed assumptions about meaning coexist in another area of pragmatic and widespread concern, here represented by Etienne Dolet's unoriginal and compendious little manual, *La Maniere de Bien Traduire*.[29]

Having been ridiculed by scholarly critics in the late 1530s

---

[28] His works on this subject are briefly exemplified and described by S. K. Heninger, *The Cosmographical Glass* (San Marino, 1977), pp. 170–71.

[29] Lyon, 1540. Dolet's five succinct "rules" of translation are summarized by George Steiner, *After Babel* (Oxford, 1975), pp. 262–63, in the course of an acute analysis of Western theories of translation (Ch. 5). Steiner points out both the paucity and the persistence of ideas on the subject: pp. 238–39, 262.

for the first two volumes of his commentary on Cicero, Dolet abandoned a projected third volume and turned his attention to the embellishment of his native tongue. He offers this brief essay as an earnest of a grand design (never carried further) to form "l'orateur Francoys," in the hope that "la langue Fran-coyse . . . pourra estre reduicte en telle perfection" as Latin and Greek (p. 6). Insisting, traditionally, that the translator must have perfect command of both languages in which he works, Dolet is against word-for-word translation. The order of words should be disregarded in favor of "sentences . . . en sorte que l'intention de l'autheur sera exprimée." To render "line for line" can both "deprave the sense" and fail "to express the grace" of either language (pp. 15–16). Dolet gives a sample of what he recommends: a passage of Cicero, which his trans-lation greatly expands by incorporating an explanation of its "sense," not at all verbally accurate but, according to Dolet, "faithful" (p. 14).

Such recommendations, which go back at least as far as Leonardo Bruni,[30] implicitly contradict the received view that meaning is located in the referents of individual words. There is a larger "sense," visible in whole propositions and identified as the "intention" of the author, that the translator is after. To say this is to recognize that words are emphatically not neutral containers or merely cosmetic transmitters of a thing called "meaning" that exists outside and independent of them. The paradox is inherent in the traditional dualism of the post-Pla-tonic vocabulary of discourse, or rather, in the conflict of this theoretical assumption with the awareness compelled by the

---

[30] De interpretatione recta (ca. 1420), in Humanistisch-Philosophische Schriften, ed. Hans Baron (Leipzig, 1928), pp. 84–87. Bruni is defending in this brief and unfinished essay his own translation into Latin of the Nichomachean Ethics (1418). He insists on knowledge of the full range of writers and usages in both languages, on the recognition of "totas sententias" that are produced by such contexts, as well as on the ways in which individual use can alter them. We must distinguish, he says, "tropes and figures of speech that signify something different from the words, from preestablished custom" (tropi figuraeque lo-quendi, quae aliud ex verbis, aliud ex consuetudine praeiudicata significent). Bruni's essay, however, was never published in the period.

routine practice of translation. Remarking on the monotonous dichotomy of word/sense persistent in discussions of translation since St. Jerome, George Steiner describes the paradox as follows:

It predicates a literal meaning attached to verbal units, normally envisaged as single words in a purely lexical setting, which differs from, and whose straightforward transfer will falsify, the "true sense" of the message. Depending on the degree of sophistication available to him, the writer on translation will treat "meaning" as more or less inherently transcendental. . . . "Meaning" resides "inside the words" of the source text, but to the native reader it is evidently "far more than" the sum of dictionary definitions.[31]

Indeed, anyone who has ever studied a foreign language knows how far he can remain from the "meaning" of a sentence even when he knows the "definition" of every single word in it. One therefore wonders why, at a time when translation and language-learning itself were pursued so widely and with new urgency, this ordinary experience did not result in a more direct and sustained attack on the old semantic assumption. The answer, as I have suggested, partly lies in the character of that urgency: the pressure to show that vernaculars can "signify"—meanings, intentions, elegance, or whatever—as effectively as Latin. Yet as Latin itself was being described in the same contingent terms as vernaculars—it grows and decays; it has different levels of usage; these sociohistorical contexts are semantically crucial to its interpretation—it remains difficult to understand why statements about language seem so opaque to and uninfluenced by the actual experience of dealing with it. The discrepancy seems great enough to require another kind of explanation than that of polemical convenience, which is but the shadow of a profounder reluctance to connect the use of language with the theory of how it means.

---

[31] *After Babel*, p. 276. Steiner goes on to describe the general result as "inflationary," whereby a translation must always exceed the original by creating "for it an illustrative context" (p. 277)—which is exactly what happens in Dolet's sample from Cicero.

Despite the sixteenth-century translator's full recognition that he cannot simply transfer meaning from one word to another, but must re-create it in different words, manipulating it with a whole range of conscious devices and skills, he persists in regarding it as "transcendental." This feeling, I think, is the powerfully magical residue of the traditional process of "signification"—the process that Valla could not reformulate even after he had destroyed the basis of its operation, the process that working translators continue to assume even after they have wrestled with all the circumstances of mundane usage that do not "stand for" a meaning but constitute it. Meaning, like "truth" and "knowledge," is still *felt* to stand comfortingly above the disputatious immersion of words in the chaotic flux of times, places, and wills; to exist as an absolute, a final guarantee (or desperate hope) that the world is, at least in principle, certainly and permanently intelligible. This is the great desire of Western culture that Plato imposed on human affairs, that Aristotle further extended into the investigation of nature, that Judaism and Christianity furnished for the very process of history. In its most basic—that is, linguistic—terms, it is the wish to divide the indivisible in order to preserve the "signified" from dissolution in the unceasing, corrosive ferment of the "signifiers." This desire was not weakened by the increasing attention paid to the scope and intricacy of that ferment; on the contrary, it seems to intensify as it is threatened. Vives, as we saw, still wants to find apodictic meaning in "things," even though he is painfully aware that the only way he can approach it is by the careful observation and interrogation of words. It is the dilemma of the age. If language, in Susanne Langer's description, dreams our desires,[32] the language of discourse, the grammar of "signification," dreams the deepest desire of all: for a final repose from the frenetic inconclusiveness of interpretation. In theory this can be supplied by assertions of magic, usually as divine authority; in life it can only be supplied by death.

[32] "The Lord of Creation," *Fortune* (Jan. 1944), pp. 140–42.

Philosophers, translators, and biblical interpreters in the Renaissance were caught up in this dilemma; but Prince Hamlet, Shakespeare's greatest user of language, is made to enact it. Hamlet is nothing if not a hermeneuticist (he was even at Wittenberg). Faced with a clear assertion of meaning, he must verify it by interrogation and observation; he must then interrogate his own impulse to verification. Hamlet never doubts that he has a duty to avenge his father's death; he insists on being certain that the facts invoke the duty. Ghosts can deceive; their intentions toward us must be interpreted. Hamlet must interpret everything in a world where no text is transparent, where nothing is as it seems. He assaults the macrocosm of the universe and the microcosm of himself to yield him up their true meaning. No social hypocrisy is too small to be unmasked; no metaphysical speculation too large to be entertained. Hamlet is above all a connoisseur, a professional expert, in the use of words. He plays with them obsessively, is fascinated by their power, disgusted by their emptiness, amused by their duplicity. Words in Hamlet's mouth are self-propagating; they lead to no final clarification, but to other words. And so in his mind do meanings. (It is no accident that his play has stimulated more volumes of commentary than any other work of secular Western literature.) Hamlet composes a text to be performed, whose meaning will be the reaction of one member of the audience. Having thus resolved on the truth of the ghost's meaning, he finds no clear basis for action, but only further possibilities of significance. Encountering Claudius at prayer, Hamlet inquires what it would mean to kill him now, decides that the context would signify something other than his intention, and refrains. Ironically, Claudius's ensuing remark informs us that Hamlet has misread the context. How could he do otherwise? All he has to go on is observable language—words and gestures; he cannot read the king's mind. Still, convinced that his uncle has killed his father, he worries what this might imply about the guilt of his mother and passionately persuades her (with words like daggers) to repent.

While Hamlet has been busy interpreting everything, almost everyone else in the play is busy interpreting him. Polonius is sure he knows what Hamlet's antic behavior means—indeed, Polonius knows what life means; his resonant clichés are nuggets of fixed "significance" often ludicrously inapplicable to the situation—and dies in the attempt to verify it. Having discovered the king's death warrant for himself, Hamlet supplies that text with other referents, interprets his escape with the pirates as providential, and returns to Denmark a changed man. No longer hysterical with self-reproach, Hamlet gives up plotting, ceases trying to impose certain meanings on events, to write the script, to set the time "right." So he becomes an actor in Claudius's script, whose presence, however, will invalidate Claudius's intended meaning. Hamlet cannot provide, single-handed, the meanings that he seeks; but he remains alert—"the readiness is all"—to detect them in occasions. He interrogates Yorick's skull. The last possibility of significance to be ready for is death, and death is silent on its own meaning. But Hamlet goes right on interrogating language: he delights in the precisian pedantry of the gravedigger, violently resents Laertes' rhetoric of grief, parodies the periphrastic pretentiousness of Osric, and finally kills the king with a triumphantly ironic pun on the meanings of "union." Dying, Hamlet is adamant that Horatio live on to maintain the flow of words, to report his cause and tell his story. Hamlet dies just as he has so energetically lived, committing a speech act, telling Horatio to tell Fortinbras something, cut off in mid-sentence—"The rest is silence." The unceasing effort to interpret—to find, create, impose, verify meaning—is life; but the only incontrovertible, unalterable significance the process ever arrives at is the emptiness of its own absence: silence is death.

The play of *Hamlet* presents to the audience the same hermeneutic challenge, the same defiant opacity, that its events present to its characters. Though we may not be able to play a tune on a recorder, to "make it speak," as Hamlet says, we think we can sound not only his depths, but even fathom the universe. Hamlet sneers at those who try "to pluck out the heart" of his mystery, for it is meaning in precisely that traditional sense—as kernel, as essence, as fixed object that can be penetrated, as final interiority—that the play calls persistently into question and repeatedly shows to be unattainable. Yet Hamlet himself hankers after something like it. His mystery, I am suggesting, is the mystery of language itself as made problematic by the shifting semantic awareness of the Renaissance. The play filters the major human concerns—for justice, passion, power—common to tragedy through a central focus on the words by which they are all mediated and shaped.

As literary artist, Shakespeare has made his own discovery of the disturbing principle adumbrated by Valla: that language is cognitive, that semantics is epistemology, that meanings are made—remade and unmade by the competing wills of communities and individuals—not born. The discovery is both terrifying and glorious. The user of his native speech delights in the greatly expanded importance of his power to manipulate it; at the same time he fears that his power is impotent, this expansion a trap, a condemnation to the perpetual motion of signifiers doomed never to find peace in a signified. It is the particular distinction of Hamlet—one that he shares with his creator and others like Rabelais, Montaigne, and Cervantes—that he finds this terror itself glorious. In this sense, Shakespeare's famous quibbles (so detested by neoclassic taste) are central to his art, not as personal idiosyncrasy, but as crystallizations made by genius out of the fitfully developing linguistic self-consciousness of the whole period. Puns celebrate the Protean fluidity of signifiers, exploiting as many different semantic dimensions—of sound, of multiple definition, of etymological association, of grammatical function, of social register—as individual ingenuity can deploy. The greatest literature of the Renaissance enacts the energies and the fears produced by this new fluidity as it emerged from all the argument of the period about words.

★

Concerning vernaculars, the most complex, poised, and intelligent argument is that of Speroni's "dialogo delle lingue."[33]

---

[33] Simone, "Sperone Speroni et l'idée de diachronie," *History of Linguistic*

Not only does he bring together almost all the strands of previous controversy, giving new twists to most of them; he also introduces a new one, derived from his sometime teacher, Pomponazzi: the utility of the vernacular for the dissemination of scientific knowledge. Though himself a poet and a great promoter of vulgar eloquence (he also studied with Bembo), Speroni enlarges the debate beyond the confines of provincial, belletristic rivalry, and gives unusually full expression to the opposed lovers of Latin and Greek. His dialogue is thus a convenient digest of virtually all the issues that would continue to be disputed in the quarrel between the ancients and the moderns.

Lazaro, the defender of the ancient, starts things off by developing the stock notion of the vernacular's origin as barbaric contamination of Latin into a political attack on current speech. Present-day Italian has been wholly corrupted by ultramontane barbarisms even as Italian territories have been conquered by foreigners. No language can become glorious "that is born and grows with our calamity and still maintains itself with our ruin" (fol. 111ᵛ). The "corruption" of the vulgar in the usual sense is for Lazaro but proof "of the slavery of the Italians" (fol. 114). It is interesting that events have reversed the application of the appeal to patriotic feeling made by Bruni and Alberti when the Florentine republic was thriving. Then, such sentiments could presage glorious achievements in the vernacular; now, after the occupations by France, Spain, and the sack of Rome in 1527, the same sentiments, disillusioned, can furnish an argument for its increased degeneracy and for the consequently still purer and more elevated status of Latin. It is equally interesting that this conservative spokesman should devote himself at the outset more to attacking the new than praising the old, which suggests, of course, a climate of opinion in which allegiance to the vulgar has gained sufficient

---

Thought, ed. Parret, pp. 302–16, describes this single aspect of its importance without placing it either in the context of similar debates or in that of its own structure as dialogue. Both of these contexts are well discussed by Helene Harth, ed. and tr. Speroni, *Dialogo delle lingue* (Munich, 1975), who makes intelligent use of Apel's treatment of Speroni, pp. 216–24.

ground to require retaking. The offense is mounted from a position already much weakened. It is most interesting that the offense is predicated on the assumed connection between the political history of the community and its language. The fundamental recognition that language is a dynamic social product having social functions provides the grounds that make debate possible.

These grounds are immediately used against Lazaro by Bembo, who points out that Latin itself is barbarous if you count only its "origins," the settlers of Rome being no more than a tribe of Phrygian hunters (fol. 111ᵛ). Occupied Italy is a melancholy fact; but its language must still serve the primary purpose of communication, which is enhanced by grammatical regulation. Against Lazaro he insists that the same rules of composing and uniting words apply to the vulgar as to Latin (fol. 113ᵛ). Bembo develops this point in terms of the usual organic metaphor, slightly modified. He compares Italian to a young tree not yet producing flowers (of eloquence, naturally) or fruit, and blames this lack not on the tree but on the failure to cultivate it properly. He describes how the Romans carefully tended their language: it is a plant with grammarians, orators, and poets as its gardeners. "Every language is accustomed to yield not so much by its own nature as aided by the artifice of another."[34] The emphasis here is on the organic process as humanly directed, subject to the artistic will. Bembo concludes, however, by returning to the older, undirected sense of the metaphor as inexorable, divinely ordained cycle: some trees mature and bear quickly, then die, while others last many years but take a long time to produce, like Italian.[35] The equality between languages implied by comparing them as individual organisms (the vulgar can be pruned and cultivated as well as Latin) is denied when they are con-

---

[34] Fol. 117ᵛ: "non tanto per sua natura, quanto d'altrui artificio aiutata, suol produrre ogni lingua."

[35] Fol. 118ᵛ: "che qual arbor tosto nasce, fiorisce, & fa frutto; tale tosto invecchie, & si muoia: & in contrario, che quello duri per molti anni, ilquale lunga stagione harà penato à par fronde. Sarà adunque la nostra lingua."

trasted as species (their life cycles, their inherent "natures," differ). Human will can intervene decisively in the first process, but is impotent in the second. These opposed implications of Bembo's uses of the organic metaphor are not only an accurate summary of his actual position in the *Prose* (where he both grants the superiority of Latin and encourages the imitative cultivation of the vernacular), but will be taken up by subsequent speakers. Speroni is not simply rehashing the controversy, he is probing the implications of its terms.

A Roman courtier has intervened occasionally up to this point; it was he who first objected to Lazaro's contempt for current speech on the grounds of the simple necessity for practical use. He now objects to Bembo's imputation of "natural" superiority to Greek and Latin by comparing Latin to a decayed and rotten relic made into an idol for the superstitious. The relic and the language are equally dead; the learned speak "dead Latin words" and we "a living vernacular" (fols. 119–19ᵛ). To this Bembo replies that neither is really dead, since each can produce effects in live people, and asserts that the semiarchaic literary Tuscan of Petrarch and Boccaccio is the only variety of the vulgar worth cultivating. The courtier is innocently nonplussed at this, and forces Bembo to the admission that this vulgar must indeed be learned by study, that the last place we should look for it is in Tuscany now, where modern speech is "contrary to all rules" (fol. 120). The courtier is of course the slyly aggressive, radical, antischolarly defender of current usage as defining the vernacular. Although neither his viewpoint nor any other is finally endorsed by Speroni, he is allowed to do to Bembo's position what Bembo has done to Lazaro's: to underscore the absurdity of accepting past usage as a *limit* on present practice, whether in Latin or Italian. Bembo used the fact that language is socially dynamic against Lazaro; now the courtier uses it against him. This symmetrical argumentation in the first half of the dialogue criticizes, by seeing language as a sociohistorical product, the whole prescriptive strategy of assimilation that attempted to dignify vernaculars by fixing their forms, grammatical or literary, on the Latin model.

Once again the ground of the argument shifts from a collective perspective on language to an individual one. Rebuked by Bembo for his unwillingness to learn any variety of the vulgar by study and rule, the courtier responds by adducing the expressive power of actual speech. "At least," he replies, "I say what I have in my heart . . . I can discover and arrange the thoughts of my mind, whence arises the life of writing."[36] Badly, he maintains, would we "signify our thoughts" in any language we must learn by exercise and reading instead of by "discoursing among ourselves." We should therefore write whatever language we learn "della bocca"; and we learn it best not in the classroom but by conversing at court (fol. 121). Though he does not mention it, the courtier is here making a new inference from the old Aristotelian and Ciceronian tag:[37] if words are signs that reveal to others our internal conceits, then the fullest revelation is achieved in the words that come most naturally to us. If we express our thoughts badly in a learned language, it is presumably because we *have* them in our mother tongue. This near equation of thought and speech comes close to articulating the Vallesque epistemological insight that words constitute the thought or meaning that the ancient tag portrays them as conveying. But the courtier, who might well have stepped from the pages of Castiglione, has no epistemological pretensions and develops the point no further.

Instead, he graciously draws into the argument a listening scholar, who retells, for roughly the second half of the dialogue, the debate of his masters, Perotto and Lascari, about the

---

[36] Fol. 120ᵛ: "Almeno dirò quello che io haverò in core . . . porrò . . . trovare & disporre i concetti dell'animo mio; onde si deriva la vita della scrittura."

[37] The courtier's *sprezzatura*, which consists in being well informed without advertising it, is adroitly contrasted throughout to the academic habits of the other speakers. Earlier, for example, he has quoted Cicero's famous praises of history (mistress of life, light of the world, etc.) with a negligent, "come alcun dice," fol. 115ᵛ. That this appealing grace can also function to justify laziness and ignorance is also brought out in the course of the dialogue.

translation of ancient wisdom into modern tongues. Perotto (usually regarded as representing Pomponazzi) wants it all to be thus made available so that we can study scientific subjects without having to spend so much time learning languages; translation will produce more good "philosophers." Perotto explicitly poses the central question of the felt relationship of the Renaissance to antiquity: "Why is it that the men of this age are generally less learned in every science, and of less worth, than the ancients were?" Lascari gives him the traditional answer, a laconic encapsulation of the potent myth of historical decline, the inevitable physical, moral, and intellectual decay of the world from an imagined Edenic perfection: "What else can we say, but that we're going from bad to worse?"[38] Perotto's answer, to the contrary, is that the time-wasting concentration on Latin and Greek has prolonged our substantive ignorance. Here, in the matter of the respective efficacy of languages, is broached the confrontation of aspirations to progress with convictions of degeneracy that will motivate disputes in science, religion, and literature for the next two centuries.

Lascari takes up the organic metaphor in order to deny that languages and the knowledge they encode can be "transplanted." To see different tongues as natural species, each having its own particular conditions of growth and kind of product, is again to imply a potentially constitutive connection between words and thoughts. Before Lascari can develop it, however, Perotto intervenes with a denial of the metaphor itself. Not to be compared with "something produced by nature,"

languages are not born . . . in the manner of trees . . . some of which are feeble and infirm as a species, some healthy and robust and more fit to bear the weight of our human conceptions. Rather, all their power is born into the world from the will of mortals. . . . The lan-

[38] Fol. 124: "onde è che gli huomini di questa età generalmente in ogni scienza son men dotti, & di minor prezzo, che già non furon gli antichi? . . . Che si puo dire altro, se non che andiamo di male in peggio?"

guages of every country . . . are of one and the same value, and are framed by mortals to one end with one judgment.[39]

Perotto wants to establish this radical linguistic equality, by insisting on the single purpose of all languages and denying any "natural" differences, in order to bring them all under the dominion of a particular kind of human will: the will to "scientific," or universally valid, knowledge. His point is that any language can contain and transmit it; hence the justification of translation. Lascari continues to contradict this, insisting that Greek is qualitatively different, a healthier tree, better fitted to philosophical discourse than vulgars. He urges that "diverse languages are apt to signify diverse conceptions, some the conceptions of the educated, others those of the uneducated."[40] Perotto is impatient with words; he wants to arrive at the "cognition of things." Lascari paints a contemptuous picture of the rabble mangling the ideas of Aristotle in Lombard or Bergamasco.[41] Perotto paints a glorious and proto-Baconian

[39] Fol. 125: "non nascono le lingue . . . à guisa di alberi . . . quale debole, & inferma nella sua specie; quale sana & robusta, & atta meglio à portar la soma di nostri humani concetti: ma ogni loro vertu nasce al mondo dal voler de mortali. . . . le lingue d'ogni paese . . . siano d'un medesmo valore, & da mortali ad un fine con un guidicio formate."

[40] Fol. 125ᵛ: "Diverse lingue sono atte à significare diversi concetti, alcune i concetti di dotti, alcune altre de gl'indotti." Apel quotes the first clause of this sentence and comments that Lascari's position demonstrates "at once the deep insight of the humanists into the meaning of language . . . and their inability to recognize it as a truly historical mode of thought," p. 222.

[41] Fols. 127–28. Despite this superciliousness, there was, and is, a real problem here. Lascari's sense of the intimate connection between structures of language and thought provides his conviction that subtle philosophical arguments cannot be adequately reproduced in local, unwritten, unregulated dialects. The problems posed by the Renaissance *translatio studii* are posed in the present by the "transfer of technology." Today, the difficulties of the situation are most acute for educators in developing nations like India, and above all in Africa, confronted with a plethora of local, tribal, often unwritten languages and dialects. The questions of finding a lingua franca for education, of how to provide access to it for a multivernacular population, of whether Heisenberg or Wittgenstein can or should be translated, say, into Yoruba, have no self-evident answers.

picture of men consciously disciplining their own languages to penetrate to the universals they necessarily contain. "Nature," he avers, "in every age, in every province, and in every costume is always one and the same thing." So is the ultimate content, the signified, of all languages. Even beasts can "signify their emotions" in a great variety of sounds; men can do so much better, every man in his own speech. "Writing and languages were invented not for their own sake, but only for our utility and commodity." The kind of "commodity" Perotto has in mind is amply indicated by his explicit desire that one day, after sufficient disciplining, there will exist a "single language," allowing perfectly transparent access to things (fols. 127^v–28). He therefore concludes by pouring scorn on the arrogant, superstitious, relic-worshippers who pay more attention to Aristotle's Greek than to his science, who make language, and not knowledge, their chief object of concern (fol. 129).

The courtier rejoices at what he takes to be all this support for his own position. He vows to flee "the vexation of learning to speak with the tongues of the dead" and admonishes Lazaro to cease such vain labor (fol. 129^v). Lazaro politely declines further combat, remarking that the courtier has misunderstood Perotto and underestimated both the difficulty of science and the value of textual scholarship. Bembo agrees, admitting that perhaps even the ordinary citizen can learn to philosophize, if not poetize—which he insists can only be done in the Tuscan of Petrarch and Boccaccio. Bembo ends the dialogue in amiable inconclusiveness, assuring the courtier that "our Roman tongue" can make one "gracious" but not "glorious" (fols. 130–31).

Speroni has orchestrated the presentation of all these opposed points of view so that their similarities and divergences are permuted and recombined in unexpected ways. The paradoxes thus discovered in the movement of the dialogue as a whole crisscross the polemic stances of its participants, offering a more complex awareness of language than that of any individual argument. The basis of this awareness is the perception of semantic fluidity stimulated by the humanist observation of common usage in speech communities.

The metaphor of organic growth derived from this observation is one kind of fluid signifier that the dialogue develops in contradictory ways. As individual organism, a language can be refined and reformed according to our desires and purposes (we form its meanings); as species, it has inherent necessities beyond our control (its meanings form us). Bembo takes both positions: the first, to encourage the cultivation of Tuscan literature on the Latin model; the second, to explain the tardiness of this process and to preserve the status of the model. Perotto rejects the metaphor altogether, in order to deny (Bembo's second point) the status of model to any language and to intensify (Bembo's first point) the affirmation of the power of will. Lascari takes the second position and uses it against the first: no amount of will can alter the fitness of one language for some purposes that differ from those of another. A subsidiary irony in all this is that the same kind of metaphor that served in the previous century to legitimize and dignify vernaculars can now be made to denigrate them. By these permutations, by having the speakers' intentionally opposed points of view both meet and diverge at more points than they themselves seem aware of, Speroni's dialogue is demonstrating the fluidity of the signifiers, which all its participants are trying to congeal. That no single participant is either permitted a total victory or made to appear wholly foolish clearly indicates that their perspectives are not mutually invalidating, that the reader is invited to experience as paradox what they present as contradiction.

This is certainly what happens with the organic topos, the cumulative manipulations of which reveal the paradoxical existence of language as both enabling and constraining, both responsive and resistant to human will, allowing the individual to create meanings, but only those meanings that his speech community has made possible in the structure of his language. There is nothing inconsistent in such a complex grasp of the ways in which language as a social product is the (not at all transparent) mediator of the individual's experience of both himself and the world. In the progress of its argumentation by means of the skillful recombination of traditional terms, the whole of Speroni's dialogue is greater than the sum of its parts, offering the reader even further possibilities of recombining its terms to produce additional arguments. The text, in short, invites us to continue playing the game it has established, to continue unfolding new horizons of significance beyond those that the particular perspective of each speaker attempts to close off. The text is performing an awareness of its subject as, literally, dialogue: language as ongoing "conversation" (in the archaic sense that includes both words and acts), whose interpretation is never complete, whose meanings are not indeterminate but always determinable and yet never, finally, determined.

Let us, for example, accept the invitation to play the game with the diametrically opposed views of Perotto and Lascari. The former finds all languages to be equal in value and identical in function. The latter finds them to be different in function and therefore unequal in value. As presented in the rich context of the dialogue, neither view claims validity on the basis of abstract, logical analysis of the subject, but each is generated as a means of supporting broader attitudes and wider purposes. Indeed, the views of all the disputants (who continually criticize each others' motives) are determined not by any sustained investigation of what language is or how it works but by what each of them wants to do with it. Lazaro wants to use it as an index to political potency; Bembo to write poetry; the courtier to express emotions naturally in speech and writing; Perotto to do science; Lascari to reconstruct classical texts. The multiplicity of these unexceptionable purposes served by language makes the reader aware of its multiplicity of function and therefore suspicious of efforts to privilege one function above all others. The most concerted such effort is of course Perotto's, whose purpose makes explicit the deep desire dreamed by the traditional grammar of "signifying" for that final repose on a fixed and lasting "signified": all words do is transparently reveal their universal content. That this reductive dream will be enacted for over four hundred years as a part of the triumph of empirical science, only to be refuted by philosophers in this century, who will point out just what Speroni's dialogue demonstrates—the multiple functions of language—is an historical irony of considerable magnitude. Although Speroni is hardly responsible for this irony, he is responsible for the structure of the dialogue that suggests other ironies in Perotto's view. His limitation of language to a single function is a corollary of his conviction that all languages are of equal worth. This conviction has already emerged from the first half of the dialogue as a result of observing the historical variation and social specificity of all languages. The irony is that for Perotto this equality becomes a matter of indifference, and his argument a direct denial of both the history and the specific densities of languages. The conviction that first celebrates and legitimizes the rich variety of vernaculars ends up by simply ignoring them altogether. Perotto's yearning for a "single language" looks forward, through all the seventeenth- and eighteenth-century designs for a universal language, to logical positivism and the *Tractatus*.

These ironies—that Perotto wants that which the whole dialogue shows to be multiple to be single, and that he obliterates what its first half has shown to be central—encourage us to reconsider the opposed view of Lascari. His insistence on the unequal value of languages may be discounted insofar as it proceeds from the kind of elitist prejudice already mocked in Lazaro by Bembo and in Bembo by the courtier, and as it denies their central inference from the observation of linguistic change and usage. But Lascari's reason for this insistence—that different languages function in different ways—seems fully justified by exactly the same kind of observations, honoring and preserving the unique operations of languages as sociohistorical products. Lascari is perceiving between languages the same difference in function that the dialogue as a whole reveals within them. And difference in function may, of course, exist without at all entailing difference in value; conversely, equal value does not at all entail identical function. Although Lascari, like most people, cannot find difference between either languages or societies without regarding it as superiority or inferiority, the dialogue encourages us to do so. Its form and structure embody the de facto multiplicity that discredits both Perotto's single privileged function and Lascari's single privileged evaluation. We are thus left with the other halves of both positions, recombined into the view that all languages may be equal in value and different in function.

This view looks forward through the ideas of Herder and Humboldt to modern anthropology and the linguistic theories of Sapir and Whorf. Whorf's well-known descriptions of how the Hopi verb system differs from that of Standard Average European and his suggestion that the supposedly "primitive" system is superior for some purposes[42] can be seen as present versions of the kind of awareness generated by the fundamental humanist attention to common usage that made living languages objects of serious study in the sixteenth century. Speroni's dialogue presents perhaps the widest range of attitudes brought to bear on this new enterprise, and in such a way as to emphasize the disturbing challenge it offered to both the traditionally hierarchical and the newly scientific strategies of containment of the linguistic energies it released. The game of recombination that his dialogue invites the reader to play by employing the whole text to reinterpret its parts is (in addition to being an enactment of the hermeneutic circle) a direct affirmation of the active role of the auditor in the dialogue that is language: its meaning is not "represented" for us passively to ingest; we must reconstruct it.

There are additional semantic implications to other opposed views in the dialogue that can be recombined into an ironic rapprochement, further underscoring the persistence of assumptions subversive of theoretical orthodoxy on both sides of the controversy over vernaculars. The courtier is the most

---

[42] The relevant papers are collected and edited by John B. Carroll, *Language, Thought, and Reality* (Cambridge, Mass., 1956).

radical partisan of the currently spoken vulgar of the *beau monde*, and Lascari the crustiest conservative defender of the supremacy of ancient tongues. The insouciant voice of society here confronts the crabbed tones and austere discipline of the academy. Yet, of all the disputants, only these two—separated by the large temperamental and socio-linguistic gap between town and gown—evince an apprehension of forms of language as forms of thought, an appreciation that the specific qualities of a given language constitute unique meanings that are not directly transferable without loss to other languages. It is the fear of such loss that makes Lascari oppose the translation of classical texts; it is the impatience with such loss that makes the courtier unwilling to express himself with another tongue than his own. Once again, the reader is not obliged to accept the prejudiced or lazy conclusions of either contestant (that texts shouldn't be translated, or that Latin needn't be learned), in order to grasp the subversive assumption that words constitute meanings, which underlies the arguments of both. That this assumption is shared by the spokesmen for modern speech and ancient Greek suggests the semantic power of all languages, however differently it may be exercised, as the real basis of their equality. The common ground thus revealed between the most intransigently "ancient" and the most aggressively "modern" positions is the implicit semantic awareness generated by the humanist observation of actual usage, heard or written, which appears in Speroni's dialogue to undercut and transcend the often sterile, partisan polemics of the old versus the new. The largest historical irony for which Speroni is responsible is the demonstration that precisely this awareness is lacking in the most avant-garde dimension of the new: the confident ambitions of empirical science depend on an assumption of linguistic transparency that is very old indeed.

★

The wide-ranging sophistication, the subtle balance, and the deliberately manipulated paradoxes of Speroni's text were bound to suffer considerable loss when it became a chief instrument in the campaign of the Pléiade to legitimize the vernacular. A selection of arguments from the "dialogo delle lingue," along with sundry passages translated verbatim, was made for this purpose in 1549 by Joachim du Bellay, *La Deffence et Illustration de la Langue Francoyse*.[43] Du Bellay wants to show that all languages are equal in value and are therefore equally susceptible to conscious enrichment and varied use. The arguments that supply his aim are exclusively those of Perotto and Bembo, with a sprinkling of the courtier's. Du Bellay begins at the beginning, with the "origins" of language—not seeing vernaculars as successive corruptions of Latin, but accepting all languages as the diverse, post-Babel products of human will. "Donques les langues ne sont nées d'elles mesmes en facon d'herbes, racines et arbres: les unes infirmes et debiles en leurs espèces: les autres saines et robustes, et plus aptes à porter le faiz des conceptions humaines: mais toute leur vertu est née au monde du vouloir et arbitre des mortelz." It is thus impossible to "praise or blame" one language or another, since they all have the same origin, "c'est la fantasie des hommes: et ont été formées d'un mesme jugement à une mesme fin: c'est pour signifier entre nous les conceptions et intelligences de l'esprit."[44] In time, though, some languages,

---

[43] Ed. Henri Chamard (Paris, 1904). This edition includes the hostile and pedantic commentary of Barthélemy Aneau, *Quintil Horatian* (Lyon, 1550), who objects less to du Bellay's purpose than to his unoriginality and incompetence in pursuing it. Brunot (*Histoire*, II, 84–87) echoes these objections and generally deplores the success with which du Bellay and Ronsard claimed full credit for "renewing" the French language, although Brunot (II, 80) can point only to one barely earlier text (Jacques de Beaune's *Discours*, 1548) that urges the equal value of the vernacular. The point is less the merits, of course, than the success: du Bellay's particular plunderings of Speroni started the vernacular bandwagon in France, onto which Peletier, Tyard, and Ronsard soon climbed. The plunderings were first demonstrated by Pierre Villey, *Les Sources italiennes de 'la Deffense . . .' de Joachim du Bellay* (Paris, 1908).

[44] Pp. 47–48. Du Bellay's words are a direct translation from Speroni of Perotto's (quoted above, n. 39). Aneau claims that du Bellay misuses "fantasie" to mean "volonté"; but the substitution is strategically appropriate: since he is

by being better "regulated," become richer than others; "mais cela ne se doit attribuer à la felicité desdites langues, ains au seul artifice et industrie des hommes." All things created by Nature are the same—from the four elements to the arts and sciences—only the variation in human will makes men speak and write about them differently (pp. 48–50).

Du Bellay has played the game of recombining the variously opposed positions of Speroni's debaters in order to produce a univocal argument that vernaculars are the potential equals of Latin and Greek, requiring only careful cultivation to realize the potential. The first book of the *Deffence* elaborates this familiar assimilative strategy; the second provides tactical instructions for achieving it. The tensions, however, present in the strategy from the outset (as in Bembo's *Prose*) are intensified into palpable ambivalence by du Bellay's having elected to reproduce from Speroni's dialogue arguments whose motivation and aim are not (as Speroni had shown) compatible. On the one hand, Bembo wants to preserve the authority of ancient texts as literary models while urging the potential equivalent value of the refined and archaic vernacular that imitates them. On the other, Perotto rejects the whole notion of models, urging the capability of vernaculars to supplant ancient texts for scientific purposes. Du Bellay has indeed seized on what their arguments have in common—the insistence on the efficacy of the will to improve vernaculars—but is led by his partisan purpose to reproduce a good deal more of Perotto's position than can comfortably coexist with his adoption of Bembo's strategy. The temptation is understandable: a convenient way to cry up the vernacular is to cry down Latin and Greek; but if one cries them down too far, their status as models for imitation will be seriously eroded.[45]

---

preparing to assert the power of the poetic "imagination" to make French illustrious, he here identifies that imagination as an origin of language itself.

[45] This use of the ammunition Perotto provided is a major source of the "incoherence" Brunot complained of in the *Deffence*. But such incoherence is inherent in the terms of the assimilative strategy itself. How du Bellay continually shuffles between loving and hating the ancients, between advocating

So it is that du Bellay's customary exhortations to study and imitate the ancients sort rather ill with the tirades he borrows from Perotto on the deleterious effects of that study. It is blamed for the lack of present knowledge of the sciences, which would have been greatly increased were not so much time spent merely getting up the languages. The learning they contain must be translated into all vernaculars (pp. 133–36). Du Bellay berates theologians and pedants for keeping knowledge, like relics, closed off from common view, not permitting its delivery "de ces paroles mortes en celles qui sont vives et volent ordinairement par les bouches des hommes" (pp. 140–41). He thus varies Perotto's themes with the tones of the courtier, making a selection that continuously employs the idea of the speech community to undermine the cultural privilege of the ancient tongues otherwise necessary as models. The same combined selection produces du Bellay's observation that the vulgar is scorned "perhaps for no other reason than that we learn it in infancy and without study, the others with great pain and diligence. If it, like Greek and Latin, had perished and been put in the reliquary of books, I have no doubt that it would be as difficult to learn as they are."[46]

The legitimation of language one learns "della bocca" became of course a key item in the program of the Pléiade, and was additionally useful as a stick with which to beat their predecessors, *les grands rhétoriqueurs*. As a polemical tool, the advocacy of "natural" speech operated in the same network of ambivalence and contradiction that covered associated items in the program: imitation versus invention, divine inspiration versus conscious rhetorical craft. So in 1555 Jacques Peletier advises poets to write in their native speech, to cultivate the in-

---

"imitation" and "invention," is nicely analyzed by Margaret W. Ferguson, "The Exile's Defense: du Bellay's *La Deffence . . .*," *PMLA* 93 (1978), 275–89.

[46] P. 157. The first sentence is Perotto's; the second is du Bellay's addition of the courtier's metaphor: the passages are juxtaposed by Villey, *Les Sources italiennes*, p. 60. Du Bellay clearly enjoys articulating this kind of avant-garde iconoclasm. He also extols (pp. 161–63) Dolet's project to form "the French orator."

nate graces of French instead of trying to reproduce in it the beauties of Greek or Latin.[47] This involves employing colloquial diction and caution in creating neologisms; even the poet, Peletier explains, does not have sovereign rights over his words "because usage belongs to the community," which tends to resist coinages.[48] At the same time, however, translations are encouraged because they can add words to a native vocabulary felt to be inadequate (pp. 105–107). Similarly, the poet is to imitate the finest classical works, whence, since languages are what human will can make them, he can find rhetorical recipes by which to make French capable of everything. Having previously stressed the use of the "natural" spoken vernacular, Peletier betrays his discomfort with the *de rigueur* advocacy of imitation by attempting to modify or supplement it. After generally insisting that the poet must be widely learned, Peletier says that all his private study should be succeeded by

going to see in fact what he has seen only in writing, thus to contemplate the living images of the things of Nature. Otherwise . . . nothing will be said of him except that he speaks with the mouth of another, by rote and in debt. For how would it be possible for a man to speak pertinently of things that he has only read about? (p. 221)

Experience, it seems, must follow book learning so that one will speak with his *own* mouth. The metaphor connects the inadequacy of (still necessary) imitation with the exercise of native speech. The words that come most "naturally" to us are coming to possess an authority superior to that of the models themselves. The strategy of assimilation is gradually becoming one of competition.

[47] *L'Art Poëtique*, ed. André Boulanger (Paris, 1930), pp. 112–13, where he is summarizing du Bellay. Grahame Castor, *Pléiade Poetics* (Cambridge, 1964), discusses his concept of naiveté (p. 80) and explains the whole ambivalent program (pp. 185, 188–92).

[48] P. 119. This accurate observation did not prevent Peletier from attempting to impose on the community his bizarrely reformed spelling, reproduced in Boulanger's edition.

The tactics of vernacular liberation in France thus consolidate into univocal and therefore ambivalent expositions some of the variously opposed positions dramatized in Speroni's dialogue. Whether assimilative or competitive, the strategy continues to reflect the paradoxes and tensions between its prescriptive aim and its descriptive method. The semantic insights Valla drew from the latter, and which are implicitly enacted in Speroni's dialogue, have now receded wholly behind the polemical stress on languages as equally efficient (the new argument) means of transporting or containing meaning (the old conception). On both the literary and scientific fronts of the campaign, the traditional rhetorical (Aristotelian/Ciceronian/Horatian) definition of language prevails: words are signs that permit individual *expression*—the squeezing-out of what exists within (conceit, image, idea, feeling) that "refers to" what exists without (object, fact, reality, truth). Thus the vernacular belletrist in particular employs the observation of usage made by Horace (Peletier translated the *Ars Poetica*), which Valla developed into a revolutionary semantics, while maintaining the traditional semantics of containment and transmission. Yet even the traditional terms of "expressiveness," when used to justify the production of literature in the currently spoken language, can suggest an awareness of a more intimate bond between words and meanings than can be accounted for by the traditional theories. Peletier's metaphorical equation of our own language with our own experience suggests that their significance is mutual, that their meaning is neither discoverable nor expressible in other tongues. Linked to the increasing ambivalence toward literary imitation, such metaphors also preserved the growing sense of semantic density specific to a given language that is at odds with the cosmetic theory.

It is such metaphors, and not the theory, that indicate the character of much innovative literature actually produced in the Renaissance. Peletier's metaphor, for example, is almost a blueprint for what Montaigne gradually made of his *Essays*: in

his own words, "a book consubstantial with its author."[49]
Montaigne's attitudes toward the vernacular are especially interesting since he had the purest possible humanist upbring-
ing: Latin was in fact his "native" speech, learned in infancy
before he was ever exposed to French. But Latin was not the
language of his experience, of the unceasing process of self-
formation that became the "matter" of his book. Montaigne
retained enough humanist prejudice to see both his subject and
his medium as slightingly transient and variable: "If it had been
durable matter, it would have had to be committed to a more
stable language." His final addition to this passage summarizes
the diachronic contingency of the vernacular as a communal
product:

It slips out of our hands every day, and has halfway changed since I
have been alive. We say that at this moment it is perfected. Every century says as much of its own. I have no mind to think that of it as long
as it flees and changes form as it does. It is for the good and useful
writings to nail it to themselves, and its credit will go as go the fortunes of our state.[50]

Montaigne's self-deprecating acceptance of such change—
he writes but "for few men and for few years"—not only permits him the continual and careful exploration of his personal
vagaries, it allows him also to reject both strategies of assimilation and competition. By constantly averring that what he
writes is careless and trifling, Montaigne insists on the difference between his efforts and those of the ancients he so freely
and frankly plunders. Though his confession that "the good
authors humble and dishearten me too much" may be quite
sincere, he is still serving notice that he is creating a new literary genre with its own unique procedure and style. The model
for this genre is the humanist observation and description of
linguistic usage and change. The temporally layered, additive

[49] *The Complete Essays*, tr. Donald M. Frame (Stanford, 1958), p. 504 (II,
18).

[50] *Ibid.*, p. 751 (III, 9). The famous account of his childhood education is in
I, 26.

composition of the *Essays* records the minutest elaborations or alterations in Montaigne's reading, opinions, physical and emotional states with the same kind of attention and the refusal of an a priori system that characterized, for example, Valla's examination of classical Latin or Bovelles' of modern French. The *Essays* are a virtual etymology and historical dictionary of self; Montaigne's text simultaneously celebrates and identifies the ceaseless fluctuations of his personal identity with those of the spoken vulgar.

The self *is* the language of its own experience; Montaigne exploits and manipulates the rich variety of common usage in that language with as keen a self-consciousness as he has of his painful kidney stones. He avoids none of the phrases "that are used in the streets of France; those who would combat usage with grammar make fools of themselves."[51] While not scorning any actual usage, neither does he surrender to it (nor ever try to make it a rule), but rather makes it subject to his will. Montaigne fashions it with the same care and discipline by which he attempts, according to his favorite examples of Socrates, Seneca, and Plutarch, to fashion himself. The discipline includes, of course, recording in appropriately casual words the failures in the attempt. Hence he prefers to write without books and without literate aid or criticism: although with them the work would be better, it "would have been less my own; and its principal end and perfection is to be precisely my own." Although one of Montaigne's central themes is the difficulty or impossibility of exercising self-control, physical or moral, his text paradoxically demonstrates his sovereign control over language: it is what he wills it to be, "perfect" in its recording of his own "imperfections." Montaigne directly

---

[51] *Ibid.*, p. 667 (III, 5). In an earlier tirade against affectation, he exclaims of words, "Would that I might use only those that are usual in the markets of Paris" (p. 127), and praises the *vulgus* over the *doctus* in precisely Valla's manner: "He knows no ablatives, conjunctives, substantives, or grammar; nor does his lackey, or a fishwife of the Petit Pont, and yet they will talk your ear off, if you like, and will perhaps stumble as little over the rules of their language as the best master of arts in France," p. 125 (I, 26).

claims such control, both generally and for himself. "Handling and use by able minds give value to a language . . . by stretching and bending it." When in Italy he chatted in Italian, "but for serious discourse I would not have dared trust myself to an idiom that I could neither bend nor turn out of its ordinary course. I want to be able to do something of my own with it."[52] He transcribes a long note he once made in his Guicciardini: "for whatever language my books speak, I speak to them in my own."[53]

To make "his own" book portray "his own self" in "his own" language clearly assumes a constitutive relationship between his own use of that language and his own meanings. They are created, as his text creates himself, from within the vernacular. Montaigne does not merely assume this relationship, he states it in connection with two different and central issues in the campaign of vernacular liberation: imitation and expressiveness. Criticizing the contemporary habit of bookmaking by "concoctions of commonplaces," Montaigne is at pains to defend his own generously "borrowed ornaments." He does so first by claiming that they are intended not to conceal but to reveal him, and second by explaining how, on the other hand, he sometimes conceals them. He is happy "to hide one now and then, disguising and altering it for a new service. At the risk of letting it be said that I do so through failure to understand its original use, I give it some particular application with my own hand, so that it may be less purely someone else's."[54]

What Montaigne is altering is meaning, conceived of precisely as use and application in a context. By changing the context—taking the mildly heroic risk of misapprehension—he alters the "service" that the words perform. His recognition of how far such alteration may extend includes, by the very mention of the risk, the reader's role in the construction of "his

[52] *Ibid.*, pp. 665–67 (III, 5).
[53] *Ibid.*, p. 305 (II, 10).
[54] *Ibid.*, pp. 808–09 (III, 12).

own" meaning. As he so often does, Montaigne here antici-
pates the interpretation of his text, which is both a form of
controlling it and an acknowledgment that it will yet escape
that control. But if he has no sovereignty over our reading of
his text, he is still monarch of his uses of past texts. Montaigne's relation to these is not one of imitation (reproducing
in the vernacular the kind of literature extant in Latin), nor of
assimilation (doing to or with the vernacular what had been
done to or with Latin), nor of competition (insisting that
whatever is done in the vernacular is more authentic or useful
than in Latin), but of appropriation. Just as he "bends" his spoken idiom to his own purposes, so he refashions the words of
others with his own "hand." Montaigne habitually speaks of
the constitution of meaning in terms of tangible concreteness;
it is physical creation, literal manipulation.

As the usage of words is meaning, so is it also thinking.
Montaigne makes this point in a splendidly acute criticism of
the rhetorical tradition of eloquent "expression," which suggests the fallacy of the venerable vehicular conception of language.

I hear some making excuses for not being able to express themselves,
and pretending to have their heads full of many fine things, but to be
unable to express them for lack of eloquence. That is all bluff. Do you
know what I think those things are? They are shadows that come to
them of some shapeless conceptions, which they cannot untangle and
clear up within, and consequently cannot set forth without: they do
not understand themselves yet. And just watch them stammer on the
point of giving birth; you will conclude that they are laboring not for
delivery, but for conception, and that they are trying to lick into shape
this unfinished matter.[55]

Where the words are not found, neither are thoughts or meanings. By evoking the biological basis of our vocabulary for
mental operations, by literalizing the physical implications of
long-dead metaphors, Montaigne turns his language "out of
its ordinary course" in order to insist that the "delivery" of

[55] *Ibid.*, p. 125 (I, 26).

thought in words is not like that of a gift in a fancy box, but like the physical delivery of an infant. It is not the presentation of an object in a variable container, but the production of a fully formed and inseparable unity. Of course, the association of sexual processes with mental and linguistic ones lies dormant in most Indo-European languages. Montaigne reawakens it here as an organic image for the epistemological function of language as the enabling, "shaping" medium of thought, not as mere packaging.

The occasion of his criticism identifies another powerful psychological reason for the tenacity of the cosmetic, vehicular theory. The "excuse" he is exploding has never lost its appeal. What teacher of the humanities has not heard the eternal lament: "I know what I mean (think); I just can't say (express) it"? The fact that such "knowledge" is illusory—indeed, "shapeless," as Montaigne says— has not prevented the theory from consoling countless generations of lazy and careless writers or speakers. The demand for self-understanding entailed by the awareness that words constitute meanings is not easily fulfilled even when admitted. By not admitting it, the cosmetic theory, having assured us that the ultimate signified is in or out there somewhere, also comfortably dispenses us from the obligation of ever having to articulate it ourselves. The theory both flatters our desire for restful certainties and justifies our inability to state any.

Montaigne, however, whose whole enterprise was one of self-understanding, constantly rejected both the flattery and the desire, energetically accepting the hard labor of hammering out his own meanings in his own words. Moreover, he accepted—with both sorrow and delight—the full consequences of the new semantic awareness: that no articulation is final, because meaning is not a fixed and penetrable object, but the provisional result of the incessant and re-creative transaction between texts and interpreters. To all these activities and attitudes, Montaigne's most direct heir is Prince Hamlet.[56]

---

[56] Scholars have long noted the pervasive tonal, thematic, and sometimes

This legacy is more profound than their common thematic concerns or the fashionable ethical and metaphysical gestures that both make (neither consistently) toward stoic resignation, skeptical relativism, or fideistic conviction. The gentleman essayist and the fictional prince are most completely at one in their indefatigable interrogation of words, the promiscuous intensity of their efforts to make meanings. Both thus courageously pursue the implications of the revolutionary consciousness of language that had been latent since Valla infused it into the pedagogy and controversy of the period. Filtered in part through the new attention to vernaculars, this consciousness became the basis for the greatest achievements in vernacular literature.

Montaigne's achievement was to create a literary genre the forms of whose language are the forms of his experience of life. For him, as for Hamlet, these forms are mutually constitutive: experience is shaped by words; words are tested by experience. In Montaigne's last exploration of the meanings produced by this dialectic, he affirms the melancholy but nonetheless invigorating necessity of their ceaseless reinterpretation. He begins "Of Experience" by remarking the infinite diversity of opinions in man's search for knowledge and truth. "And those people must be jesting who think they can diminish and stop our disputes by recalling us to the express words of the Bible. For our mind finds the field no less spacious in registering the meaning of others than in presenting its own." He goes on to compare human efforts to codify laws and explicate philosophies to the attempts of children to divide and recombine a mass of quicksilver: "The more they press it and knead it and try to constrain it to their will, the more they provoke the independence of this spirited metal; it escapes their skill and keeps dividing and scattering in little particles beyond all reckoning." This concrete image for the "scattering" of

---

verbal echoes of Montaigne in the play, some of which are observed by Harry Levin, *The Question of "Hamlet"* (Oxford, 1959), pp. 59, 72–75, 103.

truth introduces a meditative series of questions and answers
that is a soliloquy on the adventure of making meaning:

Who would not say that glosses increase doubts and ignorance, since
there is no book to be found, whether human or divine, with which
the world busies itself, whose difficulties are cleared up by interpretation? The hundredth commentator hands it on to his successor
thornier and rougher than the first one had found it. When do we
agree and say, "There has been enough about this book; henceforth
there is nothing more to say about it"? . . . Do we therefore find any
end to the need of interpreting? Do we see any progress and advance
toward tranquillity? . . . It is only personal weakness that makes us
content with what others or we ourselves have found out in this hunt
for knowledge. An abler man will not rest content with it. There is
always room for a successor, yes, and for ourselves, and a road in another direction. . . . It is a sign of contraction of the mind when it is
content, or of weariness. . . . If it does not advance and press forward
and stand at bay and clash, it is only half alive. Its pursuits are bound-
less and without form; its food is wonder, the chase, ambiguity. . . .
It is an irregular, perpetual motion, without model and without aim.
Its inventions excite, pursue, and produce one another. . . . It is more
of a job to interpret the interpretations than to interpret the things,
and there are more books about books than about any other subject:
we do nothing but write glosses about each other.[57]

Montaigne does not leave the topic without wryly noticing the
extent to which his own book is a gloss on itself. But glosses
are both needful and exhilarating; the hunt for meaning, which
no sooner finds one quarry than it starts another, is life; the
"tranquillity" of achieving it a kind of death; it is not an object
but an activity; its production is reproduction. Montaigne
could well be describing *Hamlet*. Although the formal development of theories was no part of his purpose, he here makes
perfectly clear the challenge of the new linguistic awareness to
the old semantic assumptions. Based on the idea of the speech
community, the challenge postulates the crucial role of the
hearer, the interpreter, the audience—all of us—in the com-

[57] *Essays*, pp. 815–18 (III, 13).

munal manufacture of meaning. "Speech," as Montaigne says in another precise and resonant physical metaphor, "belongs half to the speaker, half to the listener. The latter must prepare to receive it according to the motion it takes. As among tennis players, the receiver moves and makes ready according to the motions of the striker and the nature of the stroke."[58] Whereupon, of course, the "receiver" becomes the "striker," appropriating the stroke with his own force; the roles of interpreter and interpreted are continuously exchanged in the language game. It should be noted that while metaphors of this kind are open-ended in their postulations of meaning as transaction, they in no way assume that it is indeterminate. On the contrary, a game or a hunt, in order to be performed at all, has both rules and constraining circumstances: we "must" play it according to these. As social process, the language game changes with time, at any moment of which the scope for able exercise of both will and skill is, as the *Essays* demonstrate, great but not infinite.

★

Although the consequences of the shifting semantic awareness of the Renaissance are most fully apprehended in its literature, we have been observing the shift as it occurs in the tensions and paradoxes of debate about vernaculars. After reaching its high point in Italy with Speroni, this debate continues there to consolidate its gains and solidify its strategies, contributing very little new to the discussion except the further refinement of its major topoi. The idea of "corruption," for example, derived from the organic metaphor to describe the origin and development of vernaculars, is extended into a deliberate paradox by Tolomei's *Il Cesano* (1555). The structure of his dialogue simply denies the prescriptive, pejorative implications of the process and reformulates it, in even more strictly organic terms, as purely historical description.

The dialogue is a conscious reprise of the main positions in

---

[58] *Ibid.*, p. 834 (III, 13).

the Italian debate, focusing directly on the "name" that should
be given to the vulgar. Bembo speaks for "Tuscan," Trissino
for "Italian," Castiglione for "Cortigiana illustre," and Ales-
sandro de Pazzi for "Florentine." Thereupon Gabriello Cesano
announces a different approach to the subject and speaks without interruption for the rest (about two-thirds) of the book.
His approach is to insist on the social origins and purposes of
languages as unique to man. He makes the Vallesque distinction that, although we make sounds "by nature," words are
produced "from human wits" (p. 40). Geographical groups of
people thus give names to things according to their needs. He
cites a number of ancient Greek philosophers as authority for
this notion, but specifically demurs, as Valla did, from the Pla-
tonic/Pythagorean mystic derivation of words from celestial
intelligences and consequently correspondent with divine harmony: "I reckon this fancy of theirs more beautiful than true,
as . . . Aristotle and the other Peripatetics demonstrate."[59]

Thus born by human effort out of human need, languages
grow and die, shrink and expand, and are constantly modified
by interaction with each other resulting from chance or conquest. Hence any single language may be entirely transformed
over a long period of time, as has happened, for example, to
Latin.[60] But this "corruption" occurs very gradually and is
hardly to be perceived. In such a way has modern Tuscan developed out of the collision of Etruscan with Latin and the subsequent mingling with barbarous tongues (pp. 45–46). Cesano
is now prepared to declare that such "corruption" is not degradation but simply necessity: nothing in nature is generated
except in such cycles of destruction and renewal. Given this in-
evitability, the whole debate turns out to be over a non-issue:
if *no* language exists in a pure and unadulterated state, the
quarrel over what to call the vulgar—which presumes the sep-

[59] P. 42: "istimo questa loro imaginatione piu bella che vera, come . . . Aristotele & glialtri Peripatetici dimostrano."

[60] P. 44: "che per lunghezza di tempo potesse una lingua a poco a poco tutta
transmutarsi & tutta rifarsi, creandosi ogni giorno qualche nuovo vocabolo, et
alcuno de' vecchi abandonandosi in quella guisa."

arateness of its varieties—is empty and vain.[61] However just this inference, Tolomei (who was Sienese) is careful to state it only conditionally, so that he can later argue for Tuscan.

Having thus sidestepped for a while the naming issue, his spokesman, Cesano, now ascends to a defense of the vulgar as such, as distinguished from Latin. He refutes the usual objections: paucity of vocabulary, lack of "rules," insufficient discrimination of cases, uneconomical expressions. On the last point, he comes as close as Speroni's courtier to identifying words and thoughts, claiming that language superior which can render the "swiftness of thinking" most immediately.[62] The native language in which we actually do think thus wins the palm even over the more highly inflected Latin. Finally, Cesano discusses at length the great literature of the Trecento to prove that the vulgar is indeed a "proper" language in its own right, and not merely a "corrupted" Latin (p. 54). Though still capable of improvement, the vernacular is fully equal to ancient tongues in its capacity to be well used, nobly embellished, and so forth, in its own way.

By recognizing the social dynamism of all languages while apprehending the semantic density specific to any single one, Tolomei has effected the recombination of Perotto's and Lascari's positions, which Speroni's dialogue invited the reader to make. Languages are, in principle anyway, both equal in power and different in how they exercise it. Similarly, Tolomei has extended the organic metaphor in both of the directions given it by Speroni's Bembo. As individual organism, the vernacular—now "in the finest flower of its age"—is to be cultivated and perfected by human will and artifice.[63] On the

---

[61] P. 48: "conciosia cosa che se non fusse lingua per se stessa ne di pregio alcuno, molto vana sarebbe hora la fatica nostra di cercar con tanta cura, come ella chiamar si debba."

[62] Pp. 52–53: "perche essendo le parole imagine del pensiero nostro, il pensiero essendo breve & veloce, certo quella lingua è di maggior lode degna, che piu s'avicina alla prestezza del pensiero, & puo con manco parole figuarci chiaramente li affetti humani."

[63] P. 55: "nel piu bel fior de gli anni suoi." Tolomei is here endorsing the

other hand, the development of the vernacular as species is that of an inescapable "natural" process—the birth and death of words—to which "no skill or human industry is applicable."[64] Tolomei thus reproduces the complex awareness of language as an evolving social product, which Speroni's dialogue enacted. Both responsive and resistant to human will, the resources of the vernacular are, while diachronically determined, synchronically determinable by the ingenuity of its users.

The revolutionary semantic implications of this awareness (in part performed by Speroni's text) are now, however, buried beneath the explicit conception of vernacular resources as merely "expressive." Speech opens our mind to those around us, and writing makes manifest our thoughts over distances of space and time (p. 68). Neither the basic perception that language is a sociohistorical product; nor the attribution of its origins to people instead of gods; nor the description of its development as a "natural" process that conscious art can still modify; nor the apprehension of an intimate connection between vernacular words, thoughts, and experience; nor the ascription of equal potential value to all languages; nor the recognition that each may have different structural and semantic capacities—none of these observations and attitudes current in the defense of vernaculars ever alters, at the level of *theory*, the received idea of the semantic operation of language as a transmitter or beautifier of what exists separately elsewhere.

This traditional view, along with the whole gamut of now established observations and arguments, is rehearsed again in Varchi's *L'Hercolano* (1570). Like Tolomei, only in a livelier manner and at greater length, Varchi wishes to demonstrate

---

point made earlier in his dialogue by Castiglione (in Speroni's by Bembo): that nature does not produce its perfect fruits without our effort—"se la cura dell' huomo non sovvenisse"—that which nature starts, art must finish: "le belle cose incominciarsi dalla natura, finirsi dall' arte," pp. 20-21.

[64] P. 47: "La dove nissun' arte, o humana industria, vi si adopera." The mortality of words harks back to Horace's leaves: the lines are quoted and Valla's use of them discussed above, p. 100.

the literary capabilities of the vernacular by expanding the kind of elaborate and technical analyses of the sounds of words made in Bembo's *Prose*. The expansion is necessary, since Varchi's purpose is more radical than theirs. He abandons the assimilative strategy for the competitive: for him, vulgar literature is finer than Latin or Greek and Dante superior to Homer.[65] Though Varchi still employs the dialogue, with rapid exchanges between eager and often easily confused interlocutors, his channeling of the issues mainly toward literature, as well as his aggressively modern stance, recalls the programmatic treatises of du Bellay and Peletier. But regardless of whether the argument is for the parity (as in Alberti or Bembo) or the superiority (as, ambiguously, in Peletier) of vernacular literature vis-à-vis ancient, the basis of the strategy is the venerable expressive definition of language as vehicle. It enables us, says Varchi, to "send out" the thoughts and feelings we have "enclosed" within us.[66] Hence that language is superior that is "richest" in expressive resources (p. 197), that offers the fullest means of egress for all the stuff inside the head.

★

If the traditional definition thus retained powerful utility for the defender of the modern—whether literature or empirical science—it remained even more staunchly advocated in the literary theory of the pure classicists. In the *Poetices libri septem* of Julius Caesar Scaliger, the most comprehensive and one of the most influential works of the century, the vehicular conception of language is the explicit foundation of the theory.[67] For Sca-

---

[65] Though Varchi's claims are more extravagant than his predecessors', his arguments are frankly grounded on theirs: Tolomei is discussed (pp. 250–52); a general debt to Speroni is confessed (p. 239); Bembo is frequently cited throughout.

[66] Varchi states this as the purpose of endowing Adam with language, p. 34: "quei pensieri, e sentimenti mandar fuori, che egli haveva dentro racchiusi."

[67] Lyon, 1561. Scaliger is discussed in the exhaustive survey of the entire subject by Bernard Weinberg, *A History of Literary Criticism in the Italian Ren-*

liger, however, words are the carriers less of thoughts and feelings than of things and actions. Not at all concerned with the
vernacular, he has no need to stress the internally "expressive"
power of words; instead, aiming to make literature a respect-
ably philosophical subject, he focuses on the externally "representative" power of words. Language simply pictures things
as they exist, literature as they don't, might, should, or could
exist (p. 1). From the ancient dualism of word/thing, which
makes of language a conveyance or copy of "reality," Scaliger
derives a definition of literature that endorses Horace at the expense of Aristotle. "Names are concepts [notiones] of things,"
and all speech is "nothing but images"—by which he means an
"imitation" of something outside itself.[68] "Because words are
the images of things, there is imitation in all speech." Hence,
of course, "imitation" will not suffice to define literature (as
much current theory, extrapolating from Aristotle's definition
of tragedy, had proposed), which thus becomes distinguisha-
ble from language not by its mode of operation but by its purpose: "to teach pleasurably" (docere cum delectatione).[69] Thus
literature is fully reaccommodated in the domain of rhetoric as
an instrumental art of persuasion. Scaliger is denying only that

---

aissance (Chicago, 1961), II, 743–50, 812. The kind of literary imitation he advocates—of static norms untainted by local or temporal variation—is finely
described by Greene (*The Light in Troy*, p. 180) and typifies that of later neoclassicism.

[68] P. 346. Scaliger is perhaps the extreme example in the period of the tyranny of reference over language: the only "profit" in any art is what it conveys
from somewhere else: "Nulla igitur imitatio propter se, nempe ars omnis ex-
tra se prospectat quod alicui conducibile sit."

[69] P. 347: "Denique imitationem esse in omne sermone. quia verba sint
imagines rerum." Scaliger has the virtue of consistency, linking these definitions of language and literature to the concomitant correspondence theory of
truth: "adaequatio notionum cum iis rebus, quarum notiones sunt." Despite
the referential tyranny, there is considerable shrewdness in other aspects of
this argument: he rules out "fiction" and "falsehood" as defining literature for
the same reason that they are also activities of language itself, like "imitation."
He then makes the converse of this point: just as not all "imitation" or "fiction" is literature, so not all literature is "imitation," some being "exposition,"
like Empedocles, or "expression," like lyric verse.

"imitation" is the *definiens* of literature. Otherwise he is eager to show how indeed poetry accomplishes what it shares with all language: his fifth book presents a vast number of passages from ancient poets exemplifying imitation; his seventh gives recipes for composing poetry on this basis. All the usual verbs he uses to describe how language works—to picture, signify, represent, or imitate—firmly locate its meaning, and a fortiori that of literature, in whatever "things" it thus variously refers to.

The semantic assumptions of Scaliger's literary theory are thus identical to those of Salutati's *De Laboribus Herculis*. Despite the intervening century-and-a-half of all the kinds of linguistic investigation and argument that have made those assumptions extremely problematic, they are still shared by the late humanist advocate of classical imitation and the early humanist practitioner of allegorical interpretation. Salutati, we may recall, defined poetry *tout court* as the use of "symbols"— that is, any word or phrase or character that "stands for" something else. On this basis he tried to make literature an independent, autonomous art, without realizing that this mode of operation, which St. Augustine ascribed to language itself, failed to distinguish literature at all from its medium. This is just the logical error that Scaliger describes and avoids by switching the definition to Horatian purpose. The mode of operation, however, remains the same for both thinkers, and in both is seen as common to literature and language. That this ancient, dualistic, vehicular, cosmetic, and instrumental mode of operation continues to dominate literary theory more than vernacular debates results from the same assimilative strategy being more stringently applied to literature than to language. Both the pioneer defender of Dante and the dedicated Latinist want to dignify literature by qualifying it as an object of serious study. Their tactics differ: Salutati removes literature from its place in the medieval trivium under grammar to set it up on its own; Scaliger puts it back in the Renaissance trivium under rhetoric. Salutati makes extravagant claims for literature as the quasi-theological container of all knowledge; Scaliger classi-

fies literature (its genres, prosodic forms, rhetorical procedures) in a quasi-scientific manner according to both historical
and systematic criteria, while retaining qualified but similar
claims for it as the conveyor of all knowledge to men.[70] What
both theorists are doing, each in the terms of his own epoch, is
assimilating literature to the most prestigious intellectual discipline of their day. When theology was the queen of sciences,
one could show (as Dante had attempted with his poems) that
literature was as richly significant, and in the same way, as
Scripture. When secular philosophy per se became fashionable, helped by the newly available texts of Plato and Aristotle
and allied in Italy with the revival of the political usefulness of
eloquence, one could show that literature was fully susceptible
both to systematic analysis and oratorical exploitation. But
whether legitimized as a theological or a philosophical study,
literature must in both cases be made to resemble a discipline
that abandons words for things, that looks through language,
not at it, for meanings presumed to be beyond it.

This seems to me the central weakness of the literary theory
of the period—apart from its general arid pedantry or naive enthusiasm.[71] The desire to dignify and revalue literature assimilated it to disciplines that assumed the dualistic transparency
or correspondence of words, which effectively prevented such
theories from interrogating the semantic operation of language. One didn't need to inquire how language meant; one
already knew. In this respect it made no difference whether the
discipline aimed at was the old theology or the new science (as
Speroni showed), whether the poet was a divine mouthpiece
or a rhetorical craftsman (or both). Such was the assimilative
pressure that theoretical statements about literature remained
confidently referential up to the Romantic period and beyond.

---

[70] Cf. Weinberg, *Literary Criticism*, II, 746, 749–50.

[71] Thomas Greene identifies this weakness as the abandonment of the earlier
humanist discovery of and response to contingent, temporal difference: "It is
rare that discussions of intertextuality acquire any vitality in the enormous
body of later cinquecento criticism. The historicism of Petrarch and Valla was
largely repressed or exhausted": *The Light in Troy*, p. 180.

Here is a typical one, made by a Scots poet and playwright about 1634: "Language is but the Apparel of Poesy, which may give Beauty, but not Strength. . . . I value Language as a Conduit, the Variety thereof to several Shapes, and adorned Truth or witty Inventions that which it should deliver."[72]

The point I wish to stress is that to see language as decoration or delivery tube is the functional equivalent of not seeing it at all. The linguistic dualism of word/meaning is therefore different from the other reigning dualistic conceptual frameworks with which it is aligned: flesh/spirit, sensible/intelligible, passion/reason. Having dichotomized their subject into competing parts, these other forms of inquiry are nonetheless centrally concerned to put them back together again, to explain the relation between them. Ontology, epistemology, and moral psychology all focus on the connection between their theoretically separated terms: how matter is shaped by mind in the cosmos; how flesh is linked to spirit in the microcosm of man;[73] how we can extract what is truly knowable from sensory impressions; how right thinking is constantly derailed by desire. Even when the link is conceived as mainly oppositional, there is at least some intrinsic interaction that must be accounted for, some kind of relation whose elucidation is the main business of the inquiry. This is not so in the case of language. The linguistic dualism (by whatever name: style/thought, form/content, matter/manner) does not identify the two terms of a dialectic, as in the other cases (or even of a combat), but merely of a metonymy. The relationship posited, instead of being mutually implicative or necessarily interactive, is simply one of temporary—indeed accidental—contiguity. Clothes can be draped on any body; a drainpipe is quite indifferent to what may pass through it. In sum, the linguistic dual-

[72] Sir William Alexander, "Anacrisis," in *Critical Essays of the Seventeenth Century*, ed. J. E. Spingarn (Oxford, 1908; rpt. Bloomington, Ind., 1957), I, 182.

[73] For example, the whole elaborate physiological theory of "spirits"—vaporous emanations from the blood to the brain—was devised to provide just such a connection.

ism offered no way at all for its terms—for words and meanings—to be functionally involved with each other.

Literary theory could therefore say a great deal about words and, with equal ease, could wholly disregard them to get on to the "matter," without in either case ever examining the relation between them. Words are detachable or negligible. It is no wonder that, as I argued earlier, this relation can only be supplied at the level of theory by magic. It is also no wonder that such theories are (and were) grossly inadequate to describe what the richest, most concentrated, and complex use of words in literature had to do with its meanings. The parenthesis is crucial: for the point is not just that the theoretical framework is fallacious in the anachronistic light of twentieth-century reflection on language, but rather that it was also defective in its own time, being unable to conceive precisely the functional relation between words and meanings that the period's greatest literature was exploring. This exploration, as I briefly described it in *Hamlet* and Montaigne, proceeds from semantic assumptions generated elsewhere than in the explicitly literary theory of the age.

This book is an attempt to identify where and how these challenging assumptions are generated, to trace their fitful and fragmentary ramification throughout the culture since their semisystematic introduction into philosophy by Lorenzo Valla. There is one such assumption that preceded and indeed inspired Valla, which would appear to offer a very broad and diffuse way of conceiving a closer relationship between language and meaning than that posited by referential semantics. This assumption is the humanist equation of "wisdom" and "eloquence," the conviction, derived from Cicero and powerfully reinforced by the discovery of Quintilian, that the good orator must also be a good man. Erected into a principle of ethical pedagogy, it insisted on the simultaneous presence of the beautiful, the good, and the true in both words and "matter." In the central humanist endeavor—education for moral ends by means of disputation—this insistence would seem to imply a relation between style and thought that was not merely metonymic, but that postulated some kind of intrinsic connection as an ideal unity.[74] The most famous statement of this ideal in English was made by Roger Ascham:

For in the rudest country, and most barbarous mother language, many be found can speak very wisely; but in the Greek and Latin tongue, the two only learned tongues, which be kept, not in common talk, but in private books, we find always wisdom and eloquence, good matter and good utterance never or seldom asunder. For all such authors as be fullest of good matter and right judgment in doctrine, be likewise always most proper in words, most apt in sentence, most plain and pure in uttering the same. . . .

You know not what hurt you do to learning that care not for words but for matter, and so make a divorce betwixt the tongue and the heart. For mark all ages, look upon the whole course of both the Greek and Latin tongue, and you shall surely find that when apt and good words began to be neglected, and properties of those two tongues to be confounded, then also began ill deeds to spring.[75]

Despite the naiveté of this bald declaration, the moral and political dimension of the ideal unity of thought and expression has been enduringly influential, especially in the Anglo-American tradition.[76] The moral bias that became strident in

[74] The conscious and not always consistent ways in which Petrarch, Salutati, and Bruni tried to reconcile the claims of "eloquence" with those of "substance" are well analyzed by Jerrold Seigel, *Rhetoric and Philosophy in Renaissance Humanism* (Princeton, 1968), esp. pp. 35, 84–85, 106.

[75] *The Scholemaster* (1570), bk. ,II, in *Prose of the English Renaissance*, ed. Hebel, Hudson, et al. (New York, 1952), p. 124. The omitted paragraph lists as examples of bad language *cum* reprehensible doctrines Stoics, Anabaptists, Friars, Epicures, Libertines, and Monks.

[76] The power of this humanist legacy, from Pope to Lionel Trilling, is obvious enough. Its particular interest today is its survival in the face of repeated twentieth-century crises. The latest of these has stimulated the reappraisal and reapplication of the wisdom/eloquence equation in the attenuated form given it by Matthew Arnold and the New Critics. Though there is nowadays general doubt "that the humanities humanize" (George Steiner, *Language and Silence* [New York, 1974], p. 61) there is still the conviction that they *ought* to, which produces attempts to say how they could: Louis Kampf, "The Scandal of Literary Scholarship," in *The Dissenting Academy*, ed. Theodore Roszak (New York, 1968); Richard Ohmann, *English in America* (New York, 1976).

Protestant humanism was but an intensification of the way in which modern history was discovered in the Latin language from Petrarch through Valla to Machiavelli as a nostalgic response to contemporary politics. The glory of ancient Rome was felt as an eternal reproach to the moral and political degeneracy of its descendents, from the split papacy of Petrarch's day to the foreign dominations of Machiavelli's.[77] The degeneracy—political, moral, and linguistic—was seen to have begun early: the golden age of perfect Latinity was that of the Republic; the golden age of Greek during the flourishing of Athenian democracy. From there it was a gradual decline into despotism, conquest, and chaos (Ascham is alluding to this traditional cliché in the second paragraph above).[78] Valla, criticizing the political ambitions of the then pope, detected the forged *Donation* in its anachronistic vocabulary and its degenerate medieval syntax. On the positive side, Bruni and Alberti found in the rise of the Roman Republic inspiration and hope for both the political and literary future of the Florentine one. Machiavelli, no conventional moralist, saw degeneracy as mere weakness, and sought to remedy it among the Italians by advocating a streamlined Roman *virtus* as the calculated acquisition and use of pure power. This failing, Speroni's Lazaro is ready to consign the Italians to the chaos of unimprovable vernaculars befitting a nation of slaves.

In short, the perception of language as a sociohistorical product (whose semantic implications we have been tracing in arguments about vernaculars) was tied from the outset to a particular view of the history of Western society. This view is

[77] This nostalgia is powerfully expressed by Petrarch's *Rime* 53, which was possibly addressed to Cola di Rienzo, whose whole career was an attempt to revive the empire by uniting all Italy under a government at Rome.

[78] In moral and political terms, of course, the humanists acquired this view of Roman history from Livy and, after the discovery of his text in 1430, Tacitus. They extended the perspective to their own day—according to Augustine's picture of the last age of the world as a downhill slide from the fall of Rome to the second coming—and, the crucial point, found it validated in the subsequent history of Latin, which they were eager to arrest and reverse.

encapsulated in the very use of the term "corruption" to describe the evolution of the vernaculars from Latin—one problem of the whole assimilative strategy. Clumsy style is coextensive with bad thinking and immoral acting both in nations and individuals. The fortunes of this equation in England were greatly enhanced by the advent of Protestantism, which allowed one to condemn medieval Latin not only because of its unclassical "form" but also because of its papistical "content."

The question is, simply, how intrinsic a connection is involved here. In Ascham's formulation, the initial exception to the rule he goes on to state implies that the connection is not intrinsic at all. Common talk, even in barbarous vernaculars, can be wise without being eloquent. Such an enormous exception was in part necessitated by the Christian tradition that honored "wisdom" as transcending abstract, intellectual knowledge to comprise practical intelligence applied especially to the moral management of life. And no one, certainly not a disciple of Erasmus and Vives, could deny even to the illiterate masses the possession of the wisdom that comes from faith and produces virtue. On the other hand, very few, and certainly not a humanist like Ascham, were willing to grant that wise common talk might have its own brand of "eloquence." The latter, as *The Scholemaster* makes clear by both precept and example, is exclusively learned, classical, and programmed; it means imitating in the vernacular the best ancient models, mainly Cicero. Thus the ideal unity applies only to the learned, particularly to the process of learning. The equation of good utterance and good matter is therefore a standard of judgment for highly formal usage; it does not even pretend to describe the wider operation of language in common speech.

It is frankly a norm, not a dialectic; it postulates no continuous interaction between its terms, but merely states their coincidence on a scale of value. The unity thus demanded is perfectly consistent with the metonymy of the traditional linguistic dualism: its terms are not united (like Montaigne's tennis players) as partners in a process, even an antagonistic one, but as contiguous objects in space. It is the unity of "fit," which suggests another reason why the common herd are excused from achieving it. Since the clothing of words is always separable from the intact body of meaning, the pleb may have no choice but to dress his in rags; the gentleman has the resources and the obligation to be tailored, shod, and gloved for presentation at court. The closeness of the "fit"—from the loose peasant's smock to the tightly bejeweled encasement and revelation of the body by the courtier's doublet and hose—is an index of social propriety and distinction. The demand for a close fit between words and matter is not a statement about the function of language, but the application of a standard—social, moral, political, and psychological—to it.

The very idea of what was "fitting" was of course the central concept of Renaissance rhetoric: decorum.[79] Again, it is a concept of the adjustment of separable objects to each other: the speaker fits his words to his subject, his audience, his occasion, and his purpose. In theory, anyway, he might convey the identical meaning to different people on different occasions in different words. In practice, however, in the endless catalogues of schemes and tropes that provided recipes for the achievement of copiousness and adornment according to ancient and/or modern models, the figures of speech were in fact presented as functionally connected with meaning. The one thing that words were supposed to fit that made this possible was purpose. Even when the purposes were confined to the three traditional aims of oratory or to any of the Ciceronian "topics," they compelled a de facto treatment of the language that realized them as, at least to that extent, constitutive of meaning. At this level, the "form" of words indeed created their "con-

---

[79] Despite much subsequent scholarly investigation of rhetoric, especially as it bears on literature, the best general discussion of decorum in English remains that of Rosemond Tuve, *Elizabethan and Metaphysical Imagery* (Chicago, 1947), Ch. 9. The place of rhetoric in Western culture is brilliantly analyzed and useful surveys of Renaissance primary and secondary material are presented by W. J. Ong in the first three chapters of *Rhetoric, Romance, and Technology*.

tent."[80] A great many of what are classified as mere figures of "speech" turn out to constitute forms of argument, indeed of "thought." The figures, however, are never fully conceived, never explicitly described, as doing this, but are talked about in textbooks of rhetoric (as well as in theories of poetry) wholly in terms of the metonymic dualism of sartorial decoration or expressive transportation.[81]

We thus find a contradiction between treating words as semantically constitutive and conceptualizing them as merely cosmetic at the very heart of one of the principal target disciplines to which vernaculars were assimilated.[82] What is described at the level of explication of what figures of speech *do* is not what is prescribed at the level of direct statements of what they *are*. This coexistence on different levels of opposed semantic assumptions—the ubiquitous tension between description and prescription—is exactly what we have observed in other areas of reflection about words, i.e., in the philosophy of Vives, in arguments to legitimize vernaculars, and in theories of translation. These areas of linguistic concern all preserve the semantic challenge that Valla first formulated, keeping it alive and available for use by attentive readers like Montaigne. What is more, the two central norms of rhetoric

[80] This is Tuve's central argument. Though she overstresses it in the direction of attributing to the rhetoricians *theoretical* awareness of the matter, the basic contention seems valid and has been virtually absorbed into present criticism of the English Renaissance. I have described it in more detail and demonstrated its usefulness for analyzing the lyrics of Fulke Greville in *The Fatal Mirror* (Charlottesville, Va., 1972), Ch. 3.

[81] For this reason Apel, *Die Idee der Sprache*, observes that the cognitive implications of Ciceronian rhetoric are never drawn (p. 153, quoted above, ch. 2), and that even poets persist in regarding their own images in the mode of medieval allegory as but concealments or adornments of separable "content" (p. 175).

[82] A parallel but different kind of contradiction in the rhetorical tradition is described and employed in Richard A. Lanham's stimulating study of Renaissance literature, *The Motives of Eloquence* (New Haven, 1976), p. 5. A fascinating, post-Derridean account of "rhetoric" as the obverse of "logic" is provided by Jonathan V. Crewe, *Unredeemed Rhetoric: Thomas Nash and the Scandal of Authorship* (Baltimore, 1982).

itself reflect the challenge in a paradoxical way—by recognizing as wish what they cannot formulate as process. The equation of eloquence with wisdom and the principle of decorum both assert as ideally inseparable what the circumscribed domain of rhetoric as style or elocution has conceived to be always separable: the words and the matter. The theoretical framework that has driven these asunder also demands that they *should* be put back together. The demand is for an apparent semantic integrity which, because it is not conceivable as such in rhetorical terms, becomes a demand for moral integrity, for behavior that is appropriate and "fitting," whether political, personal, or social. In sum, the feeling deeply embedded in the craft and practice of rhetoric that the deliberate manipulation of words was somehow coextensive with meanings is acknowledged only by being transposed into other domains and translated as a moral imperative.

However expanded by politically disappointed Italians or Calvinistically righteous Englishmen, the personal moral imperative had been there all along, in the reiterated insistence of Cicero and Quintilian that good orators were necessarily good men. Applied by and to the professionally skilled users of words, this imperative reveals the same anxiety about that skill that Plato had about the Sophists. If the orator is trained to argue *in utramque partem*, what is to prevent him from making the worse cause appear the better? Simply his irreproachable character: the ancient objection is defined away by identifying the orator's skill with his personal probity. A bad man defending a bad cause will ipso facto make a bad speech. Ascham extends this conviction further into psychology with his resonant evocation of "a divorce betwixt the tongue and the heart." To the moral congruity of words and behavior Ascham adds that of words and feelings—an interiorization of moral value appropriate to Protestantism—the requirement of sincerity. The verbal skills of his teacher and pupil are subject to this second degree of control: by studying the best thought in the best words they will not only be unable to speak well in a bad cause, they will be able to speak well only in accordance with what they actually feel and believe. To neglect words for matter is, Ascham implies—adroitly reversing the ancient objection to purely verbal skill—to make it possible to lie.[83]

The wisdom/eloquence equation therefore functions at the same time both as a covert acknowledgment of the power of words to constitute meanings and an overt attempt to control that very threatening process. The translation of semantic into moral integrity embodies the profound, ultimately Platonic distrust of eloquence itself. Built into the norms of rhetoric is a fundamental fear of just the kind of linguistic facility that the discipline is dedicated to producing. During the Renaissance, the vastly increased importance given to the facility correspondingly intensified the fear and hence the insistence on mechanisms of control. As one of these, the equation of wisdom and eloquence is the functional twin, applied to language as expression, of the traditional grammar of "signification," applied to language as reference. Words, as we have repeatedly heard, are signs of things that enable us to convey our thoughts to others. Their meanings are the objects outside of us or the images and concepts inside of us, standing in both cases securely beyond the equivocal, historically changing, potentially deceitful use of words. The purpose of the traditional vocabulary of discourse is to keep them there, safely transcending the vagaries of time, chance, and willful perversion—to all of which words are only too liable. The grammar of "signification" assures the veracity of words as accurately representing external things; the wisdom/eloquence equation assures the veracity of words as genuinely representing internal intentions. In both cases what is represented or referred to is the preextant guarantor of meaning that calls a definitive halt to all the dismaying processes by which the Protean fecundity of words threatens to multiply meanings without end.

These processes were made most visible by the newly sharp-

---

[83] On this point Ascham was a prophet: no form of lying is more "scientific," more ostensibly concentrated on "matter" to the neglect of feelings, than that which is done by statistics.

ened perspective on language as the historical product of a social community. Their energy was most apparent in living vernaculars, where, though it might proliferate unattended on low social levels, it was to be molded and controlled by assimilation to classical grammar and rhetoric in order to become more dignified and socially respectable. In England, the whole assimilative strategy—finding the vernacular capable of "eloquence" in Ascham's sense—[84] had in the sixteenth century the same impulse that it had in the previous century in Italy, never shading into the kind of ambivalent competitiveness already manifest in both Italy and France. Crossing the Channel, the basic moves and assumptions in the argument to legitimize vernaculars were harmoniously absorbed into the fabric of humanist pedagogy with virtually none of the theoretical fanfare that had established them on the continent. Beginning roughly with Ascham, who was trying to do in English what he taught his pupils to do in Latin, English writers proceeded directly to implement the strategy without bothering to defend it. Richard Mulcaster, Spenser's schoolmaster, simply declared his conviction that English was the equal in beauty and power of any language, ancient or modern; he saw its development in organic terms, with "custom" as the best guide to it.[85] Vernacular rhetorics supplied procedures and models for its ornamentation. Above all, of course, poets and translators used it, in self-conscious efforts to produce in English what had already been produced in Italian and French as well as in Greek and Latin. The only part of the assimilative strategy to generate theoretical controversy in sixteenth-century England was the question of how or whether classical meters could be used in English verse.[86]

---

[84] His efforts to achieve this in his own work and their considerable influence are well described by Lawrence V. Ryan, *Roger Ascham* (Stanford, 1963), pp. 279–86.

[85] *The First Part of the Elementarie . . .* (London, 1582), quoted and discussed by R. F. Jones, *The Triumph of the English Language*, pp. 163–65, 192.

[86] This well-known argument was mainly between Spenser and Gabriel Harvey, Thomas Campion and Samuel Daniel, though many poets practiced

The first impulse to defend vernaculars arose in fifteenth-century Italy primarily as a way to rationalize and justify the classics of vernacular literature that already existed there. The unremitting investigation of historical usage in Latin, erected into a philosophical principle by Valla, provided the catalytic agent for the intensified defense of vernacular languages in the sixteenth century. The poets of the Pléiade selectively borrowed the linguistic arguments in order to rationalize the literature they were producing themselves. The English merely absorbed the theories into rhetoric and pedagogy and set about producing a literature of their own. The absence in sixteenth-century England of any text wholly devoted to a theoretical defense of the vernacular is not due only to the ready availability of such works in Italian and French. It is due much more directly to Protestantism. The English had no need whatever to defend in theory a vernacular that was already in practice as the language of worship, Scripture, and the Established Church. The real triumph of the language first occurred in the domain not of words but of the Word. Having achieved this vital displacement of Latin, unlike both the Italians and the French, the English people from court to cottage could deal with the most important dimension of their personal experience entirely in their mother tongue.[87] Unlike the German Protestants, who enjoyed the same privilege, the English also belonged to the same nation; their vernacular was thus the language of collective, religious and political, as well as individual experience.

Though the cultural implications of these obvious differences seem so vast as to be incalculable, they can at any rate suggest powerful reasons why England, unlike Italy and

---

this form of imitation. Both practice and theory in the whole controversy are analyzed by Derek Attridge, *Well-weighed Syllables: Elizabethan Verse in Classical Metres* (Cambridge, 1974).

[87] Enough cottagers were reading the vernacular Bible by 1543 to appall Henry VIII, whose Parliament of that year passed an Act forbidding them to do so. See A. G. Dickens, *The English Reformation* (New York, 1964), pp. 189–91.

France, never developed an official "academy" to dictate rules for both language and literature. The institution of such formal control over newly legitimized vernacular energies was after all a logical conclusion of the whole strategy of assimilation. The della Crusca and the Académie Française were latent in the earliest efforts to regulate and purify actual speech; nor was the desire for such an institution, on the latter model, lacking in England. In 1667 Thomas Sprat, significantly observing the rapid development and enrichment of the vernacular during the Civil War, proposed the creation of an "English Academy" as an adjunct of the Royal Society in order to codify grammar and spelling and also to serve as "a fixt and *Impartial Court of Eloquence*, according to whose Censure all Books or Authors should either stand or fall." But even after enumerating the artistic and political advantages of his proposal, Sprat expresses little hope for its realization and dismisses it as "an extravagant conceit."[88]

His sense of reality was indeed sounder than his project. The regulatory academy actually flourished where the vernacular and its literature were less completely integrated into all levels of the national life than they were in England. Where Latin remained the language of the Church as well as of the universities, the spoken language and its literature were likewise capable of being compartmentalized as the possession of a similar elite. Restricted to the social sphere of those who appointed themselves its guardians—from Cardinal Bembo to Cardinal Richelieu—vernacular language and literature could more easily become subject to the kinds of regulation borrowed from the equally restricted sphere of Latin study. The assimilation, in short, was simply more thoroughgoing in Italy and France than it could be in a country whose native speech and literature had been legitimized not only as the possession of an educated elite but as the medium of religious experience essential, by definition, to all. By alluding to the lin-

---

[88] *The History of the Royal-Society of London*, in Spingarn, II, 113–15. Past and subsequent designs of this kind are reviewed by Spingarn, II, 337–38.

guistic energies of the Puritan Revolution, Sprat identifies the very fact that made the "English Academy" nothing more than a gleam in his eye. The impossibility that he sensed of legislating control over those particular vernacular energies is well illustrated by the career of one of his humbler contemporaries, John Bunyan. After fighting in the Parliamentary forces, the Bedfordshire tinker discovered by his own efforts in his own language in the context of his daily life the liberating power of the Word, which he subsequently preached until he was thrown for over a decade into prison, where he wrote, among a stream of devotional and polemical tracts, an account of his conversion and an allegorical fiction that immediately became classics of English literature. The exclusively vernacular culture that made Bunyan's achievement possible was no more likely to be regulated by a linguistic authority than by political and ecclesiastical ones.

Although the prescriptive part of the assimilative strategy thus failed of its institutional application in England, the descriptive part was there elaborated in appropriately radical ways. While formal arguments for the vernacular were not necessary, the observations and assumptions that furnished such arguments on the continent were diffused in Britain in the wider contexts of scholarship and educational reform. Two brief examples must suffice: one from the learned domain of historical philology, and one from the more popular concern with linguistic pedagogy.

Edward Brerewood, a professor of astronomy in Gresham College, summarized and extended for his countrymen the research of continental scholars from Biondo to Joseph Justus Scaliger on the historical development of Latin and its relation to vernaculars.[89] Citing Scaliger on the fourteen mother tongues of Europe that have no connection whatever with Latin (p. 21), Brerewood makes the assumption of the equal

---

[89] *Enquiries touching the diversity of languages, and religions through the . . . world* (London, 1614). This book appeared the year after Brerewood's death and was subsequently translated into both French and—signaling the achieved displacement—Latin.

and independent existence of all languages, which is central to his argument. His thesis is to deny what he calls the "common opinion" that French, Italian, and Spanish were produced by the "corruption" of Latin by barbarous tongues after the collapse of the Roman empire. He traces a three-stage process that presumes the vernaculars to have begun developing long before the middle of the fifth century.[90] They did not spring "from the corruption of the Latin tongue . . . but from the first unperfect receiving of it" (pp. 30–37). The invasions therefore merely continued a process already under way. Brerewood argues this point at length, deliberately refusing the pejorative view of vernaculars implicit in the idea of "corruption." "Pure" Latin was not there to be corrupted, since "there is no language, which of ordinary course is not subject to change" all by itself, independent of "forraine occasion" (p. 42). Brerewood pushes his dispassionate survey of diversity back to include languages earlier than Latin, comparing the former domination of Etruscan in Italy to that of Gaelic in the British Isles (p. 50). He hypothesizes throughout about the processes of linguistic change in a way that wholly avoids both the organic metaphor and its latent value judgments of origin, perfection, degeneration, and contamination.

Joseph Webbe (about whom virtually nothing is known) devoted an entire little treatise to the proposition that all languages should be learned by example and not by rule.[91] Ascham, as well as his mentor Sturm and even Vives, would have approved the proposition, though they would have been dismayed at Webbe's extreme and uncompromising development of it. He simply carries the descriptive method of the humanist investigation of language to its logical conclusion, divorcing it from its customary and paradoxical alliance with prescriptive aims. By so doing, Webbe presents a neat compendium of the single subversive strain in humanist thinking

[90] This theory is of course the accepted one today; cf. Migliorini, *Storia della lingua italiana*, p. 1.

[91] *An appeale to truth, in the controversie betweene art, & use; about the best and most expedient course in languages* (London, 1622).

that supplied the basic rationale for the liberation of vernaculars. He begins by declaring the object of language study to be "the whole speach of a Nation" in the full multiplicity of its uses (p. 4). He cites Valla with approval (pp. 6, 8) and uses Quintilian as a champion of the observation of speech against the prescriptions of "Leonardus Aretinus, and his Followers" (p. 22). The actual acquisition and use of a language is wholly unrelated and prior to "art": lackeys and oysterwives can "entertain you your fill."[92] Webbe's whole point, repeated in all these ways, is that the observation of actual usage is everything. "Grammarians, in th' exposition of Authours, tell their scholars, that this or that construction is by reason of this or that rule, but truth it self will tell us otherwise: for, out of those Authours, this or that was made a rule, by reason of this or that construction" (p. 32). Vives might have made this statement,[93] but neither he nor almost any humanist whose practice it summarizes would have wished to draw its furthest consequence. This is the flat denial of the very idea of correctness, as Webbe directly infers: "whatsoever is in use, is neither inconvenient, nor a Soloecism" (p. 36).

Such total insistence on "use" over "art" is the most radical extension of Valla's seminally innovative treatment of language. Webbe's position also recalls the equally wholesale rejection of any prescriptive standards for vernaculars made by Bovelles. Unlike Bovelles, however, Webbe has no reassuring grammar of mysticism to fall back on; he affirms, as Montaigne had done, the unrationalizable vitality of common speech in and for itself. All these writers bring to the surface the current of revolutionary linguistic assumptions contained within the conventional disciplines of Renaissance humanism. The assimilation of vernaculars to Latin, the doctrine of literary imitation, the moral and social ideals of rhetoric, the explicit definition of language as clothing or drainpipe—all func-

[92] Pp. 24–25. At this point, Webbe cites Montaigne, whom he is paraphrasing. The passage is quoted above, n. 51.

[93] He in fact made one very like it, quoted above, p. 121.

tion as strategies of that containment, to keep that vital flow buried and controlled. Only occasionally does it burst forth to become visible in some of the arguments about words we have examined. These are the exceptions that reveal what is hidden in the rule. The situation was aptly described by Karl-Otto Apel, who found the "essential advantage" of the humanist linguistic concept to be its "more implicit than explicit appreciation of the communally established function of language."[94]

I have attempted to isolate some theoretical moments when that appreciation becomes explicit, beginning from Valla's elevation of the idea of the speech community into a philosophical principle. His treatment of language as both diachronically contingent—the ever-evolving product of a collectivity—and synchronically cognitive—constituting at any given moment how the subject knows the world—established the dialectic whose tensions and paradoxes unfolded in subsequent debates. To describe usage and to prescribe it, to see language as the ungovernable product of collective will and as subject to the conscious craft of individual will, to see words as conveying thoughts and still to see the thoughts conveyed as inseparable from the words, to see meanings as transparently transferable from one language to another and yet to sense that such transference is always a loss—all these paradoxes are the multiple axes along which semantic awareness is shifting during the Renaissance. All proceed from the basic tension between conceiving the relation of language and meaning as cosmetic and treating it as constitutive.

I have also suggested that this shifting awareness, largely subterranean in theory, breaks forth most clearly in literature. The extent to which the period's greatest literature becomes conscious of itself as a structure of manufactured meanings, and takes as one of its major subjects the complex and problematic relations between words and meanings, is simultaneously a part of the process I am describing and its most impor-

---

[94] *Die Idee der Sprache*, p. 273.

tant consequence.[95] The alteration of semantic assumptions ultimately results in imagining new forms of life in new forms of literature—however carefully crafted their resemblance to old forms.

The most obviously "new" forms of life and literature produced in the Renaissance by the deliberate effort to revive or return to old forms were, of course, produced by the Protestant Reformation. As we have noticed, this genuine hermeneutic revolution was, in Britain, inseparable from and a cause of the triumph of the vernacular. But in general the secular theory of words had its own origin and momentum, and is separable from the divine theory of the Word on better grounds than either the exigencies of exposition or the difference in subject matter. The humanist study of language, in all the contexts we have discussed, is primarily a didactics of production: the "finding" (in the older or newer sense of *inventio*) of words that will in turn produce sound scholars, virtuous citizens, or literary artists. By contrast, the study of Scripture is primarily a didactics of reception: the correct apprehension and interpretation of divine meaning. Although both the humanist investigation of actual speech and Protestant biblical hermeneutics share the same revolutionary principle—that of a community of speakers or believers—the orientation of each is basically different. Men might create words, but only God has created the Word. The fecundity of the former process could be admired and feared, stimulated and controlled; the fait accompli of the latter could only be received and interpreted. The theory of words addressed itself to an audience of potential or compelled writers (and speakers); the theory of the Word to an audience of actual readers (and hearers). The arguments in each domain focus, in short, on the two different players in Montaigne's tennis game. To the crucial reconception of the role of the "receiver" we now turn.

[95] A consequence traced most thoroughly to date by Quint, *Origin and Originality*, in terms of the tensions in literature between the allegorical representation of the timeless and the historical exploration of the contingent.

PART III

ARGUMENTS ABOUT
THE WORD

> Those people must be jesting who think they
> can diminish and stop our disputes by recalling
> us to the express words of the Bible.
>
> —MICHEL DE
> MONTAIGNE

As humanist philology, inspired by classical rhetoric, engendered a sociohistorical semantic awareness that catalyzed the
legitimation of vernacular languages in the sixteenth century,
it simultaneously produced by means of the same awareness
new ways of apprehending the meaning of Scripture whose
revolutionary consequences were immediate and remain with
us today. My purpose in discussing some of the ensuing controversies—carried on then as now not merely by academic argument but also by shooting in the streets—is in no sense to
resolve them. It is simply to trace, in this most hotly disputed
and broadly diffused area of linguistic contention, the presence
and transmission of the whole complex of contradictory assumptions about how language means that I have called the
Renaissance semantic shift.

The beginnings of these similarly new ways of interpreting
Scripture may be located in the independent efforts of two major religious reformers in the early sixteenth century.[1] The first

---

[1] These efforts were not without precedent. Comparable ways of reinterpreting Scripture may be found in the practice of earlier reformers, like John
Wyclif, and contemporary ones, like John Colet and Lefèvre d'Etaples. I am
selecting those whose influence was the most immediate and lasting, in no

of these, Erasmus's editing and retranslation of the Greek New Testament, was directly inspired by Lorenzo Valla. The second, Martin Luther's early lectures as Professor of the Old Testament at Wittenberg, was the indirect result of the humanist discovery that the historical context of language is semantically constitutive, which Valla had sought to make into an epistemology. The subsequent apprehension of the meaning of even the divinely inspired Word in mundane ways different from the obligatory ontological "correspondence" between word and thing was not only profoundly disturbing and intensely resented; it was also an important basis for the notorious splintering among the developing Protestant sects. To open the divine text to the newly historical modes of interrogation was to perceive a temporal semantic fluidity that offered ample scope for competing attempts at determination. In addition, the particular way in which Erasmus and Luther opened the divine text to a rhetorically derived kind of emotional meaning had profound repercussions in the rhetorically linked domain of literature.

No sooner, indeed, than these new interpretive energies were released did the clamor begin for their control. Analogously to the other kinds of linguistic debate we have examined, the movement of biblical hermeneutics in the sixteenth century is from attacks on the immediate, medieval past, through the description of historically, communally, or emotionally determined meanings, to the prescription and reaccommodation of these meanings within traditional systems of control. One particular subject, the doctrine of the sacraments, especially the Eucharist—which Protestants disputed more fiercely among themselves than with Catholics—throws into high relief the general pattern of challenged and reasserted semantic assumptions. It does so for the simple reason that the

---

small part because of their assiduous exploitation of the new medium of print. Elizabeth L Eisenstein documents the growing association in the sixteenth century of print and Protestantism, pointing out that printing allowed "older evangelical drives" to be fully implemented for the first time: *The Printing Press As an Agent of Change* (Cambridge, 1979), I, 331ff.

very definition of a sacrament ("an outward and visible sign of an inward and spiritual grace") was modeled on, as well as functioned as the model for, the whole Platonic/Augustinian process of "signification" in language itself. When Luther insisted, therefore, on taking literally the famous words of institution, "This is my body," he was denying that process in a fundamental way that even some of his most fervent sympathizers could not accept. The ensuing quarrels about the literal or figurative presence of Christ in the bread and wine thus explicitly involved the relation of "sign" and "signified" that was central to traditional semantic assumptions. These arguments, in short, were not only about how to interpret a given scriptural text (a *parole*); the terms in which they were conducted also called into question both the entire semantic operation of the medium (the *langue*) and the very special status attributed to it as proceeding, however indirectly, from God.

To insist on untangling the profane history of the divine Word by applying to it all the humanist techniques of textual criticism grounded in Valla's scrutiny of "common usage" and heretofore applied in editions of classical and patristic texts was revolutionary in itself—as evidenced by the extent to which Erasmus was subjected to accusations of impiety for having done so. But this revolution was lasting: Greek and Hebrew became prerequisites for biblical study, and Erasmus was widely honored then and since for establishing the principle, in the words of Guillaume Budé, "that no man can rightly call himself a theologian . . . before . . . he has duly washed his hands in every fountain of the Muses."[2] The deeper revolution, on the other hand, inherent in the application of humanist descriptive methods to the transmission and translation of the Word, was so threatening that it was all but swallowed up in controversy. What Erasmus had begun as a scholarly practice

---

[2] *OE* 583 (*CW* IV): Erasmus's letters are thus cited by number from P. S. Allen et al., ed., *Opus Epistolarum* (Oxford, 1906–58), along with, where available, the number of the volume in *The Collected Works* (Toronto, 1974–) where an English translation may be found. The letters are numbered in the *CW* as in Allen.

the Protestant reformers pursued to the level of hermeneutic theory, where they became uncomfortable and confused. For to submit the Word to grammatical, rhetorical, and historical interrogation and hence to the multiple, semantically determining contexts of humanist philology was to invade the very stronghold of magical reference, of truth as the correspondence between utterance and fact finally guaranteed by God.

No sixteenth-century reformer, of course, wished to make such an assault on the linguistic foundations of Christianity. Rather, he wished, with Erasmus, to return *ad fontes* and to purify them from later corruption; to discover, with Luther, the joyous and liberating promises made by the Bible; to reorganize, with Calvin, ecclesiastical and political society on that basis. But the assault was implicit in his hermeneutic activity; unrecognized, but sensed as a potent threat, it may help to account for the ferocity of the debates. As a latent threat it certainly sealed the fate of the new forms of semantic awareness that produced it. Their implications had to be kept from overtly undermining the finality of the sacred semantic guarantee. In the sixteenth century, this issue was conceived of in terms of authority. Once the seamless fabric of the sacred text was torn by arguing the need to correct its imperfect human transmission, to translate it into vernaculars, and above all to interpret it less as an eternal enigma and more as a complex and imaginative record of historical human events (as "literature," in short), the problem was seen as that of deciding among the new possibilities of meaning thus offered, of reestablishing some final and divine truth. What person, group, or institution was to have the authority to say what Scripture meant? Protestants, of course, denied this authority to the Roman Catholic Church, but were then compelled to substitute another: the individual believer, the trained theologian, the congregation, Bishops, synods, and so on. So conceived, the problem was insoluble, and was disputed with a rancor appropriate to the anxiety it aroused.

The intensity of this anxiety may be gauged by the inadequacy or the incoherence of the solutions that were offered.

The neatest of these was that of the Council of Trent, which simply declared that since interpretation is the exclusive prerogative of the institutional Church, no interpretation shall be made that is contrary either to the fathers or to promulgated dogmas: consequently, "Holy Scripture can say, and by interpretation can be made to say, nothing that conflicts with ecclesiastical doctrine."[3] Thus to reassert authority by maintaining that all previous disagreements counted for nothing was a response so desperate as to border on hysteria. The issue was not at all the supposed "infallibility" of the institutional Church; for in terms of its practices, the Council of Trent produced some of the most far-reaching directives of reform in the Church's history. To urge changes in the behavior of its officers, or even in the conduct of its rituals, was no problem; but to urge changes in the understanding of its Book was literally unthinkable. The desperate response was confined to the crucial matter of semantic custody and control over the Bible. The Protestant responses to the same matter were almost as desperate, if only in their incompatible variety. The nature of their opposition to the Catholics, however, at least forced them to deal with the issue of interpretation, instead of defining it out of existence as Trent did.

The interest for us in their internecine quarreling over it is the freedom with which they availed themselves of contradictory semantic assumptions to defend now one, now another particular textual reading or specific hermeneutic instruction. What often appears in their overt disputes about what Scripture means are deeper and not always recognized differences about how it means. The Protestant search for an apodictic religious truth contra the medieval Church is exactly analogous to Vives's search for an apodictic philosophical truth contra medieval scholasticism. Their critical weapons come from the same Vallesque arsenal of observed linguistic usage and carry

---

[3] J.K.S. Reid, *The Authority of Scripture* (London, 1957), p. 121. Reid's theology is Barthian, but his assessment is accurate: cf. the Tridentine decree on canonical scriptures, fourth session, 8 Apr. 1546, in Philip Schaff, ed., *The Creeds of Christendom* (New York, 1877), II, 83.

with them the same semantic challenge that must finally be avoided or denied. A semantic assumption useful for making a negative critique must be abrogated when a positive prescription of meaning is to be upheld. Again, as was the case with legitimizing the vernaculars and assimilating them to Latin grammar and rhetoric, a descriptive method coexists in contradiction with a prescriptive aim. Thus the revolutions accomplished—in society, politics, and religious sensibility—by the stimulus of the Protestant reapprehension of the Word were permeated by the unconsummated conflict between opposed conceptions of the meanings of words. What, however, remained unconsummated in respect to Scripture had much more extensive consequences in respect to literature.

5

THE CHALLENGE FROM
ELOQUENCE

i. Erasmus and Literature

My hart the Anvile where my thoughts doe beate,   —MICHAEL
My words the hammers, fashioning my desires . . .   DRAYTON

The lifelong devotion of Erasmus to correct and fastidious
Latin was formed by Valla's *Elegantiae*, of which he made in his
youth an abridgement for students.[4] At about the same time he
wrote letters defending the *Elegantiae* against the attacks of
Poggio and praising Valla as the reviver of eloquence.[5] About
seventeen years later, Erasmus discovered near Louvain Valla's
brief application of the philological techniques of this revival
to Scripture, and he had it printed, for the first time, by Badius
Ascensius.[6] Several years earlier in Paris Erasmus had presum-

[4] Erasmus describes this effort while complaining to Peter Giles in 1530 of
its unauthorized publication in 1529: *OE* 2260. As Allen notes, the references
to its date of composition are a bit confused, but fall somewhere between
1486–88. Authorized or not, Erasmus's epitome of the *Elegantiae*, called the
Paraphrasis, had more than fifty printings by 1566: Ferdinand Vander
Haeghen, *Bibliotheca Erasmiana* (Gent, 1893; rpt. Nieukoop, 1972), Part I, pp.
152–53.

[5] *OE* 20, 23, 26, 29 (*CW* II). Erasmus also praises Valla in such terms in the
famous letter to Dorp in 1515—*OE* 337 (*CW* III)—and continues to do so
when, in 1518, he is constrained to defend his own textual work on the N.T.
to Martin Lypsius: *OE* 843.

[6] *Laurentii Vallensis . . . in Latinam Novi Testamenti interpretationem ex colla-*
tione Graecorum exemplarium Adnotationes [Paris, 1505]. The caution, thoroughness, and revolutionary practice of Valla's philology in this text is described by Robert Stupperich, "Schriftauslegung und Textkritik bei
Laurentius Valla," in *Text-Wort-Glaube*, ed. Martin Brecht (Berlin, 1980), pp.
220–33.

ably made the acquaintance of Valla's *Dialectica*.[7] The new language-based epistemology of the latter work, however, seems to have made little if any impression on him, which is not surprising in view of his intolerance for philosophical speculation in general, conditioned by his detestation of scholasticism. Erasmus was never interested in opposing the tradition he despised at the level of theory (though he appreciated those who did so, including Valla and especially Vives). His biases were those from which mainstream humanism takes its definition: pragmatic, philological, pedagogical, and ethical. All of these were activated and directed toward the purifying of the Word when Erasmus found and published Valla's linguistic observations on the Vulgate New Testament as compared with Greek manuscripts.

In his dedicatory letter of this edition to Christopher Fisher, Erasmus, by defending Valla, is articulating the motives and the principles of what will become a large part of his own life's work.[8] After sojourning in Italy to perfect his Greek and publishing successive versions of his own New Testament, Erasmus was continually constrained to reiterate the same principles in his own defense. These principles, of course, are entirely restorative and conservative, and Erasmus is at pains to derive them from the theory and practice of the fathers of the Church, who were themselves, he explains, grammarians. Knowledge of the original languages of Scripture is essential to theology. Biblical prophets and poets may have preached by inspiration alone, but interpreters require secular erudition, rhetorical sophistication (*copia*), and intelligence. Even Scripture may contain linguistic errors; that its actual words are not "immutable" is clear from the conscious emendations of St. Jerome. The necessity of detecting and correcting such errors is even greater now that the new art of printing can multiply

---

[7] In 1498 he requested and received a copy of it from the printer Robert Gaguin: *OE* 67, 68 (*CW* II). No further references to it exist in Allen's index to the correspondence.

[8] *Adnotationes*, sigs. A1ᵛ–A2ᵛ. The letter is included in *OE* 182 (*CW* II).

them by the thousand.[9] Erasmus defends Valla personally in reference to the same authorities, claiming that they were no less spiteful and scurrilous toward their opponents than he, and that his errors can likewise stimulate us to seek truth. Valla's work is thus located in a venerable historical continuum that extends from Origen to Nicholas of Lyra.

By thus defending the textual criticism of the Word even before he had attempted it, Erasmus displayed an awareness that such an enterprise would appear suspect to current theological opinion. How and why it would subsequently appear so revolutionary he could not have foreseen. Yet, as he was forming his own resolve to improve the earthly state of the divine text, he attempted not only to fumigate the controversial and heterodox reputation of Valla but also to provide grounds and sanctions for the whole enterprise. Both the grounds—that the linguistic transmission of Scripture can err—and the sanctions—that the fathers employed secular learning to improve its text—he adduces are in fact historical observations of semantic fluidity. Clearly Erasmus had a sufficient sense of the latent threat of such observations to justify them in advance and in ways so traditional as to make them seem unexceptionable.

Before producing the first version of his Greek New Testament and Latin translation in 1516, Erasmus developed his prior interest in pure Latinity into a famous textbook, *de duplici copia verborum ac rerum* (1512).[10] Frankly designed to fill the practical gaps in Cicero and Quintilian in order to teach schoolboys how to write, the very title of the book suggests no reconception of the semantic dualism of traditional rhetoric.

---

[9] Eisenstein, *The Printing Press*, I, 341–42, in discussing Erasmus as exemplary of deliberate textual restorers who were also "unwitting innovators," overlooks his specific mention here of the power of print and the intensified motive it supplies.

[10] *L* I (*CW* XXIV): Erasmus's works are thus cited by volume number from *Opera Omnia*, ed. J. LeClerc (Leiden, 1703–06), 10 vols., along with the English versions as available. There were more than 150 editions of *de copia* in the sixteenth century, as well as sundry vernacular translations and abridgements.

Straightforward instructions are offered on how to achieve co-piousness both of "words" (book I) and "matter" (book II). Though this distinction is not rigidly maintained, the book is divided into treatments of verbal variation (I) and strategies of argumentation (II).[11] It is based on the sound ancient principle that style depends on the awareness of available alternatives, and so spells out for students a copious variety of models and means of verbal ornament and argumentative procedure. The models are frankly prescriptive and privileged; Erasmus is writing an *ars*, not an historical investigation of actual use. In fact, he quotes the standard Horatian passage on custom as the sovereign of speaking (*Ars Poetica*, ll. 70–71) and explicitly dissents from it: "Since the rule of speaking is now to be sought not from ordinary people but from the venerated works of the learned, the same authority does not belong to common usage."[12]

The traditional didacticism of Erasmus's rhetoric shows us that he held, in full maturity and at the height of his powers (the *Praise of Folly* appeared in 1511), an equally traditional conception of the separable relation between words and meanings. To be sure, as is the case with the whole tradition of Cic-ero- and Quintilian-derived rhetoric, of which the *de copia* was a major disseminator, the actual recipes for variation of all kinds may implicitly treat meanings as context- and purpose-dependent. But words are still explicitly conceived as semant-ically cosmetic. The divergent assumptions that I have located in the tensions between the descriptive methods and prescrip-tive aims of rhetoric generally have been detected in Erasmus as functions of considering language as speech on the one hand and writing on the other. The experience of speech as the me-

[11] Book I contains, for example, the well-known list of about 200 ascend-ingly flowery and ingenious ways to say, "Your letter delighted me very much." The "commonplaces," where arguments are to be sought in book II, reproduce with very slight alterations and deletions Cicero's sixteen categories of "invented" arguments (*Topica* xviii.71).

[12] *L* I, 9F: ". . . *si volet usus*. Nunc quoniam loquendi ratio non a vulgo, sed ex eruditorum monumentis petitur, non est eadem consuetudinis auctoritas."

dium of social relations "presumes the unity of content and form," whereas the literary inculcation of rhetorical "variety" presumes "that fact and word do not clearly coincide."[13] Erasmus's traditional conception of language needs stressing in order to correct the recent claim, made in the most cogent study to date of his hermeneutics, that his view of it was as innovative as his language-based theology.[14] But he not only states the standard formula—"what clothing is to our body, style is to thoughts"—he amplifies it at great length in terms of cleanliness, propriety, and so forth. He goes on, in a virtuoso exemplification of the verbal variety he is preaching, to offer two additional similitudes for the *elocutio/sententia* relation: furniture and banquets. We should choose our words with the same good taste that we exhibit in adorning our bodies, decorating our homes, and setting our tables.[15] None of the relations evoked by these conventional comparisons is functional; all

[13] Dietrich Harth, *Philologie und praktische Philosophie: Untersuchungen zum Sprach- und Traditionsverständnis des Erasmus von Rotterdam* (Munich, 1970), pp. 69–70, 74. Harth endorses with respect to Erasmus Apel's analysis of the unrealized potential in Ciceronian/humanist rhetoric (quoted above, ch. 2): "Die in dieser Auffassung enthaltene Möglichkeit einer radikalen Historisierung und damit verbundenen Relativierung der Sprache und der von ihr benannten Einrichtungen, blieb Erasmus freilich verborgen," p. 76.

[14] Marjorie O'Rourke Boyle, *Erasmus on Language and Method in Theology* (Toronto, 1977). Her analysis unfolds the complex significance that radiates out, largely in terms of key metaphors, from Erasmus's notorious substitution of *sermo* for *verbum* in John 1:1. Her approach thus goes beyond the still useful analyses of J. B. Payne, "Toward the Hermeneutics of E.," in *Scrinium Erasmianum* II, ed. J. Coppens (Leiden, 1969), 13–49; and C.A.L. Jarrott, "E's Biblical Humanism," *Studies in the Renaissance* 17 (1970), 119–52. From the philological perspective, there is now a good account of E's exegesis in Jerry H. Bentley, *Humanists and Holy Writ* (Princeton, 1983), pp. 173–91.

[15] *L* I, 8A: "quod est vestris nostri corpori, id est sententiis, elocutio." Boyle quotes this phrase, construing "sententiis" as linguistic expressions rather than "thoughts," in order to urge that words may be clothing other words: pp. 51–52. In the phrase alone, the usual ambiguity of *sententia* offers some latitude for her speculations. But this is wholly foreclosed by the context—the subsequent images I cite—which makes clear that the ancient semantic dualism and ontological priority here remain quite unmodified. Boyle completely ignores this context.

present the metonymic "fit" of separable objects—the socially appropriate—as the model for relating words to meanings.

At the level of conception, Erasmus's view of language, like his defense of studying the languages of the Bible, is deliberately traditional. It did not need to be otherwise in order for the importance he attributed to language in both temporal and spiritual realms to acquire, however inadvertently, its revolutionary force. The nature of this importance derives from the central humanist preoccupation with language as the inevitable medium and mediator of all human experience. However contrary the assumptions about how such mediation operates: as conveyance or containment, by mystical correspondence or communal will; or however varied the definition of what is thus mediated: mental images or objects, concepts or intentions; language is continually felt, in Father Ong's resonant term, as a "presence." For Erasmus, this inescapable presence is the center of both his pedagogy and his theology.[16]

He begins his influential little treatise *de ratione studii* (1511) by declaring that the knowledge of words is prior to that of things. "Since things are not known except by the tokens of words, he who is not well-skilled in the import of discourse" is necessarily blind and deluded in judging things. Nothing is more foolish than to boast of neglecting words in order to look at the thing itself.[17] Erasmus thus concisely articulates what I have called the dilemma of the age, which Valla attempted to resolve and which became so problematic for Vives: the desire for the transparent cognition of things that is frustrated by the

[16] Boyle observes, for example, that Erasmus's "humanist methodology" rejects the scholastic "confidence in reason's ability to discern truth directly, without the mediation of the linguistic arts," pp. 124–25.

[17] *L* I, 521A (*CW* XXIV): "Principio duplex omnino videtur cognitio, rerum ac verborum. Verborum prior, rerum potior, . . . Etenim cum res non nisi per vocum notas cognoscantur, qui sermonis vim non callet, is passim in rerum quoque judicio caecutiat, hallucinetur, deliret necesse est. Postremo videas nullos omnium magis ubique de voculis cavillari, quam eos qui jactitant sese verba negligere, rem ipsam spectare. . . . Quid enim stultius?"

Bibliotheca Erasmiana, I, 16ff., records about 75 printings of *de ratione studii*, often attached to other pedagogical works, in the sixteenth century.

awareness of the opaque fluidity of words. The whole humanist focus on language as a sociohistorical product implied what
Valla sporadically inferred from it: that semantics is epistemology, that language does not reveal or reflect reality but
constitutes it. It is this challenge, or suspicion, or anxiety that
underlies so many of the intellectual battles of the period, such
as the humanist effort to replace the apodictic dialectics of Aristotle by the probabilistic ones of Cicero. Far from being the
merely belletristic repudiation or absorption of "logic" by
"rhetoric" that it has often been called, this effort is the more
fundamental acknowledgment that language is the shaping
medium of the whole human world, not a passive tool but an
active force. The epistemological problematics of this force,
the anguish it caused and would continue to cause other thinkers, are nowhere apparent in Erasmus. Here, he calmly maintains the cognitive dualism between words and things, giving
priority to words, in order to establish the initial basis of education as instruction in Latin and Greek grammar. He raises no
doubts or questions about how we are to proceed from knowing words to knowing things, evidently assuming that the latter will follow the former as night follows day. The rest of the
treatise tells the teacher how to use the best authors to inculcate
good morals along with good grammar, how the dangers that
may lurk in pagan texts—like the homosexual longing in Virgil's second Eclogue—are to be sidestepped and sanitized.
Erasmus was not concerned to examine the "sense of discourse" theoretically, but rather to apply it practically, to savor
the use of its textures and surfaces in everyday life, and above
all to draw the ethical and political consequences of this use by
reinforcing in both precept and example the equation between
good morals and good Latin.[18] His ever-expanding collections
of *Adagia* and *Colloquia* are ample witness to these concerns.

[18] Admitting that Erasmus eschewed epistemological and linguistic theory,
Boyle still complains that his "philosophy of language" has been neglected,
pp. 51; 53, n121. But it is no wonder, for example, that no one has studied
Lingua (L IV) in this connection, for it repays no such interest, being a moral
tract on the proper governance of the "tongue."

By simply transferring the central humanist focus on the "sermonis vim" from Latin-learning to biblical study, Erasmus precipitated a hermeneutic revolution that would prove unacceptable to his own Church but was enthusiastically welcomed by Prostestants.[19] Finding, when he retranslated the New Testament, the most forceful discourse of all to be Christ as the eternal conversation of God, Erasmus also produced an original theology. Both of these achievements resulted from applying to Scripture the kind of attention to language that Erasmus learned from Valla; neither required that he share Valla's radical reconception of language itself. With respect to theology, it was sufficient that Erasmus regard the New Testament as the supreme model of "eloquence" and therefore, though subject both to emendation and interpretation, of imitation. The means of this transference was his notorious, but wholly traditional, substitution of "sermo" for "verbum" to designate Christ (John 1:1).[20] Erasmus's revival of this ancient alternative reflects in itself one dimension of the semantic shift: the humanist practice of locating meaning less in single, discrete words and more in whole utterances and propositions, larger units that presuppose the semantic importance of usage and context. The crucial importance of these in the theology that Erasmus developed through the analogy of human and divine eloquence has been demonstrated by Marjorie Boyle.[21]

[19] Although most of Erasmus's religious writings remained on the *Index* only from 1557 to 1596, the methods of historical, textual research into the Bible that he urged with the impeccable precedents of the fathers were not officially approved by the Roman Catholic Church until 1943 in an Encyclical of Pius XII. See David Michael Stanley, S.J., "The Gospels as Salvation History," in *Christianity Divided*, ed. Daniel J. Callahan et al. (New York, 1961), p. 115.

[20] How Erasmus was constrained to defend this in the *Apologia* (1520) on grounds of both semantics (*sermo* more closely approximates the Greek *logos* than *verbum*) and authority (fathers from Augustine to Hilary preferred *sermo*) is described by C.A.L. Jarrott, 'E's *in principio erat sermo*: A Controversial Translation," *Studies in Philology* 61 (1964), 35–40.

[21] *E. on Language and Method in Theology*, pp. 73, 101, 124, et passim. She sees the substitution of "discourse" for "word" as the rejection of atomistic scholasticism, and shows throughout how completely E's theology is

To imitate the speech of God himself in our own individual (moral) and collective (political) lives was the unifying norm in all of Erasmus's work. He made the dynamic processes of language, as he traditionally understood them, as central to theology as Valla, who tried to reconceive them, had made them to philosophy.

These processes, as Erasmus applied them to the actual reading of the Bible, produced a metaphorical, eclectic hermeneutic theory and a dramatic, hortatory exegetical practice. Although Christ is the discourse of God, this discourse is obviously quite different from that of ordinary human speech, as Erasmus explains in his *Paraphrases* on John.[22] The language of Scripture is therefore "accommodated" to our mundane capacities; it must suggest in ways accessible to us what is not directly expressible. This very traditional principle was one of the bases of allegorical interpretation, and Erasmus must retain it even while he criticizes the elaborate and arbitrary allegories of medieval exegesis. Allegory is still necessary in general to preserve the absolute privilege of the divine Word, its qualitative otherness from our speech, and in particular to relate the Old Testament to the New in terms of typology. Erasmus, however, also insists on beginning interpretation by a careful weighing of the precise grammatical and historical context. The establishment of this "literal" sense (depending on the correct establishment of the text itself) is the prior basis for "figurative" interpretation.[23] Along with this humanist and

---

grounded in classical rhetoric—as opposed to the *devotio moderna* and Thomas à Kempis, whose tendency was to see the maximally spiritual life as silent. Indeed, Erasmus always preferred the translating Ciceronian, Jerome, to the rhetorician of silence, Augustine.

[22] The distinction is discussed by Harth, *Philologie und praktische Philosophie*, p. 45, and Boyle, p. 23.

[23] This Erasmian blend of philological and allegorical methods has been frequently observed: Jarrott, "E's Biblical Humanism," p. 124, distinguishes it from medieval "fourfold" allegory; Harth, pp. 156–59, from the "transcendental" logic of Hugh of St. Victor; Roland H. Bainton, *E. of Christendom* (New York, 1969), pp. 142–43, describes it; Payne, pp. 27, 41–42, finds it rather muddled, an "uneasy balance" (p. 49) between Jerome and Origen. The

disturbing insistence on the semantic principle of context, he also defended a principle of relevance or usefulness, whereby interpretations should elucidate the "philosophy of Christ," parsing the grammar and making effective the rhetoric of the divine *sermo*.[24] Erasmus's hermeneutics are frankly unsystematic; defined in opposition to the frigid and minute abstractions of scholasticism, the purpose of his exegesis (identical in this respect to his theology) is practical and moral: "to inflame our souls with desire for heaven."[25]

The same aim, which permits him to license morally allegorical departures from the "literal" sense on which he otherwise insisted, governs his own scriptural commentaries, including the vastly influential *Paraphrases* on the New Testament.[26] Aside from supplying grammatical analyses, historical background, and extended moral homilies, the characteristic Erasmian exegesis is a dramatized explication of a distinctly "literary" kind. It seeks to engage the emotions of the reader by elaborating the text imaginatively, by recreating its situation in familiar and contemporary terms, by drawing out the emotional power *in* the actual discourse—not by leaping to a presumed "higher" truth beyond or above it.[27] The contrast

---

central document is the *Ratio seu methodus . . . ad veram theologiam* (*L* v), first published in 1518, then in 1519 as the Preface to the 2d ed. of the N.T. The fullest and best analysis of this difficult work is Boyle's.

[24] Boyle's analysis of this process is persuasive, although she finds a principle of control over the polysemous linguistic accommodations of the Gospels in Erasmus's metaphor of Christ as the "orb" of all language: pp. 122–23. I do not see how a metaphor, which is itself nothing if not polysemous, can so function.

[25] *L* v, 77B: "ad caelestia inflammare animos." Erasmus may well have acquired this purpose from what Valla's notes on the N.T. called the *interior sensus*: see Bentley, *Humanists and Holy Writ*, p. 63.

[26] *L* vii. These were printed, as they appeared on separate N.T. books from 1517 to 1524, in countless editions and translations: see *Bibliotheca Erasmiana*, I, 142–50.

[27] Good examples are quoted and discussed by Bainton, pp. 144–45, who remarks the similarity of this procedure to Luther's, and Harth, pp. 161–65, who sees moving the audience, the emotional empowering—not simply the

between these methods may be exemplified by glancing at how medieval and Erasmian exegeses treated a single biblical story, that of the Gadarene swine in Mark 5:1–20. Both St. Thomas's *Catena Aurea* and the *Glossa Ordinaria* proceed by assigning spiritual "significances" mainly to the objects mentioned in the story. Thus, the city (whatever its disputed name and location) as well as the "legion" of devils signify all Gentile nations lost in sin and idolatry; the pigs signify individual sinners. With respect to actions, the pigs' drowning signifies the self-destruction of the proud, impious, and self-indulgent; Christ's refusing to allow the cured madman to follow him signifies that former maniacs are not promoted in the Church. The procedure is governed by the ancient linguistic dualism articulated in Nicholas of Lyra's preface to the *Glossa*: the literal sense is gathered from the words; the three kinds of mystical sense from the things themselves that are signified by the words.[28] Elements or incidents in the narrative are hence selected for spiritual interpretation insofar as they can suggest an allegorical (concerning our belief), moral (concerning our deeds), or anagogical (concerning our hope) abstraction.

The most striking difference between this medieval kind of commentary and the *Paraphrases* is that the latter are exactly what they are called: Erasmus sequentially recounts or summarizes the text; when he arrives at a story, he retells it. His primary focus is on the narrative *as such*, the emotional tone of its circumstances, the shape of its plot, the causal explanation of its actions. His medieval predecessors wholly ignore the story as a series of connected incidents, picking out separate fragments of it on which to develop general discourses about

---

understanding—of the past in the present as the basic motive of all Erasmus's work.

[28] This famous fourfold scheme is quoted by Henri de Lubac, S.J., *Exégèse médiévale* (Paris, 1959–64), I, 23, who fully endorses the husk-and-kernel hermeneutics that his volumes exhaustively describe: cf. I, 358, 363; II, 445, 603. The texts I have consulted are St. Thomas Aquinas, *Catena Aurea in quatuor evangelia* (Rome, 1953) and *Glossa ordinaria cum expositione lyre litterali & morali* (Strasbourg, 1501).

geography or demonology. For them, any isolated detail of the narrative can become a pretext for exposition. For Erasmus, the narrative as it unfolds can also become a pretext—not for exposition, but for further narrative, a retold or even interpolated story designed emotionally to persuade the reader of an ethical issue. Thus he excites compassion for the initial torment of the madman in order to urge that the spiritual degradation of mercenary soldiers is even worse:

if any reken this . . . a miserable, and a terrible sight, let him consydre with him selfe, howe muche more miserable a sight in the eyes of almighty God, is he that hath nothyng els of a man, but the name onely: He . . . who for small wages is hired to go to what warfare soever it be, to sle and murder such as he knoweth not, and never did him harme, to burn villages and good townes. . . . and then shalt thou evidently perceyve howe muche lesse was the fury of the man thus vexed with the devill, then of this wretched and unthrifty caytife.

Throughout his retelling Erasmus stresses the motivation of the characters, evoking and expanding on their feelings and situation. The devils' plea to Christ is compared to a band of ruffians' request to their feudal lord. Erasmus writes their dialogue: "We desire no wages, but onely that your grace wyll suffer us to raunge abrode in the countrey, and robbe and reave at oure owne peryll." The magnitude of the madman's miraculous change from chain-bursting violence to quiet submissiveness at the feet of Jesus is evoked at length and in concrete detail. Erasmus is also concerned to explain the actions of the tale, summoning the historical fact that pigs were regarded as unclean by the Jews to account for Jesus' permitting their destruction, "teachyng us hereby that for to save, even but one man, we ought not to passe upon the losse of other worldly thynges, be it never so great."[29] While Erasmus's eagerness to draw morals allowed him also to include some traditional allegorical significances, both his moralizing and his allegoriz-

---

[29] *The first tome . . . of the Paraphrase of Erasmus upon the newe testamente* (London, 1548), sigs. Ee6ᵛ–Ff1ᵛ. The original text, of which this translation is good, is in *L* VI.

ing are performed on a revolutionary new basis. The medieval tradition found scriptural meaning in the "things" that the words of the story could be said to "represent"; Erasmus found it in the story that the words told. The *Paraphrases* were advisedly named, and Erasmus explicitly claimed not to be writing what his age knew as "commentary."[30] In his exegetical practice, the meaning of the biblical text was not what it "stood for," but what happened in it.

As Erasmus applied the techniques of secular philology to the editing of the sacred text, so he applied those of secular rhetoric to its interpretation.[31] The former application revived an ancient tradition; the latter was new, and had profound semantic implications. How new it was then is not now easy to appreciate, for two reasons. First, our long familiarity with subsequent centuries of pulpit oratory[32] and literary discussion has rendered quite banal such attempts at the emotional vivification of a text, as banal indeed as Valla's pioneering observations of the semantic changes wrought by grammar. Second, both the didactic motive and its means of implementation are, taken separately, quite old. The rhetorical techniques are derived from the association of the orator and the poet in the entire Ciceronian/Horatian tradition: he is to persuade by moving the feelings of the audience.

What is new is precisely the combination, the unification of

[30] Preface to John, *The first tome*, sig. ( )5ᵛ, where he must nonetheless admit that "a Paraphrase is a kynd of commentarie."

[31] J.W.H. Atkins observed long ago that with Erasmus's N.T. "a new and illuminating approach to literature had been opened up," and went on to describe John Colet's prior use of it in his lectures on Romans: *English Literary Criticism: the Renascence* (London, 1947), pp. 57–59. By the "new approach" Atkins meant the investigation of historical context and of individual style.

[32] In sixteenth-century England the *Paraphrases* themselves were a model for this: copies were appointed by law under Edward VI and Elizabeth I to be kept in every parish church, where they served as inspiration and trots for preachers. The great extent to which Erasmus's teachings were congenial to and kidnapped by English Protestantism is concisely expressed in Nicholas Udall's Preface to the 2d ed. of *The first Tome . . . of the Paraphrases . . . corrected* (London, 1551), sig. ¢¢7ᵛ.

these means and that motive, as well as their employment in the interpretation of Scripture. To be ravished by eloquence, the archetypal humanist delight, is becoming coextensive with moral instruction. What in terms of production the discipline of rhetoric had confined to mere opinion-manipulation—the skillful arousal and exploitation of the audience's emotions— and then sought to legitimize by asserting the good moral character of the speaker, is being literally reconsecrated in terms of reception to bring about a genuine enlightenment. To urge the teaching of virtue, not in addition to, or in spite of, or wholly apart from, but rather by means of the emotional engagement of the reader was the contribution, probably original, made to secular literary theory by Sir Philip Sidney's *Apologie for Poetrie*. Writing about 1583, Sidney of course had the benefit of all the Italian arguments on the subject that did not yet exist when Erasmus was interpreting the Gospels.[33] But the new semantic dimension implied by his treatment of Scripture is precisely that presupposed by Sidney's treatment of fiction: the meaning of the text is the emotion that it effects in the reader.

In the first English critical treatise that has itself become literature, Sidney's whole defense of fiction proceeds from the assumption of original sin. Fiction is legitimized as the supreme didactic agent in a fallen world, where the final end of all learning is to "draw vs to as high a perfection as our degenerate soules, made worse by theyr clayey lodgings, can be capable of." Since this end is "of well dooing and not of well knowing onely," fiction is superior to both philosophy and history, its rivals in moral education, because it alone can "move" our infected will to moral action. Sidney repeats the standard Aristotelian/Horatian formula that poetry is an art of

---

[33] I can find none of Sidney's predecessors, as presented by Bernard Weinberg, *A History of Literary Criticism in the Italian Renaissance*, 2 vols. (Chicago, 1961), who quite articulates his exact position, which is, however, a matter of recombining the elements of a ubiquitous tradition. The *Apologie* is quoted from the edition of O. B. Hardison, Jr., in *English Literary Criticism: The Renaissance* (New York, 1963).

imitation whose purpose is to teach and delight; the innovation lies in the precise relation between *prodesse* and *delectare*. They are simply coextensive: we are not led through the pleasure of the text (the *dulce*) to the intellectual abstractions that it stands for or contains (the *utile*); rather, the delight of the story is what instructs us by moving our will. "Who readeth *Aeneas* carrying olde *Anchises* on his back, that wisheth not it were his fortune to perfourme so excellent an acte?" Sidney asks rhetorically. It is the tale itself, and not its "significance," located elsewhere, "which holdeth children from play, and old men from the chimney corner." And what the tale means is the emotional conviction it has wrought in the reader. Sidney himself wished to perform excellent acts and in fact died, famously, in the attempt to do so.[34] He cites two other tales to emphasize the well-doing that they produced. Menenius Agrippa's fable of the belly (later dramatized by Shakespeare in *Coriolanus*) as "applied by him wrought such effect in the people, as I neuer read that euer words brought forth but then so suddaine and so good an alteration." And Nathan's story of the poor man's cherished lamb (2 Sam. 12), "the applycation most diuinely true, but the discourse it selfe fayned . . . made *Dauid* . . . as in a glasse to see his own filthines." The precise semantic force of "application" dates only from the Renaissance and the practice of reforming preachers.[35] And it received great reemphasis from the importance placed by Protestants on what they called the "uses" of Scripture in preaching.[36] To make the divine Word effective in the interior and everyday lives of the audience was their impeccably Eras-

---

[34] The splendid story is told in Sir Fulke Greville's *Life of . . . Sidney*, ed. Nowell Smith (Oxford, 1907), pp. 127–33.

[35] In the hermeneutic sense of attributing a particular meaning to a statement, the *OED* finds the first use of "apply" in Wyclif, ca. 1375, and of "application" in 1493.

[36] These are summarized by William Haller, *The Rise of Puritanism* (New York, 1957; 1st ed. 1938), pp. 135–37. They focused, of course, less on explaining doctrines than on arousing emotions, aiming "to shape and direct feeling and conduct."

mian aim. The fundamental dynamic of Sidney's defense thus seems to proceed much more directly from reformed ways of treating Scripture than from Italian theoretical debates about literature. Reading and interpretation, for both Erasmus and Sidney, were to "inflame our souls."

Yet even Erasmian exegesis had been derived from the secular rhetorical/literary tradition, in which emotional arousal had long been one avenue of moral instruction. The crucial difference, as I have said, lies in making them coextensive in a way that no longer separates the words of the text from its meaning. Conventional theory maintained this separation: the "pleasure" given by the language of the text was sometimes said to accompany its moral utility; "but more usually it is reduced to the role of a means or instrument for the achievement of that utility. As a device for stirring the emotions of the reader and persuading him through examples, pleasure makes him amenable to the moral teachings that are the real end of the poet."[37] Here "pleasure" can be merely our admiration of felicitous diction; if it stirs our feelings it does so to soften us up for the "real" teaching that is carried on somewhere else in some other way. Pleasure is a "means or instrument" in the sense of a diverting tactic to hold our interest between bouts of instruction, or in the sense of an "example" that engages us and points us toward such instruction. In neither case is it specifically conceived as the "means" in the sense of the *agent* of that instruction. It is precisely the change from instrumentality to agency, from vehicle to actor at the level of moral purpose that presumes an altered semantic awareness at the level of interpretation. The conventional theory was of course the perfect sanction for the medieval habit of allegorical reading, which had also been transferred from Scripture to poetry by such as Dante and Salutati. The masses might content themselves with a delightful story, but the more discerning would be instructed

---

[37] Weinberg, *Literary Criticism*, I, 150. He is summarizing Horatian literary theory in mid-sixteenth-century Italy; but, as he remarks, the aim "aut prodesse aut delectare" was a universal commonplace.

by what it veiled, the doctrine that it could be found to "stand for." The time-honored image for this process, though it allowed that some instruction might be absorbed willy-nilly from a pleasurable tale, still maintained their separation: the sugar-coated pill, the "wholesome" hidden in the "sweet" (Sidney repeats this), which is but the ethical version of the Augustinian semantic dualism of the kernel and the husk. Sidney, however, also offers another image, which crystallizes the whole implicit shift between regarding meaning as separably contained in words and as inseparably constituted by them: he calls the delight of the text "a medicine of Cherries." The sweet simply *is* the wholesome; pleasure neither contains nor conceals profit, but constitutes it.

I am laboring this point because it illustrates so well how the Renaissance generated, out of the received linguistic concerns of the Middle Ages and the freshly examined ones of antiquity, new ways of apprehending the meaning of language that underlay the new forms of religion and literature that it developed. The particular new way employed by Erasmian exegesis and advocated by Sidneian criticism, arrived at by unifying the text's emotional power and its instructive value, ultimately postulates what might be called an "affective semantics."[38]

---

[38] By this term I understand only the revalued rhetorical process I have described. It is not to be confused with the ancient conviction that to interpret the words of the Holy Spirit requires illumination by that Spirit—a tautology repeated by Protestants and Catholics alike that can coexist with any semantic assumption made in practice. The term should also not be confused with the similar activity that Stanley E. Fish has made into an interesting contemporary theory: "Literature in the Reader: Affective Stylistics," *New Literary History* 2 (1970), 123–62. It is curious that Fish has elected to use a theory grounded in the temporal effects of language on a reader to identify a literary tradition that unfolds from the Platonic/Augustinian distrust of language itself, with the paradoxical result announced in his title: *Self-Consuming Artifacts: The Experience of Seventeenth-Century Literature* (Berkeley, 1972). A counter literary tradition, proceeding from Ovidian rhetoric, is explicitly opposed to the Platonic one by Richard A. Lanham, *The Motives of Eloquence* (New Haven, 1976). Both books, taken together, suggest the range of conflicts in literature between traditional semantic assumptions and the challenges to them that this book is describing.

This new way of apprehending meaning—that is, interpreting a text not by extracting from it kernels of abstraction but by using all of its concrete detail to move the will—results in a new kind of meaning apprehended: it becomes our emotional experience of the text. This is the kind of meaning that Luther also found in Scripture, that generations of Protestant divines expounded in sermons, and that caused so much trouble and divisiveness in Protestant hermeneutics. It is also the kind of meaning that can be found in some of the greatest Renaissance fictions. What Erasmus called the "sermonis vim" becomes in both Scripture and literature the power of language to constitute experience in and for the reader, which is its meaning.

Two brief examples of this constitutive power in two radically different Renaissance fictions must suffice to suggest the vital ramifications in literature of the kind of semantic awareness that proved, as we shall see, unsustainable at the formal levels of biblical interpretation, where it was initially practiced. At that level, it was introduced by Erasmus and Luther in specific opposition to medieval allegorizing; but allegory itself was by no means generally abandoned. An affective semantics emerges to coexist and compete with the standard modes of representing and signifying and conveying. This is exactly what happens in *The Faerie Queene*, which helps considerably to account for the slipperiness of its allegory as critics have tried to grasp it. Spenser himself speaks of allegory, in the letter to Raleigh, as a "method" for achieving the Sidneian delight that is instruction. The method, however, is subordinate (and hence can vary, as the twelvefold "Aristotelian" scheme in the letter does not appear in the poem) to the purpose. The meanings pointed at through the story are inscribed within the meaning enacted by the story. Spenser describes the latter activity, both in himself and in his poem, with a verb not of reference but of creation. "The general intention and meaning" of the whole poem he has "fashioned," he tells us, "is to fashion a gentleman or noble person in virtuous and gentle discipline." The "gentleman" is at the same time both character (Arthur and the eponymous heroes of the six books) and reader: we are made to share their moral formation. To "fashion" (*facere*) is to do what a blacksmith does with iron, to transfer to the realm of meaning the literal etymology of the poet as "maker" in as physical and concrete a sense as Montaigne's whole vocabulary of semantic manipulation. No poet creates *ex nihilo*, and allegorical significances are simply a part of the material with which he works. But the meaning he makes out of it "is best described as a developing psychological experience within the reader." The identification of this experience "with the direct experience of language" is what makes possible the interpretation of crucial episodes in the poem that have "no clear allegorical translation."[39] The meaning invoked by Sidney's and Spenser's new version of traditional didacticism is specifically an activity, a function of use, a transaction between utterance and hearer, text and reader.

It was the Renaissance revaluation of the ethical *results* of such transactions that permitted them to be redefined in practice as a new kind of genuinely semantic operation. The potency of discourse had first to be regarded as "inflaming" us for virtue instead of vice. If, to take the best-known example, the emotional response to the tale of Lancelot could produce only the commission of adultery by Paolo and Francesca (*Inferno*, v. 121ff.), that affective transaction could hardly qualify as a meaning of the text. As Erasmus reversed the value of the result, he legitimized the transaction and so reversed the kind and direction of the relation between divine and human language. Dante interpreted poetry like Scripture—allegorically; Erasmus interpreted Scripture like poetry—affectively. So when Sidney and Spenser read and wrote heroic romance, they apprehended and created meaning as a dynamic function—the emotional experience of the text which would, ideally, produce excellent action and virtuous discipline.

[39] Paul J. Alpers, *The Poetry of "The Faerie Queene"* (Princeton, 1967), pp. 14, 18. Alpers' analyses demonstrate this kind of semantic activity, which he calls "rhetorical." Lanham, pp. 172–76, compares *The Faerie Queene* with *Gargantua and Pantagruel* as texts that simultaneously invite and frustrate or ignore allegorical interpretation.

But in the hands of another writer, what affective semantics produced was a finely ambiguous form of madness: Don Quixote is the Renaissance reader par excellence, as "inflamed" for virtuous deeds as Sidney could demand. Without pausing to explore in detail the manifold paradoxes of Cervantes' text, I wish merely to emphasize that the agency of the Don's inflammation is romance apprehended in the new way, as a story whose concrete details are felt so vividly that their reenactment becomes obsessive delusion. Don Quixote is not responding to any "signified" abstractions; though he must occasionally expound, in comic exasperation, parts of the chivalric code to Sancho, his obsession is not to preach doctrines upon nor draw morals from but rather to reenact what he has read. The Don's semantic world is completely without "representation"; the objects and events in it do not "stand for" anything. They are what he has read they are; the barber's basin *is* Mambrino's helmet. Hence the necessary explanation of "enchantment" when hard knocks keep proving him wrong. Yet, as his adventures proceed, his wrongness about "facts" becomes balanced by his rightness about ideals and motives; his fictional reading of the world works its own enchantment, has its own effects (not all of them damaging) on that world. In part II, of course, the very fiction in which he appears has become a part of that world, insofar as the characters have read his prior "history." Insofar as they respond to him accordingly, the action that occurs in their "world" is constituted by that "history"—which, as the consistent mockery of the persona of Cid Hamet never lets us forget, is also fiction. In short, the whole idea of "reality," employed in all its brutal solidity to mock the fictive meaning our hero invests it with, is itself mocked, and indeed made to dissolve, in the whole narrative framework. The conventional dichotomies on which the text ironically insists—fact and fiction, real and ideal, *res* and *verba*—melt into indistinguishable unities.

The Don fairly articulates this new semantic awareness when he is pressed, on two occasions, about the actual existence of Dulcinea. To Sancho (1.25) he explains that the purpose she serves is existence enough; to the Duchess (II.32) that it is irrelevant whether she be real or imaginary. Dulcinea is literally but a word; and the comic absurdity of seeking its meaning in the object supposedly "referred to," the porcine Aldonza Lorenzo (the fallacy that the Don himself repudiates), is the cosmic semantic joke that runs through the whole novel. "Cosmic" because it presumes the Vallesque insight that collapsed ontology into semantics: the meaning, that is, the existence, of Dulcinea is indeed the use that she has in the language game of chivalry as Don Quixote plays it. To put it another way, she personifies Sidney's definition of fiction: "feigned" discourse that has "true" application.

The subject of Don Quixote, which it partly shares with the romances it partly ridicules, is the power of language to make meanings, create experience, and shape worlds. When the Don gives up the exercise of this power and subsides into the "real" world, he dies. The final paragraph of the book is an ironic elegy to the same power: Cid Hamet's triumphant address to his pen, hung up in retirement, having forever destroyed the credit of chivalry in the world. To celebrate such destruction is to refuse to acknowledge what the entire text demonstrates about the constitutive power of words. It is also a prophecy of what will happen to the consciousness of this power, as developed throughout the Renaissance, in the language theory of the next couple of centuries. As an enactment of this power, Don Quixote is a supremely Renaissance book; as the first modern novel and the last medieval romance, it builds a new mode of fiction by reapprehending the old one in terms of all the new semantic energies released in the philosophy, philology, rhetoric, vernacular debate, and religious reform of the period.

As such, Cervantes' masterpiece is one logical conclusion of the linguistic ferment I am tracing; but I have introduced it at this point because it focuses on what became in Protestantism the most problematic consequence of the affective semantics that reinterpreted Scripture and revalued literature. This is the vexed question of discriminating "literal" from "figurative" senses. One can easily imagine Sidney, for example, in a Platonic mood reacting with some horror to Don Quixote's acting out the emotional engagement recommended in the *Apologie* as the justifying and defining quality of literature. "Forsooth," Sidney might say, "this windmill-tilting rascal hath mistook me quite, for he imitates but as the slavish ape whose creeping mind cannot lift itself from the earth of the letter to the sky of the spirit, fetching down from my true commonplaces most false applications."[40] By drawing such a distinction, Sidney would claim that he never intended anyone to don armor and sally forth to perpetrate virtue. But if we were minded to defend the Don, we could claim that the words Sidney used tell us to do just that. We would then be having exactly the kind of argument that we are shortly going to examine in the case of Scripture, whose very terms—"literal" and "figurative"—are being redefined and counter-defined in the course of it.

In one acceptation or another, the distinction has always seemed necessary—a part of common usage, therefore of common sense—and the penalties for denying or neglecting it severe. The penalty for Don Quixote is madness of a comically benevolent and finally metaphorical kind. The same penalty, neither benevolent nor "figurative," was incurred by some actual Protestants who insisted, as the Don did, on behaving according to the "literal" Word. A group of Anabaptists in Zwingli's Switzerland took literally the text, "Except ye . . . become as little children, ye shall not enter into the kingdom of heaven" (Matt. 18:3). They devoted themselves to play, rolling about on the ground tossing pine cones, until in the course of their revels one of them decapitated his brother.[41] Thus to return, as did virtually all the reformers, via affective

---

[40] I concoct this speech from a few of Sidney's phrases in the *Apologie* and the *Old Arcadia* III.4. I am not suggesting that Sidney might not also have fully appreciated the paradoxes of *Don Quixote* as a whole.

[41] This anecdote is quoted from Oeschli's *History of Switzerland* by V.H.H. Green, *Renaissance and Reformation*, 2d ed. (London, 1964), p. 165. Oeschli calls them "lunatics."

semantics to some version of the "literal" sense was to conflate the common distinction at the risk and peril of apparent sanity, with consequences that ranged from the literarily sublime to the actually terrible.[42] The magnitude of these consequences is what gives all the wrangling about "literal" and "figurative" senses an importance far beyond the academy, where the wrangling continues today in more sophisticated metalanguages. Such debates about what and how language means, which were often confused and jejune, nonetheless entailed profound alterations in the conduct of life. To reorient semantic assumptions, to read differently, is to re-create both ourselves and our world.

ii. Luther and Scripture

And as there is greater power in the word than   —MARTIN LUTHER
in the sign, so there is greater power in the testament than in the sacrament.

Of all the reformers, Luther insisted the most strenuously on one "literal" sense of Scripture. What he came to include in this was a great deal more than the kind of philological attention to grammar and historical context that Erasmus advocated, from the example of Valla, as the "literal" sense. For Luther, the nexus of the problem was the Old Testament (with which Erasmus was never primarily concerned), where it had been since the earliest arguments over the establishment of the scriptural canon. Indeed, the Old Testament had only become canonical in a way that denuded it of "literal," in the sense of historical, meaning. The Marcionite movement in the second century had sought to reject it entirely, urging that since the

---

[42] I can only note the fascinating and difficult questions here raised about the inseparable connection between language and psychology embedded in classical rhetoric and modern psychoanalysis. When is a misuse of *oratio* a defect in *ratio*; when do misreadings become pathologies and how can we tell? On the particular pathology of acting out verbal expressions, see D. Wilfred Abse, *Speech and Reason: Language Disorder in Mental Disease* (Charlottesville, Va., 1971).

new law of the Gospels had simply abrogated that of Moses, all of Jewish history was irrelevant to the new dispensation. The Old Testament was canonized by insisting on its continued relevance to Christian believers by virtue of typological and allegorical interpretation. It was saved at the price of becoming a "shadow" or "figure" of the future, so that the numerous problems of its actual historical past just disappeared.[43] Thus the theological determination of what the Word means entailed the traditional theory of how words mean: by referring to something else.[44] We have already observed how referential semantics involves an infinite regress in the location of meaning; the same process merely reverses direction in the case of the Old Testament, whose meaning becomes locatable only as an infinite progress. Typology displaced the meaning of the Old Testament into the New; moral allegories into the present of the believer; anagogical ones into the prophecy of the last things. In all these forms of interpretation the words of the Old Testament are but signs whose signifieds are found or predicted only in an ever-ongoing future: they are veils to be seen through or torn away.[45]

[43] Hans von Campenhausen, *Die Entstehung der Christlichen Bibel* (Tübingen, 1968), p. 351. Of the medieval exegetes described by Beryl Smalley (*The Study of the Bible in the Middle Ages*, 2d ed. [Oxford, 1952], pp. 91–102) who did pay renewed attention to the "literal" sense of the O.T., none conceived that in itself it could have spiritual effects.

[44] An acute example of the continuing problem the O.T. posed is the "literal" eroticism of the Song of Solomon, which Castellio still wanted to expel from the canon in Calvin's Geneva: R. H. Bainton, "The Bible in the Reformation," in *The Cambridge History of the Bible* (Cambridge, 1963), II, 8–9. Seven rabbinical and eleven Christian allegories of the book are enumerated by Frederic W. Farrar, *History of Interpretation* (New York, 1886), pp. 32–33. Farrar, by the way, despite his prejudices and age, is still an excellent survey of the field.

[45] This is true in practice despite occasional theoretical admonitions, like Hugh of St. Victor's, that "it is necessary both to remain faithful to the historical sense and to understand the Law in a spiritual way": *Didascalicon*, tr. Jerome Taylor (New York, 1961), p. 123 (v.4). Even when Hugh himself notices the "historical sense," it is as a kind of obstacle to be cleared on the way to the "deeper meaning": p. 149 (VI.10–11).

The conventional attitude toward the Old Testament thereby produced, against which Luther was reacting, is concisely summarized in a treatise of Juan Luis Vives. Although Vives tried to be avant-garde in philosophy and Latinity, his exegesis is typically medieval. In Eden, he explains, man was instructed by God "without speech and letters." But all such knowledge having been lost by original sin, God supplies us with written records containing vestiges of natural law for managing earthly life, which are inadequate in our fallen condition, and are therefore supplemented by the hope of the coming of Christ. Thus Adam was the first prophet of Christ, the death of Abel a figure of Christ, Noah's ark a figure of baptism and the Church. But these significances were opaque to the Jews as well as to pagan nations, who remained unconvinced by the promise even when it was fulfilled by Christ's coming. Thus their "law is entirely a shadow," for their real history is but a figuration of Christ. The prophets are dark and difficult because they were not aware of what they were saying. Only "Christ illuminated their obscurities," without whom Judaic letters remain hard and unworthy of God or man, mere shadows and darkness.[46]

This picture of the poor benighted Hebrews, ignorant of what they could not possibly have known, shows how their historical circumstances could not remotely qualify for inclusion in the meaning of their texts. The "historical sense," traditionally a part of the "literal," has itself become figural: Old Testament history *is* figures. Vives provides additional "testimony to the loss of a meaningful distinction between literal

---

[46] *De veritate fidei christianae*, in *Opera* (Basle, 1555), II, 361, 364–65: "Deus quum hominem condidisset, edocuit illum sine voce & literis. . . . Lex autem tota, umbra est. . . . Has omnes obscuritates illustravit Christus. . . . Umbris ergo & caligini Veteris testamenti tanquam nocti tenebrae succesit sol Christi." The precisely opposite view—a radical historicism unacceptable even to the Protestantism that spawned it—which denied any Christological interpretation of the O.T. and confined its meaning wholly within Hebrew history was urged by Michael Servetus in 1542. See Jerome Friedman, "Servetus and the Psalms: The Exegesis of Heresy," in *Histoire de l'exégèse au XVIe siècle*, ed. Olivier Fatio and Pierre Fraenkel (Geneva, 1978), pp. 164–78.

and spiritual interpretation," and illustrates in the earlier six-teenth century the hermeneutic situation of the late Middle Ages: "The language used to describe the various senses of Scripture had virtually collapsed. One could no longer assume . . . that a reference to the 'literal sense' meant the historical, grammatical meaning of the text."[47] Indeed, the historical di-mension in the actual words was systematically treated by this hermeneutics as *not* a part of their meaning. It is typically par-adoxical that Vives, advocate of eloquence, editor of St. Au-gustine, and troubled follower of Valla, should entirely sus-pend his sporadic humanist awareness of the semantic importance of historical context and of words themselves when he dealt with the Old Testament. Erasmus saw the New Testament with this awareness, explicitly reconstructing its meaning in the emotional power of its eloquence. But it was Luther who developed the latter most clearly and radically into a hermeneutics that encompassed the Old Testament along with the New by apprehending the historical experience re-corded in its words as emotionally efficacious in the present of the believer. For Luther, the "spiritual" meanings derived from this affective semantics were not "figurative" but histor-ical, and therefore constituted what he regarded as the single "literal" sense of Scripture.

James Preus has demonstrated how Luther arrived at this revolutionary reading of the Bible in his lectures on the Psalms between 1513 and 1516.[48] The Hebrews, as Luther saw them, may not have had grace, but they had faith in the testimony of the promise made to Israel through Abraham. This promise, an historical event, is also being made to us by the heard Word. The promise is for the future—theirs of the advent of the Mes-

---

[47] James Samuel Preus, *From Shadow to Promise: O.T. Interpretation from Au-gustine to the Young Luther* (Cambridge, Mass., 1969), pp. 105, 176. He cites, among many examples, the assertion of James Perez that the spiritual signifi-cance of the O.T. is that it is literally about Christ, which seems just what Vives is asserting by equating the historical and the figural.

[48] *From Shadow to Promise*, esp. pp. 184–211. Luther's "Dictata super Psal-terium" are in *Werke*, IV (Weimar, 1886), hereafter *WA*.

siah, ours of His Second Coming—but it is made to and in the present of every hearer. And its meaning is the faith it invites us to place in it—a transaction not of cognition but of emotion and will. Luther explicates the praises, petitions, and confessions of the Psalmists not as semantic containers but as semantic agents. Both his principles and his procedure are exemplified in his treatment of the verse, "Thy word is a lamp unto my feet, and a light unto my path" (Ps. 119:105). Because the lamp directs the feet, he explains, "faith requires emotion, not intellect. It is not necessary that you should understand, but that you should wish; not that you should know, but that you should do those things that are heard." The light is not given to the eyes, for we are blind and ignorant. Faith does not illumine the mind, but the feelings, through which we are saved by hearing the Word, moved to follow it we know not where. God's Word is thus miraculous, unlike the language of human wisdom.[49]

This miracle, however, is not the usual magic semantic guarantee of the correspondence with things; it is rather the power of the divine discourse to arouse the affections and move the will. Luther continues to admire this power in the subsequent verses, "Princes have persecuted me without a cause: but my heart standeth in awe of thy word. I rejoice at thy word, as one that findeth great spoil" (161–62). He celebrates the great and fearful sound of God's voice, speaking, promising, threatening. He notes that the Word, not the church, defends us against enemies. He elaborates the simultaneous contrast and comparison of words and riches. He finds that the words of God strengthen the spirit more than the

[49] WA IV, 356: "Et tamen est lucerna, quia pedes dirigit et affectum, non intellectum requirit fides. Non ut intelligas, sed ut velis oportet, non ut scias, sed ut facias ea que audiuntur. . . . Sic enim fides non intellectum illuminat . . . sed affectum: hunc etiam ducit quo salvetur, et hoc per auditum verbi. Audiens enim affectus verbum incipit ire post ipsum nesciens quo. Igitur mirabile est verbum dei. . . . Non sic verbum litere et humane sapientie." (Luther's text is the Vulgate, where this Psalm, a seriatim descant on the letters of the Hebrew alphabet, is numbered 118.)

words of men weaken the flesh, and exclaims, "Wondrous exchange, that words should prevail over things, and things so potent and contrary! Thus Isaiah promises . . . by the naked word without the thing having been produced, but not without the thing to be produced."[50] The divine Word may be unique in the degree of its efficacy; but the kind of efficacy it has as well as the manner of its operation are those of ordinary language. And this manner, for Luther, is not representational. He exfoliates the felt meanings of metaphors and similes not in terms of what they "stand for," but in terms of the *actions* they imply: the light giving direction to the feet; the believer discovering a treasure. The treasure Luther himself discovered, as Preus concludes, is that "words are intrinsically causal: they cause expectation, fear, doubt, hope, or trust in the one who hears what they say. Not because a concealed grace comes with them, but simply from what they say as 'naked words.' "[51]

In this way Luther develops the "sermonis vim" that was central to humanism into an explicitly constitutive and affective semantics, liberating it by the way from any restriction to learned languages and literate elites. Words act on, produce emotions in, and should result in actions from the whole community of hearers. The kind of emotion, however, that constitutes for Luther the historical and "literal" sense of the Old Testament is produced less by its "naked words" than by his reading of the Pauline epistles, of which he had made an intensive prior study. The joyful trust in the Word that makes us all children of the promise is the primal feeling that is already leading him toward his revolutionary theology: justification

---

[50] *WA* IV, 381: "Mira permutatio, ut verba prevaleant rebus et rebus contrariis atque fortissimis! Sicut promissit Isaie. . . . Verbo inquit, scilicet nudo sine re exhibita, sed non sine re exhibenda."

[51] *From Shadow to Promise*, p. 254. We may note in addition that what Luther hears in God's voice—speaking, promising, threatening—are precisely the two kinds of "force" (locutionary and illocutionary) exercised by the "performative utterances" of speech-act theory: J. L. Austin, *How To Do Things with Words*, ed. J. O. Urmson (Cambridge, Mass., 1962).

by faith alone on the basis of Scripture alone, which is sufficient, clear, has one primary sense and interprets itself. Erasmus made mediating discourse central to his theology; Luther made the creating Word more central to his, extending its power even to the institution that was its custodian: "The church does not make the Word but is made by the Word."[52] The old theological determination of scriptural meaning entailed a referential semantics, whereas Luther's new theology seems to be entailed by the affective semantics that completely transformed the relation of the Old Testament to the New by finding its "spirit" in—not beyond—its "letter," its meanings in its words. In this context, "The old dichotomy of 'word' and 'meaning,' modeled on the sacramental sign and *res*, and described in terms of killing letter and life-giving spirit, lost its predominant role."[53]

In other contexts, however, particularly that of the sacraments themselves, the old dichotomies were not to be surmounted, and returned again and again to plague Luther's efforts to conflate them all. The potent efficaciousness of the Word as he experienced it furnished him, after 1517, with the hermeneutic unification of words and meanings that was an equally potent polemical weapon against traditional dualisms. With increasing gusto, Luther defied the authority that refused his reforms basically by insisting on bringing together all that it had kept apart: the Old Testament and the New, the letter and the spirit, priests and the laity, Scripture and common people, the rites of worship and the worshipper. In this campaign his constitutive, affective semantics became something of a two-edged sword, keenly undercutting the distinctions he wished to eliminate, but equally threatening to others that needed to be maintained. Luther's efforts to be consistent in his demand for semantic unity led him into some very curious

[52] This famous dictum is quoted by Farrar, *History of Interpretation*, in a succinct presentation of Luther's exegetic principles: pp. 325–35. Jaroslav Pelikan, *Luther the Expositor* (St. Louis, 1959), is mainly concerned with the development of his theology in the course of controversies.

[53] Preus, *From Shadow to Promise*, p. 271.

and confusing maneuvers when it came to reinterpreting the sacraments.

In accordance with the absolute primacy he gave the Word, Luther denies to the sacraments any operative power to create faith and, a fortiori, promote salvation. The Word can be heard and believed quite "apart from the sign or sacrament." To assault the orthodox position for overvaluing the mere "sign," Luther appeals to the standard form of dualism: "The sign as such is incomparably less than the thing signified." He insists that the scriptural usage of "sacramentum," however, is wholly different from "the sense in which we use the term"— that is, to designate the sign, the outward and visible water or bread. Noting that in the Vulgate the word translates the Greek for "mystery," he claims that "sacramentum" in the Bible "denotes not the sign of a sacred thing, but the sacred, secret, hidden thing itself." As such, it cannot produce faith, but requires faith to be properly received, understood, and experienced. Luther is thus retaining the sacramental dualism in order to stress the importance of the invisible mystery (which he locates in the biblical usage of the word), but is refusing altogether the usual analogy or assumed identity between this dualism and the linguistic. The "sign" is the object; it is never the word. The whole traditional process of signification is no longer applied to language: things may signify, but words act, perform, create. Hence Luther's famous and literal insistence that the real body and blood of Christ are present in the equally real bread and wine of the Lord's Supper. They are there simply because the words of institution say they are. "What does it matter if philosophy cannot fathom this? The Holy Spirit is greater than Aristotle." What philosophy cannot fathom, grammar can nonetheless assert, and Luther is at pains to show that the words, "this is my body; this is my blood," mean just what they say by analyzing the referents of the pronouns in Greek and Hebrew. He consistently follows the logic of humanist textual scholarship, which he articulates: the words of Scripture "are to be retained in their simplest meaning as far as possible. Unless the context manifestly compels it, they are not to be understood apart from their grammatical and proper sense."[54]

What Luther found this "proper" sense to be in the case of the Eucharist is a direct consequence of his constitutive semantics, his total refusal to apply the dualistic process of representing or signifying to language. Almost none of his fellow reformers was prepared to make this revolutionary distinction between sacramental and semantic operations. Thus the principal doctrinal differences that divided the Protestant movement from the beginning reflected the clash between traditional semantic assumptions and those generated by all the new forms of attention—structural, cognitive, and emotional—to language as a sociohistorical product. The arguments over how the body and blood of Christ are present in the bread and wine are arguments about how language means and how we apprehend that meaning.

Luther simply refused to apprehend it figuratively. Detesting even more than Erasmus the tradition of medieval allegory, Luther attacks the whole conception of *figura* along with the moral dualism that supported it. Arguing *That These Words of Christ, "This is my body . . . ," Still Stand Firm against the Fanatics* (1527), he denies Zwingli's contention that "is" means "represents" and Oecolampadius's that "my body" means "sign of my body." Luther insists that no figurative reading is required in order to accept the unfathomable mystery asserted by the words in their "simplest" sense, just as we accept the mysteries of the triune God and the union of two natures in Christ. His opponents had supported their figurative readings by urging the conventional moral superiority of the spirit (the intangible "meaning") over the flesh (the tangible object or "letter"). Luther completely redefines this conventional dichotomy: "All is spirit, spiritual, and an object of the Spirit, in reality and in name, which comes from the Holy Spirit, be it

[54] This paragraph summarizes the position expressed in his first major critique of the sacraments, *The Babylonian Capitivity of the Church* (1520), quoted from the American Edition of the *Works* (hereafter *AE*), ed. Pelikan and Lehmann (St. Louis and Philadelphia, 1955–73), XXXVI.

as physical or material, outward or visible as it may; on the other hand, all is flesh and fleshly which comes from the natural power of the flesh, without spirit, be it as inward and invisible as it may."[55] He is claiming that the distinction is not ontological and static, but functional and dynamic. The "flesh" is not morally inferior by nature, but with respect to the motive or purpose of its use. For Luther, flesh may be spirit ethically, just as the literal may be the spiritual semantically. Not content with coalescing the old categories in order to eliminate any need for a word to "stand for" something else, he tries to dismantle even the vocabulary of "signifying." Oecolampadius read "body" as "sign" on the authority of Tertullian's *figura*, mistakenly taken, says Luther, to mean "type," "as Adam is called a figure or type of Christ. . . . But *figura* in the Latin language does not mean that kind of type; the word *figura* is misused in such an instance." It merely means "form" as tangible shape or *gestalt*.[56]

Such an appeal to historical usage—using the classical to discredit the medieval—is, as we have seen, a typically paradoxical maneuver of humanism: describing the one in order to proscribe the other. Luther makes it here in order once again to deny that language has meaning by figural representation. He now distinguishes words from types as he before distinguished them from sacraments. And he wants to get rid of *figurae* al-

---

[55] *AE* XXXVII, 99. Luther's distinction corresponds to what many modern scholars take to be the accurate Pauline view of the matter. John A. T. Robinson, partly following Bultmann, has argued that Paul uses neither of his two Greek words for "flesh" to separate the material from the immaterial in the usual way, but rather to designate the entire person differently regarded: *The Body: A Study in Pauline Theology* (London, 1952), esp. pp. 24–25, 30–31. For evidence that Erasmus modified his standard Platonic dualism in this direction, see John B. Payne, "The Significance of Lutheranizing Changes in E's Interpretation of Paul's Letters to the Romans and the Galatians in his *Annotationes* (1527) and *Paraphrases* (1532)," in *Histoire de l'exégèse au XVIe siècle*, pp. 314–15. Also in this volume Jean-Claude Margolin finds a similar non-Platonic use of "flesh" in "Bovelles et son commentaire de l'évangile johannique," p. 243.

[56] *AE* XXXVII, 109–10.

together, to allow nothing to displace the meaning from the word. It is the absolute identification of meanings with single words that makes Luther's literalism so extreme, so unacceptable to his contemporaries, and so problematic when it came to explaining "figures" of speech. In his zeal to oppose the "figurative" readings of referential semantics, which displace meanings from words, Luther insists on such an iron-clad identity of meaning and word that it becomes impossible for him to accommodate "figurative" meanings at all in his new affective semantics. Unable to see "figures" as anything but displacements, he is driven to give a quite peculiar account of the commonest biblical tropes.

Pressed by the replies of his opponents, Luther repeats and extends his attack in the *Confession Concerning Christ's Supper* (1528). Against Zwingli, who had adduced many biblical examples of "signification" in the traditional referential way, he insists that "is" cannot mean "signifies." The reason is that Christ's parables make "common words into pure tropes—new and different words. Otherwise they would not be parables, if he used common words in their original sense." As one metaphorical example, Luther explains how "the seed is the word; the field is the world": "seed and field are tropes or words with a new application, according to the nature of metaphor. For a simple word and a metaphorical word are not one, but two words."[57] For Luther, a new "application," another meaning, requires a "different" word. Such a bizarre multiplication of words is necessitated by his rigid adherence to a constitutive semantics that is in this case fixed on single words to the exclusion of the semantic importance of use. "One word, one meaning" is Luther's principle; if the meaning of a word is altered by metaphorical use, he must postulate another word. He is driven to this pass in order to avoid admitting that field can "signify" world (or bread, body), since he is trying to deny the very process of signifying, to eliminate

---

[57] *Ibid.*, 175. "What a mad spirit . . . he must be," Luther continues, "who has to resort to this 'representation' nonsense."

the multiple "significances" imposed by allegorical reading. The only way he found to deny it was, paradoxically, to multiply words. If "field" can be used, as the parable obviously uses it, in another sense than the "original," then there must be a second word "field." Since words do not stand for meanings but are equivalent to them, one word cannot have more than one meaning. In short, Luther is trying to replace the semantic theory of representation with the semantic theory of identity that he derived from his emotional experience of Scripture. There it worked well enough, primarily because it implicitly construed meaning as a function of whole utterances: the heard promise that creates faith. But the identity between Word (as performing act) and meaning (as emotional assent) collapses into absurdity when Luther tries to transfer it to words (as lexical units) and meanings (as invariably coextensive with them).

In maintaining his semantic theory of identity, Luther is driven to further untenable assertions about the copula "to be" that became easy targets for his adversaries. Having ruled out metaphor (which ceases to exist: as words used with "new applications" are "different" words, all meanings are "literal") against Zwingli, he proceeds to rule out simile aganst Oecolampadius. For Luther, "is" cannot mean "to be like" any more than it can mean "signifies"; it must always mean "to be the same as." Again, however, he bases his argument on what he claims to be usage: the Bible never uses a trope of "likeness" for the fulfilled type, in the way that we might say of a picture, "This is Pope Julius." "Likeness" is not the relation between the bread and the body. He goes on to argue that even in common speech "is" is what he calls "substantive," and indicates "essence," not "signification."[58] Identity is the only relation Luther will allow between word and meaning, the only theoretical alternative to referential dualism he could propose. It is ironic that he proposes it on the very basis where it was most vulnerable, that of usage: his dissenting fellow reformers were

[58] *Ibid.*, 254, 257.

not slow in finding an abundance of counter-examples in both the Bible and common speech.

It is remarkable that Luther, a writer and translator of genius, should dig himself into this particular theoretical hole, should declare in principle that metaphor and simile, to the nuances of which he was in practice supremely sensitive, do not exist. Such a discrepancy is not only due to his personal convictions and their polemical exigencies. It also reflects the major problems characteristic of the shifting semantic awareness of the period: the gap between employing language in one way and conceiving of it in another, and the enormous difficulty of challenging assumptions that are embedded in the vocabulary one must use. Luther, bold and decisive where other humanists (like Vives) were timid and vacillating, chucked away the vocabulary of signification as trenchantly as he excommunicated the pope. But his replacement for it patently failed to account for semantic distinctions that were obvious enough in other contexts.

On translation, for example, Luther comments with the keen sensibility of a poet and the linguistic scholar's precise grasp of the subtle shades of meaning in idioms, wholly abandoning his inflexible demand in the case of the sacraments for word-bound semantic unity. He explicitly denies the kind of literalism he elsewhere upholds, fully recognizing that meanings are not coterminous with single words by refusing word-for-word renderings. Luther's goal is to make Scripture "clear and vigorous" to "the common man in the marketplace." For example, to translate literally the prayer to Mary, *plena gratia*, as *gnadenvoll*, would make a German, says Luther, think of a keg full of beer. Acutely aware of the necessity for varying judgments, he sometimes "must let the literal word go," but at others prefers "to do violence to the German language rather than to depart from the word."[59] He in fact praises himself and his associates for inventing "the principle of at times retaining the words quite literally, and at times rendering only the

[59] *On Translating: An Open Letter* (1530), *AE* xxxv, 188–89, 191, 193–94.

meaning."[60] As a succinct statement of the practice of any good translator, this "principle" is a de facto acknowledgment of what all the language theory of the period only fitfully perceived: that meaning is a function of use.

Luther's own theory did not perceive this either, although it was indeed revolutionary enough not to be understood even by those who continued to do battle for the basic Protestant position, the all-sufficiency of a Word-based faith. The semantic center of Luther's hermeneutic revolution was his concerted effort to replace the cosmetic view of language by a constitutive one: the total rejection of the process of representing or signifying (which entailed the dissociation of language from sacraments, types, and figures) and the reapprehension of meaning as both the affective product of discourse and, alas, inextricably bound to single words. While most subsequent reformers were inspired by the affective dimension of Luther's semantics to rejoice in hearing the Word as "children of the promise," none was willing to share the critical dimension that was its linguistic basis: his denial of meaning as reference or signification. The split between Luther and those he called the "fanatics" resulted from their immediate reassimilation of language within all the forms of dualism from which Luther had tried to free it.

Like Valla, Luther attempted a genuine reordering of the linguistic and ontological categories of his time; like Valla's, his effort was difficult, problematic, and left ample room for attack. As subsequent humanists practiced Valla's philological techniques and stylistic prejudices while ignoring his epistemology, so subsequent reformers practiced Luther's hermeneutic techniques and repeated some of his slogans while repudiating his fundamental semantic insights. Whereas Valla established the historical distance of the past from the present by observing lexical and grammatical usages in Latin, Luther discovered the historical immediacy of the past in the present by observing performative, emotion-producing usages in the

---

[60] *Defense of the Translation of the Psalms* (1531), *AE* XXXV, 222.

language of Scripture. The focus on usage of whatever kind is the basic link between humanism and Protestantism. The seminal influence of Valla and Luther in these respective movements is analogous not only in having been exercised without their most radical reconceptions of language being understood or respected but also in the attention that these reconceptions nonetheless forced onto the whole communal context of language as a semantic determinant. For usage presupposes users: Valla made the common custom of the speech community an arbiter of meaning; Luther made a more elastic and mystical notion of the "congregation" an arbiter of belief. The net effect of both thinkers was, at the very least, to have challenged the rules of the language game, to have altered the contours of what it was possible merely to assume about the relation of language and meaning, to have created a new consciousness of the necessity to interpret and interrogate words not as atemporal semantic containers but as historical semantic agents.

In sum, the linguistic assumptions that Valla and Luther attacked now had to be deliberately defended. Philosophers who wanted words to give transparent access to the knowledge of things now had to argue, like Vives, that they could, or like Bacon, that with sufficient discipline they might be made to. Theologians who wanted words to stand for unalterable spiritual realities now had to argue that they could so function. But the revolutionary semantic insights of Valla and Luther, while they did not prevail as such, established the terms of the defensive arguments against them. The very idea of usage as a semantic determinant is acknowledged by Bacon, who wants to reform and purify it, and by all the Protestants who employ against Luther the criterion that his hermeneutics gave them. In this way, claims and counterclaims about *how* language is used are the subversive strain in all the renewed attempts to say *what* it represents, preserving in the method of the arguments semantic assumptions opposed to their conclusions.

6

THE AUGUSTINIAN
REACTION

Every sign *by itself* seems dead. *What* gives it   —LUDWIG
life?—In use it is *alive*. Is life breathed into it   WITTGENSTEIN
there?—Or is the *use* its life?

William Tyndale, a scholar inspired by Erasmus and a translator of genius, whose partial version of the Bible as completed
and modified by Miles Coverdale became the basis for the
King James Version, was Luther's first prominent English disciple.[1] Tyndale, however, advocated a "spiritualist" or Zwinglian position on the Eucharist, and his arguments for it are an
exemplary illustration of how the new focus on linguistic
usage was assimilated back into the framework of sacramental
dualism from which Luther had tried to liberate it.

Tyndale began from the solidly Lutheran premise that
"Scripture hath but one sence, which is the literall sense. . . .
Never the latter the Scripture useth proverbes, similitudes, re-
dels, or allegories as all other speaches do, but that which the
proverbe, similitude, redell, or allegory signifieth is ever the
literall sense which thou must seke out diligently."[2] This "literal" sense is, as for Luther, equated with the spiritual understanding of the text: this is its single "meaning" from which all
allegories are excluded. What the latter are permitted to "signify" are merely illustrations or reinforcements of meanings

---

[1] S. H. Greenslade surveys "English Versions of the Bible, 1525–1611," in
The Cambridge History of the Bible, II, 141–68.

[2] *The obedience of a Christen man* (1528) in *The Whole Workes of W. Tyndall,
John Frith, and Doct. Barnes* (London, 1573), p. 166.

that must be found literally stated somewhere in the Bible. Tyndale thus accepts, for the primary purpose of inveighing against Catholic allegorical interpretation from Origen forward, Luther's semantic unity of letter and spirit as well as his basic affective principle that all Scripture is a testimony or "promise" of Christ. Although for Tyndale the emotional power of the heard Word remains central, it does not finally alter, as it did for Luther, the traditional semantic operation of words.

These behave in quite the old dualistic way, now grounded, however, in the new appeal to usage: "the use of Scriptures is to call signes by the names of thynges signified therby."[3] This frequently reiterated principle is the standard linguistic objection to Luther's doctrine of the real presence: "It is the common use and propertie of spech in the Scripture, to call the signe, the thyng."[4] The standard examples are: "circumcision is the covenant; the lamb is the passover." The former material objects or actions are "signs," the latter ceremonies "things." As Tyndale explicates them, both are "figures" of the later revealed "verities" of Baptism and the Lord's Supper respectively. And as figures "signify" verities, so does "such maner of spech . . . bryng the thyng signified into our hartes by such outward sensible signes." Hence "is" in the words of institution means "signifieth," according to this "common maner of spech in many places of Scripture, and also in our mother toung." Tyndale adduces several examples of the "representative" (as opposed to Luther's "substantive") copula, on

---

[3] *A treatise upon signes and Sacramentes* (n.d.), *Workes*, p. 447. This treatise was probably written in 1533–34. See J. A. Mozley, *William Tyndale* (London, 1937), pp. 260–61.

[4] *The Supper of the Lord* (1533), *Workes*, p. 468. Tyndale calls such usage a "trope"; Calvin identifies it as "metonymy, a figure of speech commonly used in Scripture when mysteries are under discussion," whereby "the name of the thing was given to the symbol" and/or "the name of the visible sign is also given to the thing signified": *Institutes of the Christian Religion*, IV.xvii.21, quoted from John T. McNeill, ed. and Ford Lewis Battles, tr. (Philadelphia, 1960). This edition usefully identifies which parts of the text first appeared and were revised in its five major versions.

the model of the pictorial usage of ordinary speech ("this is St. Catherine"): the three branches are three days; the stone is God's house; the seven fat kine are seven plenteous years, and so on.[5]

Because Luther, having rigidly fixed his demand for semantic unity on single words, could not account theoretically for figurative *uses* of language, it was easy to refute him with lists of such uses as these. His claim that the typical use of the copula in both speech and the Bible was to designate "essence" or identity was clearly unsustainable—on its own grounds. It thus became equally easy to ignore the far more important basis of his demand for semantic unity in his revolutionary distinction between the function—the mode of operation—of language on the one hand and of the sacraments on the other. Tyndale is typical of contemporary and subsequent reformers in overlooking this distinction altogether, assuming that words "signify" just as signs and figures do. It was no doubt inevitable that the ancient representational semantic model should continue to prevail, since it offered such a ready and long-accepted way to deal with what Luther's theory failed to: the multiple possible senses of single words. Neither theory explicitly conceived of these as functions of use; so to account for them as signs or symbols that stand for things was the obvious alternative to not accounting for them at all. Thus Luther's great challenge—his reconception of words as semantic agents—was largely submerged in the reassertion, on the sacramental analogy, of words as signs.

Largely, but not entirely: though Tyndale still sees words functioning as signs, he also sees their effects as more affective than representative. Biblical tropes may operate by signifying things, but they do so in order to bring those things "into our hearts." Indeed, the emotional dimension that Luther's hermeneutics shares with Erasmus's transferring the rhetorical "sermonis vim" to Scripture, whether recognized as a seman-

---

[5] *Workes*, p. 469. Calvin repeats these customary examples in a section wholly devoted to denying that *is* is "substantive": *Institutes*, IV.xvii.22.

tics or not, remained a central and divisive issue in Protestant-ism generally.[6] Tyndale, like most Protestants, did not recog-nize the emotional apprehension of the text as part of a semantics that called into question his traditional assumptions about how language means. But John Calvin, a more system-atic thinker who set himself the task of composing a more sys-tematic theology, was sufficiently aware of this challenge to offer a full-scale defense of just those assumptions.

Compiling the final version of the *Institutes* in 1559 after about forty years of controversy, Calvin was enabled to ex-pand and intensify his attacks on the sacramental doctrine of Lutherans and "fanatics" alike. Prominent among many such expansions are Calvin's efforts to deny the authority of Au-gustine to the "literalists" and to claim it for himself, on the precise basis of the linguistic/sacramental analogy. They can-not use Augustine's references to Christ's "flesh and blood" in the Eucharist to support their "real" presence, Calvin insists, because the Saint "explains himself, saying that sacraments take their names from their likeness to the things they sig-nify."[7] Calvin thus goes to the heart of the matter, opposing the Lutheran demand for semantic unity with the authority of the most prestigious thinker to have naturalized the whole vo-cabulary of signification in Christianity. The crucial question was whether this vocabulary applied equally to the operation of both words and sacraments, whether both were "signs." Luther had said no, finding in the performative and creative power of the Word a kind of operation (different only in degree from that of ordinary words) distinct from "signifying." Cal-vin, and most other Protestants, said yes. Although all ac-cepted, contra the Catholics, Luther's distinction between sac-

---

[6] All the arguments about inspiration—of both the writers and the readers of the Bible—as a way of seeking and verifying interpretive authority were one consequence of the new importance placed on the emotional apprehension of the Word. All agreed that one had to have the Spirit to interpret the Spirit; but few if any could agree on what constituted evidence of its possession.

[7] IV.xvii.28. Augustine is everywhere in Calvin's expanded 1559 attack on the subject: IV.xvii.19–34.

rament and Word in terms of power, none saw this power, as he did, as differentiating sacraments from words in terms of semantic operation.

Calvin thus repeats, with the help of Augustine, that the faith-creating Word is alone efficacious, that without the promise, the "visible sign" in the sacrament is meaningless (IV.xiv.4). Justification and sanctification can occur without either sign or sacrament (IV.xiv.14). But what is thus different in efficacy is still identical in function. Calvin quotes Augustine explaining the relation of Old and New Testament sacraments: only the signs have changed; the thing signified remains the same. "It is the same with different signs as it is with different words; for words change their sounds from time to time; and words are nothing but signs" (IV.xiv.26). There can be no clearer revelation of the primordial motive for retaining the whole traditional process: the thing signified, the meaning, must be placed securely beyond the temporal flux of the mere signifiers. By insisting on a more intrinsic, even indissoluble, connection between words and meanings, Luther had endangered this privileged location of meaning above or beyond its mere "conveyors." But the semantic unity he postulated, as applied to the sacraments by means of the "substantive" verb "is," while vulnerable to his own criterion of usage, had ironically solved the major problem that remained in Calvin's traditional semantics—that of the infinite regress. Calvin, sticking very closely to the Augustinian position, can accept neither the Lutheran literally "real" presence nor the purely "figurative," symbolic, "commemorative" view of the Zwinglians (the position Calvin calls "fanatic"). In other words, he insists on a kind of union between the bread and the body of Christ (the sign and the signified) that is neither identity nor representation, but somewhere between the two.[8] The bread is not equated with the body nor does it arbitrarily stand for it: there

[8] All Protestants rejected the Catholic doctrine of transubstantiation, whereby the bread is held to be changed (in "substance" but not in "accidents") into the body of Christ by the priest's consecration of the host.

is rather an Augustinian "likeness" between them, what Calvin elsewhere calls "the affinity which the things signified have with their symbols" (IV.xvii.21). There is a mystical participation of the sign in the thing, of the temporal, material symbol in the eternal, spiritual signified: this is the central principle of Augustinian semantics that will become Coleridge's definition of the symbol and be thence transferred from Scripture to secular poetry.[9] Calvin frankly confesses the principle to be a mystery that surpasses understanding (IV.xvii.31–32). So indeed it is: the crucial connection between sign and thing, whether sacramental or semantic, is magic. As the sacramental union has for Calvin "no natural analogy,"[10] so the semantic union can have no natural explanation. Both are quite as mysterious as the incarnation itself.

By thus reaffirming the traditional Augustinian assumptions, Calvin perfectly illustrates the regressive magic entailed by the dualistic process of signification. Throughout his discussion he has inveighed equally against the Catholics for supposing a "magic incantation" to be at work in the celebration of the Eucharist and against the Lutherans for supposing the immediately "literal" and inexplicable union of bread and body. Instead of the latters' hasty presumption of a "miracle," Calvin boasts of giving a "sound understanding" and implicitly rational interpretation of the words (IV.xvii.25). Ultimately, however, Calvin must assert exactly what his Lutheran opponents do—a magical bond between sign and thing. All that his interpretation allows him is to postpone the assertion, to relocate at a more distant point in the signifying process just what he has forbidden Luther to assert without benefit of that process. Luther insisted on the "unfathomable" sacramental magic directly, at the outset, not by imposing the same magical semantic process on words, but, quite the contrary, by interpreting their meaning wholly as a function of

[9] See discussion above, ch.1, pp. 27–28, 37.

[10] Ronald S. Wallace, *Calvin's Doctrine of the Word and Sacrament* (Edinburgh, 1953), p. 165. The necessary mystery is that the terms of the dualism must be simultaneously kept distinct and seen as essentially conjoined: p. 197.

their grammar and usage. Though his conceptions of the latter were too narrow to be adequate or convincing, Luther's brilliant intuition of semantic unity deliberately refused to divide words from meanings in the traditional way that began the regress to the magical agency necessary to reconnect them. Calvin reasserted this traditional way with the massive testimony of its greatest Christian spokesman, St. Augustine.

Calvin's Lutheran opponents were not slow in pointing out that both he and Augustine must finally assert the same mystery that they do. Their opposition, however, does not extend to the rejection of the linguistic dualism, but merely denies its application to the sacraments. They reject the analogy without questioning the process. The general acceptance of Calvin's firm reestablishment of this process thus ensured that the new kinds of semantic awareness inherent in both the philological and emotional apprehension of the Word in Protestant hermeneutics would remain submerged beneath the traditional conception of words as "signifying" things. At the level of theory, most forms of Protestantism—especially the English varieties of Calvinism—potently reinforced the magical referentiality of words that Luther had refused. Perhaps no one but Luther could have been content with an unrationalizable mystery, accepted by faith, that set words free from their obligations to correspond with or signify things, finding the semantic operation of both words and the Word to be intrinsic, affective, and subject to the arguable, multiple determining contexts of history and human purpose. Paradoxically, the absolute trust that Luther placed in the mysteries of the Spirit (as heard, literally, in the promising Word) enabled him to demystify language itself, opening the sacred text in ways so threatening that they could not be tolerated.[11] Calvin re-rationalized the mysteries by re-mystifying language. And this effort to resecure semantic control over the Bible by reassert-

---

[11] Luther's whole separation of sacramental, spiritual magic from semantic processes explains (what has irritated and puzzled some of his commentators) "how he could place in Scripture a confidence so absolute, and yet subject it to a criticism so fearless"—as Frederic Farrar put it, *History of Interpretation* (New York, 1886), p. 338.

ing the ontologically correspondent "signification" of its words that Luther had denied is characteristic of the subsequent development and increasing formalization of Protestant theology.

Within the Lutheran camp, one of the most assiduous formalizers was Matthias Flacius Illyricus, who devoted a treatise to the defense of the real presence perfunctorily against the Catholics and primarily against other Protestant positions.[12] In general, Flacius' argument merely repeats and develops Luther's insistence on accepting mysteries that God can perform but we cannot explain, and on there being consequently no need to depart from the "simplest" sense of Christ's words to a figurative sense. To so depart, says Flacius, is "shamefully" to contradict the son of God, to deny his actual words by saying, "This is not your body, but only a sign of your body."[13] He explicitly attacks the analogy that Calvin cited from Augustine, but only to deny its application to the words of institution. Trying to reclaim Augustine's authority for the Lutheran position, Flacius takes up the question whether

the name of the thing signified may be attributed to the sign by this "metonymy" of theirs. Augustine says, first, that the sacraments have a certain likeness with the things of which they are the sacraments. How is this against us, or for the absence of the body of Christ from the Supper? We too affirm that the holy Supper, or the external eating of Christ's body, has some likeness with its spiritual fruit, of which it is properly the sign or remembrance, as Christ himself most clearly asserts.[14]

[12] *Refutatio sophismatum et elusionum, quae pro sacramentario errore contra sacrosanctum Testamentum Christi afferri solent* (n.p., 1567). The basic biography and bibliography of Flacius remains Wilhelm Preger, *M. F. I. und Seine Zeit*, 2 vols. (Erlangen, 1859–61). The fullest analysis of his work is Günter Moldaenke, *Schriftverständnis und Schriftdeutung im Zeitalter der Reformation, Teil I: M. F. I.* (Stuttgart, 1936).

[13] *Refutatio*, sig. A8ᵛ: "Nullum vero dubium est, omnes eos indigne sumere, qui filio Dei dicenti de dato cibo, Hoc est corpus meum, corde et ore contradicunt, dicentes, Non corpus tuum, sed tantum signum corporis tui est."

[14] Sig. B5ᵛ: "ut nomen rei signatae signo tribuatur per istorum Metonymion.

"Primum dictum Augustini est, quod Sacramenta habeant quandam simi-

Flacius does not bother to specify this "likeness"—to distinguish the Lutheran postulate of identity from the Zwinglian of representation or the Calvinist of participation—in his zeal to refute the entire argument "from the analogy of signified things and the exchange of names." On the evidence of John 6, he excoriates his opponent for concluding "insolently that the words of Christ must be interpreted by the analogy of the sign and the thing signified rather than by (so he blasphemes) the 'superstitious observance' of the words."[15] In order to deny the analogy in the case of the sacraments, Flacius adduces the ambiguity of "sacrament" itself—as external object, internal mystery, and the ritual act that unites them. "You have not yet demonstrated," he jeers, "that in the sacraments the name of the thing signified is to be attributed to the sign, much less that the bread is the sign or the sacrament and the body the thing signified. But on the contrary, that the bread is not the sacrament has been sufficiently shown above by your own definition."[16] Insisting on sacraments as actions, Flacius is able both to cite one reformer against another and to get round the difficult matter of the "substantive" *is*. Circumcision and the lamb of God are not signs; they are "really" the acts of covenanting and expiating.[17] Luther's required semantic identity is

litudinem cum rebus, quarum sunt Sacramenta. Quid hoc contra nos, aut pro istius absentia corporis Christi a Coena? Et nos affirmamus sacram coenam, seu illum manducationem corporis Christi, habere aliquam similitudinem cum eius spirituali fruitione, cuius proprie est signum aut mnemosynon, ut clarissime Christus ipse asserit."

[15] Sigs. B6ᵛ–B7: "ab analogia rerum signatarum, & nominum permutatione. . . . Concludit audacter verba Christi ex Analogia signi & rei signatae potius, quam ex verborum (ut ipse blasphemat) superstitiosa observatione exponenda esse." His opponent here, identified by Dr. Irena Backus, is one Abdias Liberinus, whose largely Zwinglian arguments Flacius quotes from *Syntagma Universae de sacrosancta coena domini* [Zurich, 1567].

[16] Sig. B8: "Nondum enim monstrasti, in sacramentis signo nomen rei signatae tribui, multo minus panem esse signum aut sacramentum, & corpus esse rem significatem. At contra panem non esse sacramentum, satis supra ex vostra propria definitione ostensum est."

[17] Sigs. B8–C1ᵛ. The same point is twice repeated later, as is typical of Flacius: F5–F5ᵛ, G2ᵛ–G3.

quietly shifted away from ontology to function: Christ "is" the lamb because both are propitiatory sacrifices.

For all his efforts, however, to defend these "literal" readings, Flacius never attacks the signifying, "figurative" model of discourse, never distinguishes (as Luther did) between objects that "signify" and words that work in some other way. He does, however, raise the question about language that is at the center of the whole dispute: how to identify tropes in the first place. Responding to Calvinist jeers at the Lutherans' "ignorance" of tropes, he exploits the inconsistency between what his various Protestant opponents find "figurative" in the words of institution: some located the metaphor in the verb ("is" means "signifies"), some in the noun ("body" means "sign of the body"). These adversaries, says Flacius, have not discovered "in which word of the words of the Lord's Supper there may be a trope, nor even what this trope may be. . . . Which trope is it? How do you prove it? How do you fit your trope onto the true sense?"[18] In context these questions are merely rhetorical and return Flacius to his basic Lutheran point that the exercise of God's power needs and can have no "figurative" explanation. But for all his opposition to Calvin on this point, he is quite willing later on to quote against the Catholics Calvin's whole Augustinian scheme of signs and signifieds that are called by each other's names.[19]

Such eclecticism in the interest of both polemic exigency and Protestant system-building is extended to remarkable degrees of theft and incoherence in Flacius' best-known work,

---

[18] Sigs. F6ᵛ–F7: "neque in qua voce verborum Coenae Domini sit tropus, neque etiam quis sit ille tropus. . . . Quis tropus est? Quomodo probas? Quomodo ad verum sensum tropum tuum attemperas?"
We shall shortly see how in another context Flacius tried to answer these ever debatable questions. The recognition of a trope is still an issue in competing contemporary theories on the subject, which claim philosophical importance and which may be sampled in two collections of essays: *Critical Inquiry* 5 (1978), 3–176; and *Metaphor and Thought*, ed. Andrew Ortony (Cambridge, 1979).

[19] Sigs. I2–I3ᵛ, I4ᵛ.

the *Clavis Scripturae, seu de Sermone Sacrarum literarum.*[20] This huge and chaotic compilation of "rules" for the understanding of the Word—precisely because it is gathered by express citation and, in at least one case, by silent plagiarism from a great range of secular and sacred, ancient and modern, sources—is a perfect example of the general reembedding of Lutheran and Erasmian insights into the traditional semantic model and the consequent transmission of opposed assumptions about how language means. The whole work is an attempt to systematize the revolutionary application of humanist linguistic analysis to the Word. Its Erasmian rationale is that since our understanding of the Word is necessarily mediated by written words accommodated to our capacities, the Scriptures require investigation in terms of their historical contexts and by means of all the techniques derived from secular philology and philosophy.[21] That all these semantic openings of the sacred text greatly resist being systematized is the central problem of Flacius' effort and of Protestantism itself.

The tensions produced by such resistance are apparent in Flacius' initial statement of theological rules that are to govern the entire activity of interpretation. He begins from the modified Lutheran principle that Scripture is not "exclusively" to be understood and explained by the intellect. But this leads

---

[20] 2 vols. (Basle, 1567). The first volume is an encyclopedia, alphabetically arranged, of scriptural and theological matters; the second volume contains seven treatises on various aspects of interpretation and extensive indices. Both volumes comprise about 1800 folio pages, were designed for students, and were steadily reprinted for over a century. The book is frankly a compendium, a Protestant handbook, of the humanistic, text-centered Erasmian and Lutheran impulses to reform. Moldaenke, who is generally concerned to demonstrate its theological cogency, observes its "prolixity and formlessness," p. 148. Olivier Fatio has shown that a substantial portion of *de ratione cognoscendi sacras literas, tractatus I*, is lifted verbatim from Andreas Hyperius: "Hyperius plagié par Flacius: La destinée d'une méthode exégétique," in *Histoire de l'exégèse au XVIᵉ siècle*, ed. Fatio and Pierre Fraenkel (Geneva, 1978), pp. 362–81. Fatio also observes the repetitiousness and disorder of Flacius' prose, p. 375.

[21] Moldaenke gives a good analysis of the paradoxes confronted by Flacius' hermeneutics between historicity and timelessness, imperfect Scripture and infallible Word: pp. 265–69.

him to no formulation of the role played by the emotions nor by affect-producing words, but merely to the universally accepted hermeneutic requirement of the Holy Spirit. The meanings that concern Flacius, as a textbook writer, are intellectual constructs. Though he of course assumes the faith-creating promise, its affective dimension is never developed in Luther's direction as a semantic process in human language. Though Scripture is to interpret itself as an all-sufficing whole, learned authorities past and present are also to be consulted—except the fanatics, Schwenkfeld, and the pope (*Clavis*, ii, 6). The end of scriptural study is practice, not theory, so that while all human learning is necessary, it is not sufficient (ii, 14–15). Nonetheless, within the framework of the "analogy of faith" and the correct (i.e., Lutheran) understanding of the relation of Law and Gospel, Old and New Testaments, all the secular arts of discourse are to be fully deployed (ii, 9–10). A general knowledge of contexts, both linguistic and historical, is to guide our examination of details (ii, 7–8). Grammar and style are to be continually observed, so that we may have accurate definitions of "words and things" along with proper discrimination of "terms and significances, sentences and meanings" (ii, 10).

In setting out these now fundamental Protestant positions, Flacius most frequently cites St. Paul, who is followed by Plato and Cicero, with occasional mention of Aristotle. The massive synthesis he is attempting is the intellectual, academic legitimation of the Protestant reapprehension of the meanings of Scripture. Its effect on the new kinds of semantic awareness that prompted it is analogous to that of the assimilation of vernaculars to the powers and descriptive canons of Latin. The treatment of meaning as a function of social use and the apprehension of it as the arousal of emotion are both submerged into the theoretical framework of referential semantics, which is a part of the tradition that confers respectability. To become objects of serious study, vernaculars had to be made to resemble Latin; to become part of theology, Protestant hermeneutics had to be attached to the traditional linguistic concepts of the academies. In both domains, original intuitions of the semantic unity of words and meanings are digested, with more or less difficulty, by systems of dualistic thought. We have seen how Vives thus appropriated the ideas of Valla. Flacius does just the same thing, often with similarly indigestible results, with those of Luther.

Flacius' typical maneuver is to make a flatly radical Lutheran assertion and proceed immediately to deradicalize it, to hedge it about with qualifications until it all but disappears. He performs this operation in little and in large on the difficult question "of the multiple meanings of sacred letters." Like Erasmus and unlike Luther, he criticizes the whole tradition of allegorical interpretation not as false in kind, but only in degree. With the help of Melancthon and Augustine, he faults the allegorizers simply for overhastiness in the pursuit of figures to the undue neglect of the literal and historical sense. He then repeats Luther's radical formula, but with a qualifying clause that quite prevents its development into Luther's total denial of multiple meaning: "one definite, certain, and simple meaning must everywhere be sought, closely following the precepts of grammar, dialectic, and rhetoric." Flacius also repeats the by now commonplace Vallesque principle that "that meaning is to be retained which the custom of speech provides." "Retaining" it, however, we are told in the next breath, does not preclude going beyond it: "allegory follows the literal meaning." Allegory can consist of *exempla* or images or stories and can be used for a variety of purposes.[22]

Flacius then presents, citing biblical precedents, an example of how Scripture might be thus allegorized to make one of his favorite Erasmian points:

Christ somewhere alludes to the story of Jonah; he interprets the account of the serpent lifted up in the wilderness. Paul in Corinthians interprets the veil by which the face of Moses was covered. We see them reinterpret those places I have mentioned, disclosing great mat-

[22] II, 51–52: "unam quandam ac certam & simplicem sententiam ubique quaerendam esse, iuxta praecepta Grammaticae, Dialecticae & Rhetoricae. . . . illa sententia retinendà est, quam consuetudo sermonis parit. . . . Allegoria sequitur literalem sententiam."

ters as depicted by these images. For, employed in the right place, they bring both grace and light to speech: as if one in commendation of languages and arts would compare them to baskets—the humanistic disciplines—in which were collected the remains of the five loaves. As the loaves signify the word of God, so the baskets signified languages and arts, in which men preserve the word of God. Therefore the humanistic disciplines are not to be rejected by a Christian man, since they are the vessels in which celestial doctrine is preserved. Or if anyone is to speak of twofold justice, civil and spiritual, let him say that the tablets of Moses were inscribed within and without, in order to signify that one part instructs in the justice of the heart in the sight of God, the other part in external or civil justice. Or, that there were two tablets because the former contains spiritual justice, which we properly transact with God, the other, precepts of corporal and civil life. The former contains theology, or spiritual life; the second is politics. And thus these tablets embraced the whole life of man.[23]

Now, the exact status of the "signifieds" that Flacius here assigns to the loaves, baskets, and tablets is wholly unclear and

---

[23] II, 52: "Christus alicubi alludit ad historiam Ionae: interpretatur serpentem exaltatum in deserto. Paulus in Corinthiis velum interpretatur, quo facies Moysi tecta fuit. Hos videmus versari intra locos illos quos nominavi, & maximas res quasi pictas his imaginibus ostendere. Afferunt enim, in loco adhibitae, & gratiam & lucem orationi: ut si quis in commendatione linguarum & artium, comparet ad cophinos, in quos colligebantur reliquiae quinque panum, disciplinas humaniores. Cum enim panes significent verbum Dei, cophini significabant linguas & artes, quibus inter homines asservatur verbum Dei. Non igitur aspernandae erunt homini Christiano disciplinae humaniores, cum sint vasa in quibus coelestis doctrina conservatur. Aut si quis dicturus de duplici iusticia, civili & spirituali, dicat Tabulas Moysi intus ac foris scriptas fuisse, ut significaretur, eas partim de iusticia cordis coram Deo praecipere, partim de externa ac civili iusticia. Aut, ideo duas fuisse Tabulas, quia prior iusticia spiritualem, qua proprie cum Deo agimus, continet: altera, praecepta de vita corporali ac civili. Prior continet Theologiam, seu vitam spiritualem: secunda, politica est. Itaque hae Tabulae complexae sunt totam hominis vitam."

This example, as well as the preceding discussion, is a general introduction to the section "de multiplici sacrarum literarum sensu" (II, 49) and appears to be Flacius' own work. The subsequent detailed discussion is an announced borrowing from Hyperius, *De Theologo, seu de ratione studii theologici libri IIII* (Strasbourg, 1562), bk. II, ch. 35. For the unannounced borrowings that occur later and continue to the end of Flacius' *tractatus I*, see Fatio, "Hyperius plagié."

is never examined. Do these figurative "meanings" that "follow" the literal one exist on the medieval level of tropology? Flacius has earlier deplored the standard four levels of interpretation (II, 51). Or are these "meanings" merely an application or "accommodation" of the words to the use of life? Flacius goes on to explain the four levels he had apparently rejected, calling the tropological one an "accommodatio" (II, 56).[24] Does allegory therefore produce "meanings," or simply "uses"? Is it only a figure of speech (Flacius quotes this definition from Augustine, II, 57) or an interpretive method (as his own example assumes)? [25]

The answer to all these questions is, of course, yes; Flacius is presenting an historical compendium of hermeneutics, which can in principle exclude nothing. The famous "analogy of faith" (whereby no interpretation of Scripture may contravene the articles of faith), accepted by all Protestants and by many later scholars as such a principle, cannot and does not so function, because the only admissible source of the articles of faith is the scriptural text whose interpretation they are supposed to adjudicate.[26] All the sectarian quarreling is precisely about the establishment of these articles by means of the very process

[24] Part of the problem is that at this point Flacius is reprinting Hyperius's straightforward presentation of traditionally multiple senses (*De Theologo*, pp. 363–64) with no evident concern for its inconsistency with his own introduction.

[25] Moldaenke, trying to explain all this confusion away (pp. 241–49), claims that Flacius regarded "allegory" *only* as a figure of speech grammatically considered, which is manifestly not so. He also claims that Flacius regarded Scripture as not having multiple "senses" but only multiple "uses." Flacius indeed says this at one point; but the problem is that, at some point, Flacius says or quotes or steals everything. On his conflation of his own distinction between "type" and "allegory," see William G. Madsen, *From Shadowy Types to Truth* (New Haven, 1968), pp. 30–31.

[26] That we can only know the Spirit "on the basis of that which the Spirit is to interpret" has been rightly identified as a major problem in Calvin because it is "a completely circular argument": H. Jackson Forstman, *Word and Spirit: Calvin's Doctrine of Biblical Authority* (Stanford, 1962), pp. 83–84. But the problem is characteristic of Protestantism itself.

they are presumed to control.[27] Although Flacius may not like the opinions of the fanatics, Schwenkfeld, and the pope, his hermeneutics gives him no grounds whatever for rejecting them. And only his opinions seem to separate him from, say, Hugh of St. Victor on the whole matter. Hugh, too, paid lip service to the initial observation, advised by Augustine, of the literal and historical sense, just as Flacius repeats throughout this discussion the more radical Lutheran insistence on "one simple sense." Luther, as we saw, had plenty of trouble using this as a principle of exclusion, but at least he tried to. For Flacius, and for the whole tradition of academic, Protestant scholasticism he so conglomerately represents, almost any meaning, at the level of interpretive theory, will do.

And whatever the meaning or its status, the linguistic process of its apprehension is quite explicitly that of "signifying." Flacius does not merely assume the Augustinian semantic model; he gives a lengthy résumé of it from *De Doctrina Christiana* (II, 103–05). It was partly for this reason that the *Clavis* could gain wide currency as a hermeneutic textbook even in Calvinist countries, although Flacius himself remained an arch-Lutheran in doctrinal controversies. In England, for example, one Thomas Wilson wrote a popularized vernacular hermeneutic handbook, frankly declaring that "For most of these [293] Rules . . . I am beholden to Flaccius Illiricus."[28] Wilson tries much harder than Flacius to stick to the Lutheran formula of the "single literal sense," though the senses that he finds are Calvin's.[29] But with respect to the semantics of human language, all can comfortably share the full range of Au-

---

[27] For example, in the vexed case of what we are to believe about the Eucharist, Calvinists often rejected the real presence as contravening the "article of faith" that Christ is resurrected and sits on the right hand of the Father (*ergo* he can't be in the bread). To this Lutherans responded that, according to the "article of faith" that the triune God is omnipotent, it is blasphemy thus to limit his power over his own body (he can be in as many places as he likes).

[28] *Theologicall rules, to guide us in the understanding . . . of . . . scripture* (London, 1615), sig. A3.

[29] Hence he declares that the literal sense of "this is my body" "must be refused, and a figurative improper sense is here the true sense," p. 113.

gustinian dualisms that Luther had rejected. Wilson takes this range as a controlling principle in all Scripture: the visible is to the invisible as flesh to spirit and words to sense; words are but "barke, ryne, or bone, the meaning within is as the roots, and juice, or as the marrow."[30]

At the same time as Flacius is content to reproduce the ancient theory that severs words from what they "stand for," he is nonetheless sporadically aware that there are problems here, that words constitute our only access to the Word as well as to things. The mediating centrality of language with respect both to the world (in Valla's epistemology) and to the Lord (in Erasmus's theology) produces in Flacius the kind of ambivalence that I have called the dilemma of the age: the desire to arrive at certainties by means that are necessarily and increasingly recognized as contingent. The confusions and inconsistencies in Vives's entire noetic program are manifest in Flacius' introduction to his fourth treatise on figurative language, called "prolegomena troporum":

> Words are tokens of things, and conversely words are said to be understood in place of matter, and conversely are also called the tokens of things. Things and words assist one another mutually without any conflict so that you may the more easily understand the one by the other. However, it is things that should be judged by words, rather than words by things. For speech has been devised and exists in order to reveal the secrets of one mind to others, as much as to describe external things and to lead the listener to awareness of them.
>
> We must, however, take care lest someone adhere to words so superstitiously that he sacrifices the force of things themselves. The use of speech is in fact quite diverse, and often departs considerably from common meanings; for there is hardly any locution or even word which cannot sometimes admit some ambiguity. Indeed, no one can always speak so diligently and clearly, but that sometimes a hearer or reader—even a not wholly stupid one—may be wont to lose his true meaning.
>
> On the other hand, it is not uncommon that knowledge of the things talked about offers great help to the understanding of speech. Therefore the nature of the thing must be inquired into most dili-

---

[30] *Ibid.*, p. 46.

gently and earnestly, and its substantive properties must be considered—which admirably illustrate each other. This matter we have treated elsewhere.

Moreover, the greatest care must be taken lest anyone construct whatever pleases him in the Scriptures and afterwards violently twist the words to his own construction. Heretics have always done this and those that misunderstand the Scriptures, declaring that words must be bent to things, not vice versa. . . .

Nevertheless, since speech and even single words, especially when understood figuratively, are to be judged on the basis of the nature of the thing and of the matter treated, we must take care to observe the nature of things as divine signs, so that we may reach thereby the understanding of figurative language.

Close to this subject can be regarded the controversy of words and sense, which will perhaps be treated more fully later. This indeed is usually anticipated chiefly in the argument that we should not heed words so much as the mind of the speaker—which is quite rightly said, if anyone can perceive the mind of another in any other way. For whence is it more rightly apprehended than from his own words, with which he himself wished to express it?

The accurate meanings of words must be distinguished so that we may distinguish their literal from their figurative senses; further, that we may also classify the literal ones; for the literal sense can also sometimes be subdivided.

Figurative meanings are to be even more accurately subdivided, so that we may certainly know by which trope each word in the intended structure will have changed from its innate and essential meaning to this or that tropic one. Thus also the degrees of these tropic conceptions, of their divergences from their usual meaning, must be considered so that we may adroitly discern for what reason and how far it has gone, withdrawing as it were from its native place.

A name attributed to several things different in some way does not directly signify different things. For it can be that those different things have some common ground, as in the case of the genus and species vocabulary. Thus one concept, "sadness," signifies sadness in respect to God and secular sadness. Thus many kinds of delight, fear, zeal, and similar things belonging to one genus are indicated by one concept and a common name.[31]

---

[31] *Clavis*, II, 211: "Verba sunt notae rerum, & contra. Verba dicuntur pro subiecta materia intelligenda esse: & contra etiam verba dicuntur notae rerum. Omnino citra omnem controversiam mutuam sibi operam res & verba prae-

It will require over three centuries for theology and philosophy to formulate as the "hermeneutic circle" the kind of linguistic dilemmas confronted by sixteenth-century reformers—out of which Flacius has here created a hermeneutic merry-go-round. In his usual rambling and hasty way he sum-

---

bent, ut alterum ex altero tanto rectius intelligas: potissimum tamen res ex verbis iudicandae sunt, nam ad hoc ipsum sermo institutus est & habetur, ut tum occulta alienae mentis alii patefaciat, tum etiam externas res depingat, & auditorem in ipsarum noticiam perducat.

"Videndum vero est, ne quis nimium superstitiose adhaerens verbis, rebus ipsis vim inferat. Sermonis enim valde varius usus est, ac saepe non parum a communibus significationibus recedit: nec ulla ferme locutio, aut etiam vox est, quae non aliquando aliquid ambiguitatis recipere queat. Nemo etiam tam diligenter ac semper perspicue loqui potest, quin interdum auditor aut lector, etiam non omnino stupidus, a vera eius sententia aberrare soleat.

"Contra tamen non raro rerum, de quibus agitur, noticia magnum adiumentum adfert ad sermonis intelligentiam. Quare natura rei diligentissime at verissime cognoscenda est, coniunctae eius noticiae proprietates cohaerentes expendendae, quae sese invicem mirifice illustrant, de qua re alibi dictum est.

"Videndum autem iterum atque iterum est, ne quis sibi in sacris Literis fingat res, quales ei libet, & postea violenter verba ad suum sensum torqueat: sicut semper haeretici, & etiam omnes male eas intelligentes fecerunt, clamitantes, verba ad res, non contra inflectenda esse. . . .

"Quia vero nihilominus sermo ac singula etiam verba, praesertim figurate accepta, sunt ex natura rei ac materiae de qua agitur, iudicanda: videndum est, ut rerum naturam veluti divina quaedam vestigia observemus, quo per eam ad sermonis figurati intelligentiam perveniamus.

"Vicina huic materiae videri queat controversia de verbis ac sensu: de qua forte postea suo loco plenius agetur. Solet vero illud praecipue in ea disceptatione praecipi, ut non tam verba quam mentem auditoris [sic: corrected in later edd. to "dicentis"] attendamus. Quod quidem rectissime dicitur, si quis alia ratione eius mentem percipere potest: nam alioqui unde ea rectius, quam ex eius propriis verbis, quibus eam ipsem et exprimere voluit, accipietur?

"Discernendae vero sunt accuratae significationes vocum, ita ut discernamus proprias a figuratis. Praeterea ut etiam proprias dividamus: nam etiam propria significatio aliquando subdividi potest.

"Multo magis figuratae significationes accuratissime subdividendae sunt, ita quidem, ut etiam sciamus, per quem tropum a genuina ac maxime propria, ad hanc aut aliam tropicam una quaeque vox in proposito textu migraverit. Quin etiam gradus illarum tropicarum notionum, aut a significatione declinantium expendendi sunt: ut solerter animadvertamus, qua nam occasione, & quousque tandem illa a sua, quasi nativa sede recedens, progressa sit.

"Non mox vocabulum, pluribus rebus aliquo modo differentibus attribu-

marizes both the traditional semantic assumptions together with the challenges to them that arose in the Renaissance from the fundamental awareness of sociohistorical usage as a semantic determinant. Thus, words stand for things; yet things— whether internal intentions or external objects—are only to be known "on the basis of words." But words are ambiguous; we need to know the "substantive" nature of things in order to understand speech. Yet, this knowledge is often subjectively arbitrary and can distort words. Despite this, words must still be judged "on the basis" of things as divine signs. The things, however, that are the intentions of others can only (perhaps) be apprehended in their words. Words have literal and figurative meanings, both of which require classification. The figurative ones are departures from "innate" ones, which can denote common qualities.

Like Vives, Flacius slides constantly back and forth between conceiving of words as standing for preextant things and creating them as objects of knowledge, between conceiving of meanings as contained in words and created by their use. Language is not here being described as semantically cosmetic and treated as semantically constitutive; it is consciously regarded as both. The implicit contradiction between linguistic theory and practice has become explicit in this theoretical farrago of common sense and confusion. It seems apparent that the immediate reason for Flacius' all-inclusive mixture, the motive of the hermeneutics that excludes nothing, is the utility of now one, now another, semantic conception in doctrinal controversies. For example, the primacy of words over things (even when divorced from Luther's extreme principle of "one word, one meaning") was needed to support the real presence, while the primacy of things over words was necessary to interpret scriptural statements that were obviously false, immoral, or

---

tum, diversa significat. Potest enim fieri, ut illa diversa communem quandam rationem habeant: ut sit in vocibus generum ac specierum. Sic una notione Tristicia significat tristiciam secundum Deum, & tristiciam seculi. Sic multiplex dilectio, timor, zelus, & similia in genere una notione communi vocabulo notantur."

contradictory (most of which cases occur, says Flacius in the words of Hyperius, in Canticles: II, 59). It was very useful to locate meanings sometimes in words, sometimes beyond them, as well as to consider meanings sometimes as "innate" and sometimes as a function of use. Usage itself, whether of communities or individuals, and particularly the "deviant" usage of tropes, though often clearly regarded as a semantic determinant, is never quite formulated as such but is rather explained in the dualistic terms of conventional rhetoric: words used figuratively stand for something else than they usually do. Such uses both in and of the text (like Flacius' interpretation of the loaves and baskets) count sometimes as meanings and sometimes merely as applications or accommodations. "Senses" are both distinguished from "uses" and identified with them.

This richly permissive riot of conflicting positions is but an intensified reenactment of the semantic situation we have observed in the philosophy of Vives and in the campaign to legitimize vernaculars. In all three cases, original contemporary insights into the power of language and its users to make and unmake meanings are uneasily or unwittingly reincorporated into the traditional dualistic semantic models (of Aristotelian metaphysics, Latin rhetoric, or Augustinian hermeneutics) in defiance of which these insights were generated. The challenges to orthodoxy became orthodox and were thus preserved, at the cost to them of blunting their force. Their teeth were drawn, but at the cost to orthodoxy of stretching it so thin in the effort to cover everything that it lost any definable shape. It is this fluid situation that Bakhtin described as the "exceptional linguistic freedom" that offered itself for exploitation to great writers. What it offered to common readers in their most widely shared textual encounters in an explosively literate Europe—to schoolboys at their Latin, believers at their Bibles or at sermons, citizen consumers of national literatures—was a semantic field of centrifugal energy, threatening at every moment to whirl the fabric of meaning into shreds unless arrested by a higher power.

To have traced the development of the same systematic semantic ambivalence in three primary areas of the Renaissance preoccupation with language—humanist philosophy and rhetoric, vernacular polemics, and Protestant hermeneutics—in books that formed public tastes and trained its teachers, provides evidence, I believe, for a generally shifting consciousness of meaning that, by the later sixteenth century, is divided by conflicting assumptions almost to the point of schizophrenia. The reader is invited, on the one hand, to study in the classroom, to enjoy in literature, and to take with salvational seriousness in Scripture the proliferation of meanings in whose creation he participates with no apparent limit other than individual ingenuity. He is enjoined, on the other hand, that meaning resides only in realms of objective fact or divine ordination, access to which is arduous, to be rigorously controlled, and which exist quite apart from the power of him or his language to add or detract. He is repeatedly told that words stand for such things; and he is repeatedly shown that the use of words can create what would not exist without them. Semantic assumptions that were at least occasionally perceived as incompatible by greater thinkers, like Luther and Calvin, were anxiously or carelessly conflated by lesser ones, like Vives and Flacius. And it was the lesser ones who educated the educators who taught the people from podium, pulpit, and folio.

Flacius is particularly rich in conflations of the latter sort. We have observed how he ignores Luther's affective semantics even while defending the real presence, and happily adopts as a general principle the one he refuses to apply to the Eucharist: the sacramental/linguistic analogy of Augustine and Calvin. Similarly, he takes up (possibly by borrowing it from Vives) the epistemological problem at the heart of the whole Vallesque revaluation of usage, without seeming to be aware that it is either epistemological or a problem. One of his "principles" for interpreting tropes is that "discourse accords with human opinion and perspective, not with the existence of the things." Under this rubric Flacius reports that

Plato writes in the *Cratylus* and Aristotle in the *Metaphysics* that there were philosophers who said that no object existed of itself or by its own nature, but only as it appeared to men, for man was the measure of all things—among whom they name and refute the most able Protagoras. . . . Certainly Hebrew discourse often speaks of things entirely according to the cognition, judgment, or opinion of contemporaries, rather than according to the existence of the thing itself, whether or not the truth of the thing agrees with that cognition of men.[32]

He goes on to give scriptural examples of such locutions that deal more with "human cognition and judgment than with things themselves." The examples show, however, what is evident from the second sentence above: that Flacius has no inkling of the issue here, for "cognition" and "truth" remain wholly separate and unproblematic. It is not merely that Flacius is dismissing the discredited notion of Protagoras, but that he mistakes a statement about what language does for a statement about its subject matter. His examples are verses *about* perception or opinion-giving. Flacius raises the question of how language functions only to construe it as a question of what language contains.[33] It is a miniature example of the whole process of assimilating the challenge of a dynamic and

---

[32] II, 304: "Sermo secundum speciem aut hominem opinionem, non secundum rei existentiam. Testatur Plato in Cratylo & Aristoteles in Metaphysicis, fuisse Philosophos, qui dicerent nihil rerum per sese suave natura esse, sed pro ut homini videantur, tale etiam existere. Hominem enim esse mensuram omnium rerum: inter quos illi potissimum nominant ac redarguunt Protagoram. . . . Certe sermo Hebraeus saepe admodum secundum cognitionem, iudicium aut opinionem praesentium hominum de rebus magis loquitur, quam secundum ipsius rei existentiam, sive rei veritas conveniat cum illa hominum cognitione, sive non."

The same report about Protagoras was made by Vives and is quoted above, ch. 3, n. 57.

[33] He has the excuse of the ambiguous preposition, *secundum*, whose classical sense—from "follow" as "dependent" or "based on"—is required by the idea, but whose medieval usage is attested (by the *Lexicon Minus*, not by Du Cange) in the sense of "concerning" or "as to." Flacius uses it in the latter sense here and elsewhere (as when he names the subjects of his own treatises in the Preface, II, sig. α2ᵛ).

constitutive semantics into the static and cosmetic model. Thus, Flacius is here offering discriminations of the subject matter of biblical discourse, which can be about opinions when it is not about things.

Even such discriminations, however, can be extended to become implicit acknowledgments of the semantically determining power of contexts. This occurs, for example, when Flacius presents as another "rule" the commonplace rhetorical observation that "discourse regards not only the thing but also the ideas of the hearers."[34] He cites from Luther the example of Paul's calling the law "weak and beggarly" (Gal. 4:9), pointing out that Paul is not speaking of the nature of the law "in itself" (which has always the power to convict us of sin) but rather of the "presumptuous hypocrites" who would be justified by it. So Paul is reprimanding the "abuse" of the thing itself rather than characterizing it. On the other hand, Flacius also interprets Paul's words as characterizing the thing: the law whose "nature" is powerless to effect salvation (II, 309). Flacius thus equates the "true use" of the thing with its "nature," understanding the weakness of the law not only as a rebuke on a particular occasion but also as a partial definition of the object itself.

Almost all of Flacius' examples are, naturally enough, polemical points against either the Catholics or the "fanatics." For this purpose it is convenient but not sufficient merely to employ now one semantic assumption, now another; a final sanction for the meanings thus discovered is required. And that sanction remains, with respect to the interpretation of language, where Plato had placed it: in the ontological correspondence with "things." No matter how assiduously usages—grammatical, historical, or metaphorical—were observed in the text, and no matter how ingeniously uses—applications and accommodations—were made of the text, all of these had eventually to conform with the truth of a priori, God-given objects. The observation of linguistic use and con-

---

[34] II, 307: "Sermo non tantum rem, sed et cogitationes auditorum spectat."

text could not in any case be allowed to generate its own semantics. If use is often seen as meaning, that meaning must finally be seen as objectively referential. To be "true," a use must correspond, as Flacius insists, to the "nature" of the object.

While this kind of semantic closure was polemically and theoretically necessary to the entire enterprise of Protestantism, the methods of that enterprise continued in practice to open the sacred text to all the various forms of semantic determination borrowed from humanist scholarship and rhetoric. Flacius is ever eager to demonstrate the Erasmian point that Scripture is even more "eloquent" than literature—not on the basis of its divine origin but because its language does more of what all language does. That is, Scripture "contains" more than ordinary speech or secular literature; it is more tightly packed with a greater "density of both things and meanings" (II, 311); it is, in a word, supercopious. Flacius gives an elaborate comparative analysis of Virgil's *Eclogues* and Paul's Epistle to the Romans, arguing that what Paul lacks in "grace," he makes up for in "matter" (II, 313–14). Paul, and Scripture generally, packs much meaning into few words; this normative principle is quoted from Cicero and Horace (II, 315). The rest of Flacius' treatise exemplifies tropes mainly from Paul, some from Psalms, with comparative excurses on Virgil and Demosthenes as analyzed in the commentaries of Scaliger. The next treatise in the *Clavis*, "on the style" of Scripture, is wholly devoted to "vindicating" it from the contempt of those who admire only Cicero (II, 340–341). The vindication proceeds by showing that, although Scripture contains all the levels of style prescribed in classical rhetoric, it is mostly sublime, and is therefore as complex and as efficacious in its power to move us as any profane literature.

Such a thoroughgoing assimilation, with respect to reception and interpretation, of the Word to words did not pass unopposed by some of the more radical sects who were beginning in the 1560s and 70s (in France and England) to be known as Puritans. But the constant recourse to secular philology and literature to elucidate Scripture remained typical enough of

Protestant establishments of all stripes to become a stock charge against them by Catholic controversialists. The semantic model of this assimilation remained that of cosmetic containment; but the practice of interpretation and the arguments it occasioned were conducted in terms that both perpetuated and defied that model. Meanings remained "significations," but were routinely observed to vary as functions of sociohistorical use and emotional tone.

One such argument is driven expressly to defend the general Protestant practice of applying secular semantic determinations to Scripture. William Fulke, a Calvinist defending the English versions of the Bible against their Catholic detractor, must deal with the repeated accusation that Protestants are continually consulting profane writers and ignoring the "Ecclesiastical use of wordes."[35] In reply Fulke urges the fact of historical semantic multiplicity and the principle that context is at least partly determining: "if the Scripture have used a worde in one signification sometimes, it is not necessarie that it should alwaies use it in the same signification, when it is proved by auncient writers that the worde hath other significations, more proper to the place, and agreeable to the rule of fayth." He also urges the fact of historical semantic change against relying only on the fathers, since they "oftentimes used wordes, as the people did then take them, and not as they signified in the Apostles tyme." He exemplifies such changes in Greek words and concludes: "It is not a faulte therefore, prudently to seeke even out of prophane writers, what is the proper signification of wordes, and howe many significations a woorde may have" in order to discern which is "moste apte" for the context and "moste agreeable" to the Holy Spirit (*A Defense*, p. 71).

[35] *A Defense of the sincere and true Translations of the holie Scriptures into the English tong, against the manifold cavils, frivolous quarels, and impudent slaunders of Gregorie Martin* (London, 1583), p. 69. Despite the title this debate is more serious and better-mannered than many. Fulke here reprints, refuting it paragraph by paragraph, Martin's *A Discoverie of the manifold corruptions of the holy Scriptures by the . . . English Sectaries* (Rheims, 1582).

That meanings are made by communal usage and are hence subject in interpretation to historically informed choice are the working assumptions that the Reformation inherited from humanist scholarship. They imply a constitutive and functional semantics that conflicts with the traditional representative and cosmetic model. This conflict surfaces in one of the most extended arguments that Fulke has with Martin about translation, which demands full attention to present as well as past usage. The issue is the Protestant rendering of the Greek *eidolon* as "image" (1 John 5:21). The Catholic Martin, of course, insists on making a distinction between "images" as objects of permitted worship and "idols" as objects of excessive and impious adoration. He finds the distinction in common speech: "who ever heard in English that our money, or bellie, were our images?" (p. 89). Fulke must admit this semantic distinction of usage, while trying to obliterate it by an appeal to the nature of things: "I confesse the use of the English tongue, in these speaches, is rather to call them idols, than images, and to extend the name idol (which is alwaies taken in the evill parte) to that which the word image can not so aptly signifie: yet in trueth of the thing there is no difference betwene idol and image" (p. 90). Martin keeps hammering the point that Protestants willfully or ignorantly confuse the semantic distinction that he locates precisely in contemporary English usage. Fulke keeps conceding the usage ("this Englishe worde idoll is by use restrayned, onely to wicked images," p. 108) and asserting that the objects are still the same. Martin's points are cogent enough, however, that Fulke cannot rest his case on this time-honored assertion of referential semantics that the meaning of the word *is* the object it "refers to."

Their confrontation admirably illustrates what the Renaissance discovered about language and left for Wittgenstein to demonstrate: that meaning is a function of use. "Idol" and "image" may indeed "refer to" the identical object, as Fulke says; but the *meanings* of those words, the opposed evaluations of that object, are far from identical, as Martin insists. To answer him, Fulke must here abandon the assumption that meaning equals the object and defend the rendering of "image" on the basis of historical usage: "The Greeke worde . . . signifieth generally all images" (p. 108). To this Martin objects that the "common use" and "accustomed signification" of the English word is more to be regarded in translation than the "originall propertie" of the Greek word literally rendered, and further insists that in its context it is pejorative, not general, and therefore to be rendered as "idol" (p. 113). Fulke must agree that the use in context is pejorative, while insisting that "the originall propertie" of the term so used is not. Having thus accepted the semantic criterion of use that Martin has urged all along, Fulke's final appeal is to history: "you must regarde howe the wordes were used in time of the writer." He then makes a summary that tries to have it both ways, glossing over the fact that he has lost his initial point: "in S. John, seeing at that tyme that he wrote, *eidolon*, signified an image generally, it may be translated, an image, generally, and seeing he speaketh of the unlawefull use of images, it may also be translated an idoll, as the worde is nowe taken to signifie."[36]

It is pleasantly ironic that the Catholic has here employed against his Calvinist opponent the semantic criterion that furnished the basis for the Protestant reapprehension of the Word. More important, however, is that these polemicists are having a real argument because they agree on one kind of evidence that will verify or falsify each other's positions. And this evidence is simply the Vallesque observation that the use of words—communal and individual, past and present—rather than their putative ontological correspondence, determines their meaning. At one point, Martin and Fulke even reach explicit agreement on the "principle" of translation that Luther prided himself on inventing, which required an ad hoc weighing of the claims, resulting from attention to usage, between fidelity to the historical or etymological sense and to that of

---

[36] P. 114. We should note that Fulke is compelled to this equivocation in order to defend all the generations of English translators, since "idols" had already been substituted in the Geneva Bible for the "images" of Tyndale and Cranmer: see the parallel texts in *The English Hexapla* (London, 1841).

current custom. Martin again makes the general criticism that Protestants desert "the usuall signification" of words in contemporary speech for their now inapplicable "originall propertie" (p. 131). Fulke agrees in principle that current usage may indeed take precedence over etymological purity, "that words taken by custome of speech into an Ecclesiasticall meaning, are not to be altered into a straunge or profane signification." But he is also constrained to preserve the possibility of such "alteration": "when . . . termes are abused by the custome of speech, to signifie some other thing, than they were first appointed for, or else be taken ambiguously for divers things: we ought not to be superstitious in these cases, but to avoide misunderstanding, we may use words according to their originall signification, as they were taken in such time, as they were written" (p. 132). By itself, this de facto acknowledgment of the dialectic between "past significance and present meaning" (in Robert Weimann's phrase) results from the fundamental perception of semantic change and produces the kind of research and argumentation that we have learned—but only since the Renaissance—to take for granted in the interpretation of any text.

But what this perception produces in Fulke's argument with Martin is merely a methodological agreement that remains, of course, impotent to reconcile their different versions of divine truth. "Use" all too easily becomes "abuse" as observation, ever inadequate to sustain prescription, must slide back into postulation of referential meaning in order to close the door on the flux of functional meaning that observation has uncovered. The "custom of speech" was by now a critical weapon wielded by everyone; but neither it nor the constitutive semantics it implied could furnish the ultimate validity claimed by all parties to biblical disputes. This was still sought in the nature of "things" as "signified" by the words that "corresponded" to them. Fulke has renewed recourse to this kind of assertion (no matter that it had failed him before) to defend the Protestant rendering of "church" as "congregation." These terms, he declares, are semantically equivalent: "the difference is only in sound of words, not in sense or meaning" (pp. 141–42). And this difference, he goes on to explain, is merely that of a reversible metonymy, the exchange of names between the container and the contained. It is therefore "all one . . . to say my congregation, or my Church."[37] Fulke's conclusion is belied by his own printer's capital letter in this brusque evasion of all the distinctions—semantic, actual, and normative—among forms of ecclesiastical organization and government. How one translated *ecclesia* was a semantic choice of the highest political importance—especially in England, where the difference between conceiving it as an institutional hierarchy or a communion of saints would become one of the causes of the Civil War.[38] Fulke's reductive dismissal of these profound differences highlights the polemical utility (if not cogency) of the appeal to reified, referential meaning. It serves to claim authority by masking political motives as ostensibly objective facts and by denying the interpretive obligation, elsewhere accepted, imposed by recognizing the semantic criterion of usage in context. Meanings—so fluid when located in words— had finally to be fixed in some more stable sphere.

The means of so fixing them lay ready to hand in the traditional dualistic theory and technical sophistication of rhetoric, which was capable of making a vast range of subtle distinctions in the use of words without endangering the privileged location of meanings. Fulke's reversible metonymy is the same "figurative" operation that allowed Luther's opponents to refute his doctrine of the real presence and thus evade the challenge of his affective semantics. Where Luther had found a unity, Calvin found a metonymy of a specifically mystical, Augustinian kind. Calvin's successor in Geneva, Theodore Beza, spilled much polemical ink in defense of his master's Eucharistic doctrines, intensifying the ancient analogy between

[37] Pp. 147–48 [misnumbered for 145–46, which are skipped].
[38] See John F. H. New, *Anglican and Puritan: The Basis of their Opposition, 1558–1640* (London, 1964), pp. 40, 45, 52–54.

the sacraments and language.[39] The main issue is the nature of the union between the sign and the thing. Since, "as Augustine rightlie teacheth," there must be "a certeine analogie, proportion, and agreement betweene the things signified, and the signes themselves. . . . it behooveth the signes so to agree with the things signified, that they may represent to mens minds that which they signifie."[40] The adverb for this union is "sacramentallie" (as against Lutheran "really," Catholic "substantially," and Zwinglian "commemoratively"). Beza explains its operation as that of language itself: the physical word or sign represents, by having a partial and mystical correspondence to, the meaning or thing signified. The classical definition of language is pressed into service as an explanation of the Calvinist doctrine of the sacraments: "Such thinges as are in the voice or words are signes of the affections, that are in the soule or minde. There is the selfe same consideration to be had of the sacraments."[41]

Beza thus makes explicit in a cruder form than Calvin the analogy implicit in regarding both sacraments and words as signs. Whereas Calvin had described the sacramental union as a mystic participation of the sign in the thing signified that had "no natural explanation," Beza supplies one: this union is just like that of words and meanings. For Calvin and Augustine,

---

[39] Beza was influential, and was frequently translated for a popular audience in England, owing to his hospitality to the Marian exiles and subsequent friendships with the leading Cambridge Puritans.

[40] *Two very lerned Sermons*, tr. T. Wilcox (London, 1588), p. 57. Beza made the same Augustinian/Calvinist point that sign and thing are both distinct and conjoined, even as their names may be metonymically exchanged, in *A briefe and pithie summe of the christian faith*, tr. Robert Fylls (London, n.d.), fols. 67–67ᵛ. His original works on the subject are included in *Tractationes Theologicae* (Geneva, 1582), 3 vols.: "de hypostatica duarum in Christo naturam unione" (III) and "defensio sacramentalis coniunctionis corporis et sanguinis christi cum sacris symbolis, adversus Matthiae Flacii Illyrici" (II). One of Beza's English acquaintances, Thomas Cartwright, summarized the same doctrine in a popularized catechistical tract, *A Treatise of Christian Religion*, 2d ed. (London, 1616), p. 213.

[41] *Two very lerned Sermons*, pp. 67–68. Just so are Christ's body and blood "sacramentallie signified," p. 63.

sacraments were a special kind of sign; for Beza the analogy between them and words, and the consequent remystification of language, is complete. Whether partial or complete, however, as a semantic assumption the analogy can do no more than assert the magical conjunction of what it has separated in the first place. The need for such reassertion—the focus of these disputes on the exact relation of signs and things, words and meanings—was produced by the semantic challenges latent in the scholarly and interpretive practices of Erasmus and overt in the more radical teachings of Luther. Rejecting in their different ways the tradition of medieval allegory that postulated a whole hierarchy of transcendent meanings beyond the words of the text, both reformers sought instead to elucidate the meanings they experienced in the words of the text. For Luther, this effort had resulted in a total refusal of the sacramental/linguistic analogy and a brilliant, if problematic, reconception of the semantic union as identity. Although neither of these most radical Lutheran positions was ever accepted, developed, or fully understood—even by the church that came to bear his name—his fundamental insistence on finding the meaning of the Word in the words of Scripture, encapsulated in the principle of "one literal sense," became an inspiration, a polemical weapon, and a source of difficulty for Protestants everywhere.

The difficulty proceeded, as in the case of Flacius, from the wish to accommodate under the Lutheran formula all the traditional kinds of "figurative" meaning that Luther himself had ruled out. William Whitaker, a moderate and learned Anglican, wrestles with this problem more cogently than Flacius did, attempting to maintain a clear distinction between the "single" meaning and its plural "applications."[42] But the semantic model to which Whitaker appeals to save "the whole entire sense" is precisely the Augustinian and Calvinist one of

[42] *A Disputation on Holy Scripture against the Papists* . . . [1st ed. Cambridge, 1588], tr. William Fitzgerald (Cambridge, 1849), pp. 405–07. Madsen, *From Shadowy Types to Truth*, p. 32, draws this contrast more sharply, regarding Whitaker as "a much more powerful mind" than Flacius.

participation of sign in thing. Whitaker defines the single sense, which is capable of various applications, as "that which arises from the words themselves, whether they be taken strictly or figuratively." As Luther had insisted that the spiritual understanding of the Word was an intrinsic and indivisible part of the literal meaning of the words, so Whitaker includes biblical types as parts of "the whole entire sense." Typology is thus semantically distinguished from allegories, which are not part of the sense but merely "applications" of it. For Whitaker, moreover, the moral implications of the text, like types, are also "one and the same with the literal sense." And he explains their semantic operation as bringing to light the "thing signified" that was hidden in the "sign." Taken together, these give us the "whole complete sense" that, while spiritual, is not "different" from the "really literal; since the letter itself affords it to us in the way of similitude or argument."

Whitaker's procedure again shows how Luther's original demand for semantic unity is both compromised by and preserved in the traditional network of dualistic semantic assumptions. Meanings must now be sought *in* words, must be "single" and "literal"; but words are still "signs" that signify "things." The new desire and polemic is for unity; but the unity is arrived at and explained as the magical "conjunction" of the terms of the old duality.[43] In short, the new semantic identity is asserted in terms of the old semantic process. Letter and spirit together are to make one meaning—not by the Lutheran apprehension of words as performing affectively, but rather by the Augustinian conception of words as corresponding to, by somehow participating in, things.

[43] Charles K. Cannon, "William Whitaker's *Disputatio ad Sacra Scriptura*: A Sixteenth-Century Theory of Allegory," *Huntington Library Quarterly* 25 (1962), 129–38, urges that it prefigures the post-Coleridgean notion of the unity of form and matter, overcoming the shell/kernel theory of language and literature. Though Cannon well perceives the issues, he overlooks their origin in Augustine as well as their centrality in Lutheran/Calvinist debates and so considerably overestimates both the originality and the merits of Whitaker's position.

The genuine and lasting revolution in Protestant hermeneutics, predicated on the humanist treatment of language as a sociohistorical product, was the revaluation of the "literal" sense—the insistence on locating whatever kind of value and meaning in "the words themselves" and regarding it as at least partly determined by context. Although controversy and confusion over what was "literal" and what "figurative" was perhaps as great by the late sixteenth century as it had been in the late middle ages,[44] the scholarship of Erasmus and the polemics of Protestantism did produce one permanent clarification. However "spiritual" the "literal" sense was taken to be, it had henceforth to include, not exclude, both grammar and history. This redetermination of the "literal" in the temporal flux of grammatical and historical meanings, which established the basis for all subsequent textual interpretation, found both example and sanction, as Erasmus had to keep insisting, in the fathers. But such revaluation of Scripture, like that of secular and vernacular literature, did not necessarily entail reconsideration of semantic processes. The theory of the Word, like that of words, remained ontologically bound despite its assimilation of all the interpretive practices that construed meaning as a dynamic function of linguistic usage and human purpose.

[44] Madsen demonstrates that "by the middle of the seventeenth century the distinction between the Catholic theory of manifold senses and the Protestant theory of the one literal sense had, for all practical purposes, become meaningless": *From Shadowy Types to Truth*, pp. 38–39.

7

EPILOGUE

And I can see it in various aspects according to   —LUDWIG
the fiction I surround it with.   WITTGENSTEIN

The Renaissance discovery of history as linguistic change—
first in Latin, then in vernaculars—aroused great fascination
with the idea of origins and hence with the biblical account of
creation. Commentaries on Genesis proliferated, and the origin of language became a favorite subject of humanist speculation. This domain of interests provides a final example of the
semantic challenge posed and defeated at the level of theory—
indeed of the whole collision between contradictory assumptions produced by regarding language as a human activity on
the one hand and a divinely established code on the other. In
Genesis 2:19–20 the origin of language is portrayed in God's
parading all the animals before Adam "to see what he would
call them: and whatsoever Adam called every living creature,
that was the name thereof."

The ancient and general agreement on the interpretation of
this episode remained unaffected by the Reformation. "Tradition had long accepted the naming of the animals as a sign of
man's domination over them and as a proof of his wisdom";
sixteenth-century commentaries share the belief that, in the
words of John Donne, "Adam was able to decipher the nature
of every creature in the name thereof."[1] That prior knowledge

---

[1] Arnold Williams, *The Common Expositor: An Account of the Commentaries on Genesis 1527–1633* (Chapel Hill, 1948), p. 81.

The patristic compendium in the *Glossa* had stressed man's dominion over all creatures; Nicholas of Lyra emphasized that Adam had conceptual knowledge (*noticiam*) of their "natural properties."

of their natures was a prerequisite to giving them names is spelled out by an English compiler: "by this imposing of names upon the creatures, appeareth the great knowledge and wisedome of man. . . . for names were given at the first according to the severall properties and nature of creatures."[2] The source of this extraordinary knowledge is specified by Milton's Adam as he recounts the experience:

> I nam'd them, as they pass'd, and understood
> Thir Nature, with such knowledge God endu'd
> My sudden apprehension.
> [*Paradise Lost*, VIII.352–54]

Although the biblical text, of course, makes no mention of such infused knowledge as a precondition for name-giving, the ageless word-magic that sees naming as controlling has become the cognitive power explicit in the commentaries. Their consensus admirably illustrates the philosophical formalization of the atavistic potency of words, the transposition into a conceptual necessity of the magical displacement of the felt power of words into things. The names that correspond to the possession of the object, by this basically Platonic maneuver, have become those that correspond to the accurate knowledge of the object. In both kinds of operation—what the utterance confers (power) or what must be conferred before the utterance can occur (knowledge)—words are taken to be either the magical equivalent of the object or the magical encoding of its nature and properties. Words, to be meaningful, must be mysteriously bound to a given ontology, presumed consubstantial or congruent with reality. Adam must "know" before he can "name," and his naming is evidence of such knowledge.

In the face of this apparently unanimous imposition on the

---

[2] Andrew Willet, *Hexapla in Genesin* (London, 1608), p. 37. Willet could easily be paraphrasing Luther, whose interpretation of the episode remained wholly traditional—postulating Adam's "natural knowledge" of the beasts' "properties" as a precondition for giving them "fitting" names—from his early lectures (*WA* XIV, 125–26) to his late commentaries (*WA* XLII, 90) on Genesis.

biblical myth of the a priori metaphysics that reduces language to copying (or imitating, representing, signifying) what is presumed to exist, there is in the Renaissance, so far as I know, but one dissenting voice. Charles de Bovelles, concluding the treatise in which, as we saw, he developed the notion of the speech community into a total denial that vernaculars could be standardized or reduced to rule, clinches his argument by making the revolutionary inference from the story in Genesis that "From the will of the first parent, Adam, arose, God willing, the first language of the world":

From his will, indeed—God permitting—there is no doubt that the language of the human race proceeded, which otherwise would have been uniform up to now, and alike everywhere in the world, except that the spirit of God at the building of the Tower of Babel set it asunder into the innumerable languages of the world. Since it is indeed written that in the beginning God led all the living creatures of the earth to Adam, to see what he would call them; and what he called each was its name. Furthermore, even his wife, because she was taken from the flesh and bone of the man, he called woman in the sight of God. This cloaks for us a twofold mystery. First, because it teaches that it was the first parent, by the gift of God, who of his own will, instituted the world's first language, as, following God's command, he gave a name to every single living being. Second, because it shows that man was endowed by God with free will and was given the high honor of naming, as he saw fit, every substance that was created for his sake. For as the free and spontaneous origin of all substances depended on the will of God, so God willed and decreed that the origin of all names, words, and appellations should arise from the choice of man (namely the first parent).[3]

---

[3] *Liber de differentia vulgarium linguarum* (Paris, 1533), p. 46: "Ab arbitrio primi parentis Adae primam voluntate dei emanasse mundi linguam. . . . Huius enim ab arbitrio, permittente deo, prima non dubium est humani generis lingua manavit, quae alioqui hactenus uniformis, & ubique forte terrarum par esset, nisi hanc spiritus dei in aedificatione Babylonicae turris, in immensas huius mundi linguas dissecuisset. Scriptum est enim quoniam in initio adduxit deus cuncta terrae animantia ad Adam, ut videret quid vocaret ea: & omne quod vocavit est nomen eius. Nam & hic, uxorem etiam suam, quia ex ossibus, & carne viri sumpta esset, viraginem coram deo appellavit. Id quidem

Bovelles here finds a rationale for the irrepressible variety of vernaculars by ignoring altogether the traditionally imposed metaphysics of a priori "knowledge." Names are "arbitrary," not mystical encodings of reality. To locate the origin of language in human choice is to insist, as Lorenzo Valla had, that linguistic processes are contingent on human purposes, that meanings are made and not born. And, as Valla had also done, it is to remove from the linguistic field its magical guarantor of truth and meaning.[4] God created the world, but he left man free to name it. A comparable demystification of the operation of language was attempted by Luther, who found the meaning of words not in what they signified, on the sacramental model, but in what they created as acts and feelings. Both the Vallesque perception of language as a sociohistorical product and the Lutheran apprehension of its meanings as affective relieved words of their duty to copy or encode a preextant "reality" and deprived them of their divinely guaranteed ability to do so. While Bovelles' reading of the scriptural story may be unique as a commentary, its motives and implications reflect all the challenges to orthodoxy that stimulated the entire period's reapprehension of both words and the Word.

We may observe that Bovelles, though no Protestant, offers a good deal more "literal" interpretation of the text than the traditional glosses did. He stays closer to its rather simple terms, neglecting the remoter implications of power and knowledge to focus entirely on the narrative fact of God's consent to man's exercise of will. In their turn, however, the im-

---

duplex nobis mysterium tegit. Primum, quod doceat stetisse in primo parente, & munere dei, primae totius mundi linguae voluntariae institutionis arbitrium, ut qui sua singulis animantibus, iubente deo, nomina posuerit. Secundum, quod testetur donatum a deo hominem esse libero arbitrio, impensumque illi hunc honorem, ut singulas mundi substantias, propter hominem factas arbitrariis nominibus imbueret. Sicut enim ab arbitrio dei, libera & spontanea substantiarum omnium origo pependit, ita nimirum voluit sanxitque deus, omnium nominum, vocum & appellationum origenem ab hominis (nempe a primi parentis) arbitratu proficisci debere."

[4] Valla's brief mention of Adam's naming in a crucial passage of the *Dialectica* is quoted above, ch. 3, n. 31.

plications of thus discovering the origin of language in human choice can easily be made to reaccommodate the ideas of power and knowledge. That is, the "literal" reading that excludes one set of "figurative" significations (a prior ontology) may yield another and opposite set (a posterior ontology). The same relation that tradition found in the story—the immemorial intuition of the potency of words as control of or congruence with things—may be accounted for by reversing it: the knowledge that yields the name becomes the name that yields the knowledge. Thus, the act of naming *is* the act of knowing; words are indeed coextensive with the world; they make it what we know it to be, give it the shape it has for us, and allow us to control it. But this would be a different knowledge of a different world—the variable one constituted by language, not the immutable one to which language must, however inexplicably, conform. Semantics would be epistemology, and the creative power of the divine *logos* would be demystified into the profane but no less creative power of the human community to manufacture meaning. It would be the world of Montaigne, Hamlet, and Don Quixote, the opaque but exhilarating theatre whose pageants come to no final certainty but death. It would be the world we actually live in, which became imaginable in the modern West as a result of all the forms of the Renaissance interrogation of language that we have examined.

From humanist philosophy, philology, and rhetoric appeared the following challenges to referential semantics: Valla's explicit identification of semantics with ontology; his elevation of "common usage" into a philosophical principle and his practical analysis of it as a semantic determinant. This new treatment of grammatical and sociohistorical contexts as semantically constitutive crystallized into the legitimation of vernacular literatures and speech communities, and was developed by Erasmus and Luther into different versions of affective semantics in Scripture. The reactions against all these moves toward a variously relational semantics were victorious at the level of theory, but the linguistic energies thereby released were fully manifested in literature. The historical importance of these moves is that they had never before been made on such a scale. Whatever semantic insights one may detect in poets or philosophers prior to Valla had never coalesced into the linked series of challenges to the sign/thing model which pervaded Renaissance culture, being embedded in its interpretive practices even when repudiated in its theories. Such challenges become visible only when we ourselves refuse the domination of that model.

I introduced this outline of my argument as a "reading" of Adam's naming of the animals in order to illustrate how assumptions can determine meanings. The fictions we surround things with—that is, the contexts that interpreters bring to words—are what reveal their meaning to us. This process is ironically confirmed by the contradiction between the historical development of Protestant hermeneutics and its central principle. The development is the reaccommodation of traditionally "figurative" (or any multiple) meanings within an expanded, but solidly based "literal" sense. The principle is that Scripture interprets itself, that the "express words" of the Bible scrutinized by and for themselves will yield clear and certain meanings. The contradiction between the two is that the ease with which the first may be and was accomplished reveals the fallacy of the second.

Just as I, making the revolutionary semantic assumptions derived from Valla that underlay Bovelles' new "literal" reading, was able to include in that reading an opposite version of its traditional "figurative" significance, so Protestants, making traditional Augustinian semantic assumptions, could include in a declared "literal" reading of the text most of its old "figurative" meanings. The status of these latter could remain more or less entirely vague, as in Flacius, or could be demoted from "meanings" proper to "applications," as in Whitaker. But in either case traditional figurative discourse, regarded as signifying in the traditional way, was found quite compatible with the revived literal (as historical and grammatical) sense. The "express words" of the text, even when focused on with philological sophistication and Protestant passion, will continue to yield whatever kind of meaning one assumes language has. Whether Adam's power to name the animals was cognitive or voluntarist, or whether Christ's equation of his body with bread was substantive or symbolic, cannot be decided on the basis of the text alone. Depending on one's assumption—that words constitute or are cosmetic to meanings—the meaning will alter; but in no case does any meaning determine or declare itself. In all of these Protestant polemics, and in many modern ones about literature and history, their subject matter—the "express words" of the text—is constantly mistaken for their arbiter.[5] The evidence in the case cannot also be its judge. The common inspiration, given by Luther to all forms of Protestantism, that Scripture interprets itself was a ringing battle cry to liberate the Word from the monopoly of the Church; as a principle it is political, not hermeneutic. For example, in the face of all the equally good (and equally vitriolic) arguments that "this is my body" is to be interpreted literally or figuratively, the universal insistence that Scripture interprets itself is farcical. Everyone claimed it to justify his own liberty of interpretation; but any given interpretation was determined by more and other factors than the text itself.

Crucial among these, as I have tried to show, were the conflicting assumptions about how language means, whether embedded in analytic procedures or articulated as polemical ones. Not all the common methods and principles that Protestants inherited from humanist philology and rhetoric could compel them to a common interpretation of the Word. They shared enough, though, to have a few genuine arguments about it. No party to the controversy over the Eucharist lacked either definitions of tropes, or elaborate "proofs" of their presence or absence in Scripture, or rules for establishing the relation between figurative and "true" senses. Moreover, most parties were agreed on what would constitute primary evi-

---

[5] For a discussion of this kind of error as it has affected Renaissance scholarship, see my review of P. O. Kristeller, *Renaissance Thought and Its Sources* (New York, 1979), in *Bibliothèque d'humanisme et Renaissance* 43 (1981), 167–71.

dence: grammatical usage and historical context. Their real arguments proceeded from the new, direct, and affective attention to the text and concerned the appropriateness or primacy of applying one context or another to its interpretation. To allow secular contexts as a semantic determinant of the Word was the revolution and the threat; and it was no help at all to attempt to close the debates thus opened by declaring that the text was its own context.[6] All went right on to construe differently their shared evidence and to construct different proofs out of their common materials for the different kinds of meaning they heard, saw, and felt in the sacred text. They were able thus diversely to apprehend it precisely because texts do not apprehend themselves.

The closure vainly asserted in argument could only be reimposed by authority. The spirit of Luther must have been mightily dismayed when the faculty of Wittenberg decreed in 1638 that to criticize the solecisms of New Testament Greek was blasphemy against the Holy Ghost; in his own church, the typographical errors in Luther's German Bible were steadily reprinted on the grounds (which he himself had vehemently denied) that every syllable of it was the direct product of divine inspiration.[7] Thus did Protestantism, like the Council of Trent, seek to control the linguistic energies that the first and greatest reformers had released by simply repressing what it could not resolve. The irony of the situation had earlier been appreciated by John Hales, a cultivated and urbane Regius Professor of Greek at Oxford, who pointed out that division from Rome on the basis of returning to Scripture made no sense if the reformed churches now do just what Rome did: set up their glosses as canonical.[8]

[6] The fact that adversaries agreed on this fallacious principle, each attempting to use it against the other, could produce occasionally frank bewilderment and perplexity as to where indeed they disagreed. See the excellent analysis of the contention between Whitgift and Cartwright by John S. Coolidge, *The Pauline Renaissance in England* (Oxford, 1970), Ch. 1.

[7] F. W. Farrar, *History of Interpretation* (New York, 1886), p. 374.

[8] *A sermon . . . concerning the abuses of obscure and difficult places of . . . scripture* (Oxford, 1617), p. 32.

It was nonetheless the enduring achievement, and I believe the defining quality, of the Renaissance to call the canonical into question. The semantic challenges that underlay the primary linguistic preoccupations of the period made the transparent congruence of word and fact, which Dante had been able merely to presume, henceforth problematic. The awareness of language as the necessary mediator of all experience, desire, and knowledge, sacred or profane, had become sufficiently diffused throughout the culture to require refutation as theory and to produce revolutions in the practice of reading and writing. The validity of such awareness, made possible by regarding language as constitutive of rather than cosmetic to meaning, is ironically confirmed by the very efforts made to deny it. In Protestantism these took the form of postulating the self-interpreting text and reasserting the Augustinian view of words as signs that mystically participate in or stand for a semantic elsewhere. If meanings were indeed separable and intact objects that came wrapped neatly or sloppily, transparently or obscurely, in words, then it would have been impossible to raise the semantic questions that produced all the debates on the salvific efficacy of the heard Word, the nature and operation of the sacraments, the profane transmission of the divine text, and the relevance of secular history and literature to its interpretation. Precisely the *kinds* of textual disagreements that Protestants had with Catholics and with each other demonstrate the fallacy of the semantic model that yet withstood their challenge. The ultimate paradox in the Protestant reapprehension of the Word is that the debates it occasioned—and their resistance to closure—can only be accounted for by the semantic assumption that those debates had to reject in theory. As Montaigne perceived, the endless glossing of books by books, the whole history of interpretation, demonstrates that language is neither a garment nor a pipeline, but an activity. The use of words collectively and individually constitutes their meanings, which must therefore be constructed by speakers and texts and reconstructed by listeners and readers. No better analogy for the semantic transaction has yet been offered than Montaigne's tennis game, in which victory—making sense—is always possible but never guaranteed and never permanent.

Although the consequences of this new semantic awareness were most fully drawn and exploited in the greatest literature of the period, they were, and remain, obviously unacceptable to any ideology that claims to furnish certain and unalterable truth. The Renaissance saw the beginnings of the long transition from one dominant form of such ideology—Christianity—to another—empirical science. To both forms, the spectacle of fluid signifiers was finally an embarrassment, something to be admitted only as preparatory to wiping it out. What I have called the dilemma of the age—the search for absolute knowledge by means increasingly recognized as contingent—was temporarily resolved by finding ways to deny or sidestep the contingency. But the dilemma did not thereby disappear; it merely slumbered until, reawakened by the appreciation of contingency in twentieth-century philosophy, linguistics, anthropology, and science itself, it has become the dilemma of our age, too.

★

Today, however, the over-appreciation of contingency in post-Romantic humanistic and literary scholarship has inverted the form that the dilemma retains in philosophy and science. There, the problem is still how to arrive at predictable certainties by the contingent means of one discourse or another—what I earlier called the positivist delusion. Modern criticism of literature and the arts has, on the contrary, rejoiced in contingencies and the fluidity of signifiers, replacing cognitive certainties with autonomous texts and art objects—the aesthetic delusion. Both delusions employ referential semantics to postulate the transcendental status of their opposed claims to truth: the discourse of science is to represent eternal fact, that of poetry to incarnate eternal value. Relational semantics finds both claims fallacious for the same reason that the Protestant claim of self-interpreting Scripture proved farcical:

nothing constitutes its own context, and no object or utterance is ever context-free. If it is, it is either nonsense or simply unintelligible.

What Protestants claimed for Scripture is precisely what post-Romantic poetics, inspired in part by the Renaissance wish to revalue art, claims for literature: its absolute autonomy. The self-interpreting text made up of words that mystically participate in the immutable essences they stand for is the post-Romantic literary Gospel—the secularized version of Protestant Augustinianism.[9] As we have seen in actual arguments about how to interpret the Word, appeals are constantly made to all sorts of contexts, which amply contradict the theoretical assertion constantly reiterated that the text declares its own meaning. Just the same thing occurs in much modern discussion of literature, history, and art, in which claims of theoretical autonomy can never be sustained by the practice of analytic argument. But there is a more exaggerated form of the claim to autonomy characteristic of modern humanistic scholarship that reassumes the cultural pose of its originators.

Paul O. Kristeller was voicing a cherished assumption of current "liberal arts education" when he praised the Renaissance for discovering "the autonomy of *culture*" (my italics)—that is, its existence and pursuit independent of religious and political pressures.[10] Both the nostalgic tone and the self-defensiveness of this posture are direct descendants of the way in which Renaissance humanists defined themselves as guardians of "humane letters" against the narrow aridity of scholastic logic on the one hand, and the godless materialism of Averroistic science on the other. For the modern student of the "humanities," only the names have changed and the enemies list grown somewhat larger. We suffer not only the narrow, moralistic utilitarianism of the philistines and the supposedly valueless empiricism of science, but the additional predations of educationist administrators, interfering politicians, and occa-

[9] This transference is described in ch. 1, pp. 27–28, 37.
[10] *Eight Philosophers of the Italian Renaissance* (Stanford, 1964), p. 94.

sionally revolutionary students. (Though we should recall that neither the Middle Ages nor the Renaissance was unprovided with reactionary university authorities, capricious princes, and often rebellious students.) This beleaguered but not unflattering self-image of the Renaissance humanist has produced in his modern epigone virtually the identical kind of tone and tactics. An admiring nostalgia for a remote past, which is felt to be superior to and is used to criticize the present and the more immediate past, is focused upon the verbal and artistic expression of that period, resulting in a program to recover or revive its forms of expression in some supposedly "purified" state. The general attitude, for example, of Petrarch's famous avowal in his "Epistle to Posterity"—"I devoted myself . . . to the study of ancient times, since I always disliked our own period . . . and I always tried to transport myself mentally to other times"—is shared by Douglas Bush when he recommends Renaissance literature to "modern readers" who, thanks to it, "can at least live part of their lives in a finer air than their own."[11] The Renaissance admiration for the archaic style of Ciceronian Latin along with the whole question of etymological purity in the use of words finds a modern parallel in the efforts of many latter-day humanists to preserve the very term "culture" (in its deific Arnoldian sense of high cultivation and refined artistic achievement) from its more inclusive and relativistic use in anthropology.[12]

The self-legitimation and self-protection of this humanist posture, then and now, is obvious. The professional *laudator temporis acti* asserts the "autonomy of culture" against other in-

[11] *Letters from Petrarch*, tr. Morris Bishop (Bloomington, Ind., 1966), pp. 5–6; Bush, *English Literature in the Earlier Seventeenth Century*, 2d ed. (Oxford, 1962), p. 424. Hardin Craig, one of the pioneer historicist critics of the period, frankly averred that modern philosophy "lacks the unity, the integration, the intelligible practicality of the philosophy of the Renaissance," *The Enchanted Glass* (New York, 1936), p. 264.

[12] Though this battle is long lost, it leaves traces. See the account by Benjamin Nelson and Charles Trinkaus of why Jacob Burckhardt's *Kultur* was translated as "civilization" in the title of his great work, *The Civilization of the Renaissance in Italy* (New York, 1958), Introduction, i, 6–7.

terests, tastes, and forces that seem to threaten him: formal lo-
gicians or mindless empiricists, tyrannical rulers or Senator
Joe McCarthy. The threats may be real or imagined; the point
is that in either case what is asserted as a desideratum is thereby
revealed to be most emphatically not a fact. Culture, even in
the deific sense, is never autonomous. Neither its existence
(the production of ideas or art objects) nor its pursuit (their appreciation or study) is ever independent of social pressures. To
seek freedom from some particular form of iniquitous control
is understandable and necessary. But to generalize an argument for such freedom into a concept that guides interpretation and historical investigation is utterly fallacious. The actual
situation was finely described by R. R. Bolgar at the end of his
magisterial survey of classical learning in the West:

It was always some urgent practical need that set the scholars to their
task and gave their curiosity . . . a definite and fruitful purpose. It was
always some practical need, to preserve some desired *status quo*, that
acted as a bar to the pursuit of researches which went beyond what
was immediately useful. The history of learning is not a free field. It
is the history of society.[13]

The neglect of this obvious truth has emerged as the most
glaring theoretical weakness in the largely formalist orientation of most modern criticism of both literature and visual
art.[14] Such an orientation is obliged to assume, if not explicitly
to defend, the "autonomy" of the art object.[15] In the sustained

---

[13] *The Classical Heritage and its Beneficiaries* (Cambridge, 1954), p. 379.

[14] Although Arnold Hauser's full-scale polemic for the sociological and
psychological causation of stylistic change in art, *The Philosophy of Art History*
(London, 1959), has not found particular favor among art historians, some of
his principal positions have been incorporated in later work: for example, his
attack on Wölfflin's hypostatization of stylistic elements is continued by Michael Levey, *High Renaissance* (Harmondsworth, 1975). Hauser's insistence on
relating style to a wider cultural context is partly reflected in the general approach of the Penguin series, *Style and Civilization*, to which Levey's volume
belongs, and was further extended in the approach of Michael Baxandall,
Painting and Experience in Fifteenth-Century Italy (Oxford, 1972).

[15] The profound theoretical difficulties of defining these objects, particu-

assaults that formalism has lately undergone, especially in literary theory, the autonomous art object has been an early casualty. Or so it would appear at first glance, when the formerly sacrosanct "text" is offered by Derrida as something for the reader to "deconstruct," or by Barthes as something that "deconstructs" itself, or by Kristeva as something that reflects the infinite possibilities of all language.[16] Moreover, the structuralists are highly sensitive to the operation of "ideologies," that is, of sociolinguistically imposed patterns of significance, in interpretation. In fact, the whole thrust of their program is precisely to escape from such impositions by becoming aware of their "operative conventions."[17] Recognizing the actual impossibility of escape either from history or language, structuralist (or more accurately, post-structuralist) criticism seeks nonetheless to "imagine" or "dream" the escape partly by regarding the text as merely a nest of self-referring codes. The text is described in metaphors that postulate its absolute indeterminacy: Barthes' onion of many layers but no center, Kristeva's mirror that reflects whatever is before it, J. Hillis Miller's host/parasite that feeds on and begets other texts.[18] Interpretation consequently becomes the reader's account of his own process of reading; indeed, the liberation of the reader's creative freedom is a primary goal.

To pursue it, however, by asserting the indeterminacy of the text, or of the body of texts called literature, is to preserve almost intact the kind of autonomy demanded by formalist aestheticism or Protestant hermeneutics. Indeterminacy itself—the quality of being without limits—is surely autonomy of a high order. For the *nouvelle critique*, literature is finally inde-

---

larly in the attempt to give them some distinctive ontological status, are revealed by Richard Wollheim, *Art and Its Objects* (New York, 1971).

[16] The development of French structuralism as it bears on literature is most informatively reviewed and sympathetically criticized by Jonathan Culler, *Structuralist Poetics* (London, 1975).

[17] Culler, pp. 252–53.

[18] On Barthes and Kristeva: Culler, pp. 259, 246–47; Miller, "The Critic as Host," *Critical Inquiry* 3 (1977), 439–47.

pendent of everything except the reader, whose paradoxical task becomes to recognize but "resist" (Derrida's term) the conventions operative in his own language and that of the text. Though the humanist posture, largely shared by (now old) Anglo-American New Criticism, was one of reverence toward the text, the general tone of much of the *nouvelle critique* is designedly irreverent. Though the humanist worships the ancient, the post-structuralist enthusiastically defends the modern.[19] But both assert or assume the existence of texts independent of an historical or linguistic context that could control their interpretation. Functionally, each theory requires us to ignore or to "resist" any such context. That the *nouvelle critique* at least acknowledges its existence, whereas the New Criticism had officially to deny it (often while admitting it in practice), seems to make little difference at the conceptual level.[20] Again, an argument for freedom—of the text or of the reader—generates a desideratum, manifestly not a fact, that is then regarded as a characteristic of the object itself. Again, the polemical posture moves from self-legitimation to self-aggrandizement, much more overtly for the post-structuralists than for the humanist: he was but the keeper of the flame; they have become its creators.[21]

But we are still assured that formalism, and with it the au-

[19] See Frank Kermode's refutation of Barthes' falsely chronological distinction between "lisible" and "scriptible" texts, in which he also observes that much structuralist theory is in fact a polemic against academic criticism: "The Use of the Codes," in *Approaches to Poetics*, ed. Seymour Chatman (New York, 1973), pp. 78–79.

[20] The nature and extent of the New Critics' formalism was an issue in a recent argument between René Wellek and Gerald Graff—*Critical Inquiry* 5 (1979), 569–79—in which Graff observes, citing R. S. Crane, that polemical tactics, however necessary, "should not be permitted to dictate our understanding of what literature is" (574).

[21] It is probably no accident that the most radical theories of textual indeterminacy, as well as some of the most extravagant polemical gestures, should come from France, where the opposition, in the form of a highly centralized educational system that dispenses a fairly rigid canon of literary texts along with traditionally canonized judgments on them, is a good deal more entrenched and monolithic than in America, Britain, or Germany.

tonomy of art, is dead.[22] It is important to observe that such reports may be slightly premature in order to recognize in these discussions the persistence of false oppositions that echo back to the Renaissance and beyond: ancient versus modern, words versus matter, aesthetic appreciation versus historical knowledge. The polemical exigencies of particular times and places have repeatedly misconstrued as contradictory what in fact are complementary. This is fatally easy to do because the ordinary use of "opposition" of course includes both kinds of relation. There are opposites that are mutually exclusive (i.e., genuinely contradictory, like open–shut, black–white), and there are opposites that are mutually implicative (like two sides of a coin, or a street).[23] The relation between the opposites of the first class, though it may exhibit degrees, is such that they cannot exist at the same time in respect to the same object; the relation between those of the second class is that they must: we cannot have one without simultaneously having the other. When relations of the second sort are mistaken for the first, enemies are made of complementaries whose necessarily mutual presence is thus misconstrued as hostility and erroneously generalized as contradiction. The perception of difference, by which we know all things, is mistaken for antagonism.[24] The ancient is only knowable in terms of the modern, and vice versa. Words do not exclude the "matter" they are often said to express; they bring that "matter" into consciousness. And because they do, attention to the patterns they form ("aesthetic" appreciation) does not preclude attention to the histor-

[22] It is even possible nowadays merely to assume this and go on to review the alternatives, as Edward Wasiolek does in "Wanted: A New Contextualism," *Critical Inquiry* 1 (1975), 623–39.

[23] A much more elaborate and precise classification may be found in C. K. Ogden's still useful *Opposition* (Bloomington, Ind., 1967; 1st ed. 1932).

[24] Father Ong points out that the venerable "opposition," subjective-objective, is similarly ill-founded. Of the sense of touch he writes: "When I feel this objective something 'out there,' beyond the bounds of my own body, I also at the same instant experience my own self. I feel other and self simultaneously. This is how I can differentiate them." *The Presence of the Word* (New Haven, 1967), p. 170.

ical contexts in which they function. Both kinds of attention are required by the same object, the text, and are part of the same process, interpretation.[25]

For this reason, any theory of literature that exalts one part of the process at the expense of the other, or any theory of language that severs words from "matter," or any theory of culture that uses one epoch as a stick to beat another, mistakes the nature of the phenomenon it purports to explain simply by leaving out, if not denigrating, one of its constituent parts. Hence it requires, and will inevitably receive, correction from a counter-theory that in its turn will cry up the omitted or denigrated part. The trouble with this procedure is that it never gets anywhere; like a seesaw it remains forever fixed in the same place, one end going up as the other comes down. The quarrel between the ancients and the moderns, for example, since its reinvigoration on a variety of fronts during the Renaissance, is certainly one of the most unproductive arguments in the history of thought,[26] except at those moments when it provokes parody or satire, like Swift's *Battle of the Books*. Whenever veneration of past models gives way to prescription of rigid limits on present activities, the modern will quite naturally defend his liberty by attacking what would constrain it. If the modern is sufficiently absolute in his claim to freedom, the defender of the ancient will be able to retort that some constraints are necessary if one is to be merely intelligible. The understanding of the subjects at issue is not advanced by such embattlement, which must conceive as separate and opposed what in fact can only exist as functions of each other.

The case is the same in formalist theories of art that postulate

[25] I am here summarizing points demonstrated in a different way by John M. Ellis, *The Theory of Literary Criticism* (Berkeley, 1974), pp. 146, 203, et passim.

[26] A good analysis of the quarrel, which makes clear the various self-contradictions on both sides and urges its importance as the inadvertent discovery of historicism, is given by Hans Robert Jauss, "Aesthetische Normen und geschichtliche Reflexion in der 'Querelle des Anciens et des Modernes,' " as the introduction to Charles Perrault, *Parallèle des Anciens et des Modernes* (Munich, 1964), pp. 8–64.

its autonomy either to assert its value or to concentrate attention on its "intrinsic" qualities in reaction against theories that
stressed its "extrinsic" ones—moral, historical, biographical,
or whatever. Thus the old New Criticism has been opposed by
theories that seek to bring back what it deliberately left out:
authorial intention, the experience of the reader, historical
contexts.[27] Thus the *nouvelle critique* is criticized for its lack of
"principles of relevance," of norms or controls without which
reading becomes impossible.[28] The effect of this seesaw motion is formally stated in Arthur K. Moore's careful conclusion
that such theories "appear to be individually defective and mutually invalidating." Whether old or new, Moore continues,
theories of literature

can never have been valuable as limiting concepts but only as propositions congenial to supervening cultural theories. As such, they have
not been true warrants for methodical observation but, rather, dubious excuses for accommodating literature to various notions of the
contemporary real. If analytical criticism has surpassed rank impres-
sionism, the gains have been owing more to improved reading than
to improved theory; for theory has most evidently provided a pretext
rather than a regulative principle. In truth, the function of theory has
usually been to determine literature as evidence or expression in relation to ideology and in some instances to provide such barriers to
alien modes of inquiry as enable the critic to assume a priestly role and
to mediate the mysteries of the literary imagination without serious
competition.[29]

[27] The rich variety of these as well as other challenges is presented and de-
bated at length by the international participants in the Bellagio Symposium of
1973, recorded in *New Literary History* 7 (1975), 1–233.

[28] The quoted phrase is Culler's objection to Kristeva, p. 250; the general
objection is fully deployed by Wayne C. Booth and M. H. Abrams in a symposium on "The Limits of Pluralism," printed in *Critical Inquiry* 3 (1977), 407–
38.

[29] *Contestable Concepts of Literary Theory* (Baton Rouge, La., 1973), pp. 209,
218. Independently of Moore and more brutally, Ellis finds theoretical polemics between 1949 and 1974 "intolerable," resulting in "almost a spectator sport,
rather than a field of inquiry," pp. 9–10. Grounds for this dismal view, if any
are needed, may be found in a volume like *Art and Philosophy*, ed. Sidney Hook

The treatment implied by this diagnosis is not, as it might first tempt one to suppose, that theory be abolished (although this has been seriously proposed),[30] but that it begin from premises that do its subject fuller justice, that at least avoid cutting the subject up into falsely competing parts. Such premises can be found in two seminal works that have emerged from very different traditions of thought: one from the linguistic analyses of the later Wittgenstein, the other from the social analyses of European Marxism.[31] More striking than the difference between their approaches is their common insistence on the nature of language and literature as social activities, their common denial of the formalist-historicist "opposition," and their common perception that literary texts are simultaneously both the products and producers of the whole cultural community, past and present, in which they exist.[32] Such premises can supply a "true warrant" for the accurate observation of what has been called the "dual status" of literary works as originating in the past and functioning in the present,[33] thereby requiring for their interpretation the continual

---

(New York, 1966), which records a symposium among twenty-eight eminent critics, philosophers, art historians, and musicologists, in which all the respondents deny almost all the arguments in all the papers, no one can agree what "interpretation" is, and from which the only inference would appear to be, in the words of one exasperated participant, that "one can talk about art without being able to talk about the talk about art," p. 271.

[30] By Steven Knapp and Walter Benn Michaels, "Against Theory," *Critical Inquiry* 8 (1982), 723–42.

[31] The first is Ellis, *The Theory of Literary Criticism*; the second is Robert Weimann, *Structure and Society in Literary History* (Charlottesville, Va., 1976).

[32] Weimann sees the relation between "past significance and present meaning," or *Entstehungsgeschichte* and *Wirkungsgeschichte*, as the central concern of literary study, pp. 14, 187. A similar emphasis on the historicity of understanding is found in German hermeneutics generally: cf. Gadamer's discussion of hermeneutic "application," i.e., the need to make past texts function in the present, *Truth and Method* (New York, 1975), pp. 289–324.

[33] To do justice to this "dual status" is the aim of Michael McCanles, *Dialectical Criticism and Renaissance Literature* (Berkeley, 1975), who develops a concept of dialectic expressly to rectify the formalist-historicist "opposition," which he cogently reviews and criticizes: pp. 1–10, 227–28, 241–73. McCanles

relation of formal features both to the history that produced the text and the history that the text, together with its generations of readers, produces. Finally, such premises prevent us above all from isolating the text in some "aesthetic" never-never land, directing our attention instead to the whole "system of communication," the "social and linguistic conventions" only within which is the text successively reinvested with meaning.[34]

It is the inescapable necessity of such conventions that makes the fashionable notion of textual indeterminacy so oddly perverse, at the same time as it may be a legitimate protest against one or another form of textual overdeterminacy institutionalized by academies. In any case, arguments for freedom, whether Lutheran or Derridean, are political; they cannot supply means, principles, limiting or unlimiting horizons of interpretation. Without relations there can be no semantics; without systems, contexts, and conventions, no meaning. The actual issue in genuine arguments about interpretation is not the "express words" of the text considered in either a putative vacuum or a postulated infinity. The real issue is rather how and why we select contexts, employ assumptions, and apply conventions to surround the text with the fictions that enable us, in the ceaseless historical dialogue of glosses on glosses, to construct and reconstruct meanings.

That the mirage of textual autonomy, pursued with equal vigor and similar disappointing results in both Protestant hermeneutics and modern post-Romantic (or post-structuralist) formalism, has enticed us for so long suggests how dismayingly little we have learned about language and meaning since the Renaissance. That we still seek to impute a sacred status and privilege—for whatever reason or from whatever source—to some uses of language; that we still worry about how to identify and define a trope; that we still thirst, like

acknowledges a specific debt to the first essay in Weimann's book, "Past Significance and Present Meaning in Literary History," which had previously appeared in *New Literary History* 1 (1969).

[34] Ellis, *The Theory of Literary Criticism*, pp. 142–46.

Hamlet, for meaning in some pure and isolated state—whether in a providentially guaranteed or a wholly indeterminate cosmos—all testify to the continuing power of language to bewitch our intelligence by the desires it dreams. The sacred, autonomous word—whether located in the Bible or in Baudelaire—is but the transference to language of the independent, transcendent status imputed by referential semantics to meaning. Words and texts—as we are by now rather weary of hearing—are "self-referring," the mystical signs of their own substance. Whether this assertion is made by the divine metonymy of Augustine or the profane metaphor of Barthes, the venerable process of signification is still at work—either displacing meanings beyond words or displacing words beyond contexts. To maintain reference as self-reference is to reinforce the privilege that the whole vocabulary has always claimed for whatever is "stood for."

The inability even of theories that revel in iconoclasm and delight in the free play of signifiers to jettison the very notion of "standing for" recalls Saussure's inability to scrap "sign" even after he had defined it to the vanishing point. The tyranny of reference, the ineradicable dream that language has got to represent something, if only itself, produces a predictable sadness at the heart of all the revelling even in those who know it to be a dream. In others, the sadness is a kind of despair that language appears incapable of moving beyond itself to grapple with such problems as historical change and causation.[35] Such sadness is but unnecessary nostalgia for what the vocabulary of reference has always promised and never delivered: the meaningful elsewhere that words merely stand for. Language is not our prison; we are jailed only by the referential description of itself that it palms off on us, by the false (and theoretically Platonic) promise of a more salient, other realm of which words are the mere shadows. Only by crediting this land of Oz can

---

[35] Fredric Jameson is a victim of the latter sadness who well describes the former as it occurs in Derrida's insistence that we cannot do without the concept of "sign": *The Prison-House of Language* (Princeton, 1972), pp. 185–86.

we feel sad, betrayed, and resentful that we are forever excluded from it.

Language does not keep us out of the world, it lets us into it, allows us to possess it. Language is our only means of such possession; it's all we have and all we need. It does not represent things we cannot grasp; it gives shape and significance to things so that they can be grasped. And the more kinds of discourse we learn, the more communities of discourse we master, the richer we can make our possession of all the worlds shaped by those discourses. We could be more cheerful if we remember the exhilarated passion with which Montaigne, Cervantes, and Shakespeare formed such worlds for us to possess and explore. We have only to appreciate the multiple functions of language in the human community to embark on the adventure of interpretation that Montaigne identified with life itself, the unending discovery of the universe that only language can make articulate—"the buzzing world and lisping firmament."

INDEX

A

Abrams, M. H., 301n
Abse, D. Wilfred, 235n
Académie Française, 200
Accademia della Crusca, 143n, 200
aesthetics, 71–72
Agricola, Rudolf, 114
Alberti, Leon Battista, 137–39, 157,
  185, 192
Alexander, Sir William, 189
allegory, as interpretive method, 48,
  73, 78, 187, 223, 228, 231, 264;
  scriptural, 32, 221, 262–63
Allerton, D. J., 41n
Alpers, Paul J., 231
Alphonso V, King of Aragon and
  Sicily, 90
Aneau, Barthélemy, 169n
anthropology, 3, 167
Apel, Karl-Otto, 20, 64n, 81, 114n,
  135n, 157n, 162n, 195n, 204,
  217n
Aquinas, Saint Thomas, 223
Aristotle, 93, 94, 95–96, 97–98, 107,
  117–18, 123, 129, 153, 162–63,
  182, 186, 219, 242, 261, 272
Arnold, Matthew, 191n
art, 66, 296; as autonomous, 43, 71–
  72, 74–75, 78, 294ff. See also lit-
  erature
Ascham, Roger, 198, 202; The
  Scholemaster, 191–93, 196–97
Atkins, J.W.H., 225n
Attridge, Derek, 199n
Augustine, Saint, 28, 38, 73, 187,
  192, 221n, 253–56, 257, 264,
  271, 280, 304; de doctrina christiana, 32, 265
Austin, J. L., 240n

B

Backus, Irena, 258n
Bacon, Francis, 50–51, 69, 115, 249
Bainton, Roland H., 112n, 221n,
  222n, 236n
Bakhtin, Mikhail, 135, 140, 270
Baldwin, C. S., 80n
Baron, Hans, 138n, 139
Barthes, Roland, 297, 298n, 304
Baxandall, Michael, 296n
Bembo, Pietro, 135n, 157, 200;
  Prose, 141n, 143–44, 170, 185
Bentley, Jerry H., 113n, 217n, 222n
Beza, Theodore, 279–81
Bible, 32, 85n, 179, 211, 304; Eng-
  lish, 250, 277n; exegesis of, 221,
  222–25, 228, 237–40, 244n; Gal.
  4:9, 273; Gen. 2:19–20, 284ff.;
  Gen. 4:26, 73; German, 291;
  Glossa Ordinaria, 223, 284; John
  1:1, 217n, 220; 1 John 5:21, 276;
  Mark 5:1–20, 223–24; Matt.
  18:3, 234; O.T., 235–38, 240–41;
  Ps. 119, 239–40; 2 Sam. 12, 227;
  Song of Solomon (Canticles),
  236n, 270; Vulgate and Greek
  N.T., 214. See also Scripture
Biondo, Flavio, 137n, 201
Black, Max, 19, 60n
Boethius, 91
Bolgar, R. R., 296
Booth, Wayne C., 301n
Bovelles, Charles de, 150, 175, 203;
  liber de differentia vulgarium lin-
  guarum, 146–49, 286–87
Boyle, Marjorie O'Rourke, 217n,
  218n, 219n, 220, 221n, 222n
Brerewood, Edward, 201–202
Brink, C. O., 100n

Library of Congress Cataloging-in-Publication Data

WASWO, RICHARD.

LANGUAGE AND MEANING IN THE RENAISSANCE.

INCLUDES BIBLIOGRAPHICAL REFERENCES AND INDEX.

I. SEMANTICS—HISTORY.   2. LANGUAGES—

PHILOSOPHY. I. TITLE.

P325.W35 1987   401   86–22492

ISBN 0–691–06696–5 (ALK. PAPER)

RICHARD WASWO is Professor of English
at the University of Geneva. He is the author of *A Fatal Mirror: Themes and Techniques in the Poetry of Fulke Greville*.